SOCIAL PROGRAM IMPLEMENTATION

SOCIAL PROGRAM IMPLEMENTATION

This unique collection brings together articles forming a comprehensive study of social program implementation.

Implementation — best described as the stage between policy decisions and operations — presents the often extremely difficult problem of translating general statements of policy into concrete actions consistent with original intent. The articles are of two types. First are case studies of the implementation of federal programs and projects in the fields of education, community development, and income transfers. They show the extent to which a) vaguely drawn, often contradictory legislation and plans make the intent of programs and projects difficult to translate into workable field operations and b) bureaucratic/political disagreements, frequently across several layers of government, can undermine original objectives. The second group of articles treats implementation as a conceptual problem for policy analysts and administrators. They discuss both the means of carrying out implementation analysis and assessment and the implications of implementation studies for the execution of social policy analysis and research, including evaluative research.

This timely and informative study brings together valuable information for the public administrator, political scientist, educational researcher, sociologist, economist, and social worker.

This is a volume of

Quantitative Studies in Social Relations

Consulting Editor: Peter H. Rossi, University of Massachusetts, Amherst, Massachusetts

A complete list of titles in this series appears at the end of this volume.

SOCIAL PROGRAM IMPLEMENTATION

Edited by
WALTER WILLIAMS
Graduate School of Public Affairs
  and Institute of Governmental Research
University of Washington
Seattle, Washington

RICHARD F. ELMORE
Graduate School of Public Affairs
University of Washington
Seattle, Washington

ACADEMIC PRESS   New York   San Francisco   London
A Subsidiary of Harcourt Brace Jovanovich, Publishers

ACADEMIC PRESS, INC.
111 Fifth Avenue, New York, New York 10003

United Kingdom Edition published by
ACADEMIC PRESS, INC. (LONDON) LTD.
24/28 Oval Road, London NW1

Library of Congress Cataloging in Publication Data

Main entry under title:

Social program implementation.

    (Quantitative studies in social relations series)
    Includes bibliographical references.
    1.   United States—Social policy—Addresses, essays,
lectures.   2.   Social action—Addresses, essays, lectures.   3.   Education and state—Addresses, essays, lectures.   4.   Evaluation research (Social action programs)
—United States—Addresses, essays, lectures.   I.   Williams, Walter.   II.   Elmore, Richard F.
HN65.S576   1976   658'.91'309173   75-40618
ISBN 0–12–756850–6

CONTENTS

v

II.   EDUCATION PROGRAMS

7. Is Real-World Experimentation Possible? The Case of Educational Performance Contracting   149

Edward M. Gramlich and Patricia P. Koshel

8. Implementation as Mutual Adaptation: Change in Classroom Organization   167

Milbrey McLaughlin

III. COMMUNITY-ORIENTED PROGRAMS

9. Making a New Federal Program: Model Cities, 1964–68   183

Edward C. Banfield

10. Washington: Angry Citizens and an Ambitious Plan   219

Martha Derthick

IV. TRANSFER PAYMENT PROGRAMS

V. IMPLEMENTATION ANALYSIS AND ASSESSMENT EFFORTS

LIST OF CONTRIBUTORS

Numbers in parentheses indicate the pages on which the authors' contributions begin.

BERNARD A. BANET, High/Scope Educational Research Foundation (125)

EDWARD C. BANFIELD, Department of Government, Harvard University (183)

MARTHA DERTHICK, The Brookings Institution (219)

RICHARD F. ELMORE, Graduate School of Public Affairs, University of Washington (101)

EDWARD M. GRAMLICH, The Brookings Institution (149)

PATRICIA P. KOSHEL, Consultant, Washington, D. C. (149)

MILBREY McLAUGHLIN, The Rand Corporation, Santa Monica, California (167)

JEROME T. MURPHY, Graduate School of Education, Harvard University (77)

JOHN PINCUS, The Rand Corporation, Santa Monica, California (43)

BERYL A. RADIN, Lyndon B. Johnson School of Public Affairs, The University of Texas at Austin (243)

DAVID P. WEIKART, High/Scope Educational Research Foundation (125)

WALTER WILLIAMS, Graduate School of Public Affairs and Institute of Governmental Research, University of Washington (3, 15, 267)

ix

PREFACE

Implementation is fast becoming the newest shibboleth among academics and policy analysts concerned with complex social programs. Defined most simply as the stage between decision and operations, implementation can range from the trivial case of one individual's deciding to do something and then doing it to a lengthy process among many actors across several layers of government. But whether we are talking about simple or complex cases, the fundamental implementation question remains whether or not what has been decided actually can be carried out in a manner consonant with that underlying decision. More and more, we are finding, at least in the case of complex social programs, that the answer is no. So it is crucial that we attend to implementation.

Yet both editors of this volume greet implementation's sudden popularity with mixed emotions. On the one hand, our separate experiences have led us to view implementation as the crucial barrier to improving the quality of social programs. We are intrigued by how long it has taken for the saliency of implementation to emerge and pleased that the long neglect of this critical topic is ending. On the other hand, we are leery of the consequences that can follow from a faddish concern with the problem. There has been a disturbing tendency toward faddishness in policy analysis that carries with it the danger of unrealistically high expectations about progress—a headlong leap into an area and then discouragement because unrealistic goals were not fulfilled. Hence the study of implementation, which will require extended and often tedious efforts, stands the risk of being cast out prematurely as an unproductive research area because it does not yield a quick payoff.

The failure to focus on implementation has blighted not only program administration but also policy research and analysis. In the former case, policy ideas that seemed reasonable and compelling when decisions were made often have become badly flawed and ineffective programs as they drifted down the bureaucratic process. It is not just that the programs fall short of the early rhetoric that described them; they often barely work at all. Ignoring implementation has been equally disastrous for research and analysis. *Indeed, it is possible that past analysis and research that ignored implementation issues may have asked the wrong questions, thereby producing information of little or no use to policymaking.*

A principal theme of this volume is that implementation problems in the social policy areas are *the* major substantive (as opposed to monetary or political) hurdle to better programs in the future. Our position is summarized by these three statements:

1. The greatest difficulty in devising better social programs is not determining what are reasonable policies on paper but finding the means for converting these policies into viable field operations that correspond reasonably well to original intentions.

2. The major problem of social policy analysis has been its failure to attend to the implementation feasibility of its recommendations.

3. The prime difficulties with social experimentation have been organizational: foreseeing the need for an experiment in sufficient time to meet decisionmaking demands, designing the experiment, getting it into the field, and determining if it is working well enough to provide a valid basis for testing policy questions.

In studying implementation, it seems certain that the real benefits will come, if at all, from thorough, painstaking studies of a process and its many actors—a process that may stretch from the upper reaches of Washington bureaucracy to a local project, with a number of intermediate stops. More specifically, people must investigate who has what responsibilities and how these responsibilities are carried out by key actors including several agency headquarters' offices, federal regional offices, subnational governments, and program and project sponsors and operators. Only when we look in detail at the interrelationship of decisionmaking and implementation will we be able to unravel some of the mysteries of putting programs in place. *Researchers must understand that the study of implementation is likely to require time-consuming and tedious activities that are not likely to bring striking breakthroughs in terms of understanding or techniques. However, it is an area in which unstinting hard work should over time bring large payoffs—if only we have the patience.*

The purpose of this book is to stimulate concern for and inquiry into the area of implementation. We see it as part of a growing effort to (1) increase awareness of implementation in large-scale public bureaucracies and demonstrate the need to build implementation into the structure and process that make up the organization's policymaking apparatus; (2) stimulate research on implementation by people in a variety of academic disciplines; and (3) encourage the development of techniques to carry out implementation analysis and assessment in organizations.

Some comments are needed on the chapters in this volume and the intended audience. The typical chapter is a detailed analysis of a specific case of social program implementation. In some instances the cases begin with a presidential initiative and demonstrate either how the politics of compromise produces a vague, almost unworkable program that becomes even more confused as it moves into the field (Model Cities) or how even the strongest of presidential desires can be undone completely by community groups (new towns in-town). In other instances the focus will be upon social field experiments where one might anticipate, because of the research character of the activities, that there would be a much stronger concern for the issues of specification and implementation. Here, too, we will see that politics and bureaucracy impinge. Wherever the case study starts, there is complexity, and it is through the careful and detailed analysis of process that we come to see many of the subtle elements of implementation.

Fortunately, many of these cases make interesting reading. There is a goodly dose of political and bureaucratic intrigue and a fair amount of humor. In fact, some of the most absurd things imaginable happen as decisions move toward operations. The chapters, however, are not presented mainly for their entertainment value or as illustrations of the foibles of government. In total, the chapters provide a number of insights that should prove useful in devising more sensible implementation strategies and in determining research and analytic needs.

This book is intended for overlapping groups in government and the social science research community, including policy planners (analysts), administrators who carry out programs, researchers engaged in social policy studies such as field experiments, and those concerned directly with the study of implementation issues. An earlier volume in the "Quantitative Studies in Social Relations" series, *Evaluating Social Programs,* edited by Peter Rossi and Walter Williams, also was intended to reach a broad group of government people and academicians. The editors observed in the preface to that book that "if one is to understand the complexity of evaluation research, he must confront both methodology and politics." The same may be said about implementation. However, and this is a point worth emphasizing, the present volume does not contain the kind of methodological chapters that in the earlier volume made life difficult for those whose methodological skills were low. The complexity of implementation arises more from the force of politics and bureaucracy than from any of the more traditional statistical issues treated in the earlier book.

Yet, and this too is a critical point, the present book clearly is intended for social science researchers. As an example, take the case of a social field experiment. In such research it is necessary to develop a design to test the hypotheses at issue, to put into the field a project that in its operational dimensions reflects the underlying hypotheses, and to hold the design so as to provide a valid test of hypotheses. In the animal laboratory or in a highly controlled human setting such as a mental institution, meeting these requirements may not be hard at all. In the relatively uncontrolled world of social programs and policies, politics and bureaucracy intrude. Time demands, pressures from outside groups, bureaucratic recalcitrance, and the like are the big issues, not the sample design or the statistical test.

Researchers will have to learn about an entirely different set of threats to the validity of an experiment or an evaluation. They also will need to devise new techniques or learn to use present ones differently in implementation analysis and assessment. Techniques are important. Research on implementation can be quite rigorous. The problem is to get the techniques to work in the complex world of bureaucracy and politics.

One final warning: Implementation can be a terribly unsettling area. At times there are strong reasons for optimism. For example, both editors think that there can be a very high payoff to implementation research, but there is certain to be much frustration. *Even if our research tells us what to do about implementation, we still may not know how to implement our findings.*

Perhaps most frustrating of all, there will seldom be clean and neat answers to implementation issues. Take the question of specification, the spelling out in some detail of how the program should operate. As Milbrey McLaughlin observes in her paper in this volume: "There is general agreement that a major component of the 'implementation problem' has to do with inadequate operational specificity. There is debate concerning *who* should make project operations more specific, *how* it can be done, and *when* specificity should be introduced." One thing can be said with near certainty about the "who," "how," and "when" questions: The answer will vary from case to case; and in specific cases, there seldom will be a simple, sharply delineated answer. When a project involves multiple layers in an organization, responsibilities almost certainly will be shared. The correct answer usually will be of the "Goldilocks" variety: One party should do just the right amount and then stop, and the next party should do just the right amount, and so on.

This is not to argue that we cannot devise helpful approaches to implementation. We are convinced that we can. The point, however, is that we will be limited by the realities of the field; there almost never will be any sure technological fix. Problems of implementation are ultimately problems of politics and bureaucracy. As long as this sobering fact is kept in mind, we believe that useful research can be done and that implementation in social programs can be improved significantly. We are not defeatists, just realists.

I

AN OVERVIEW
OF IMPLEMENTATION

1

INTRODUCTION*

Walter Williams

The verb "implement" has two principal meanings: "to provide or equip with the means of carrying into effect," and "to carry into effect." Implementation in an organization can involve both a *continuing* effort over time to raise the capability of that organization or associated organizations to carry out programs or projects, and a *one-time* effort to put an organizational decision into place. Increasing an organization's implementation capacity will be treated briefly in this volume, but it is the latter process, trying to move from a decision to operations, that will be the main concern. At issue is the universal problem of putting a decision into effect. All of us know that deciding to quit smoking or to lose weight, sad to say, is only the first small step toward a solution. In a complex organization such as a government agency, the same mundane distinction between a decision and its implementation pertains, although many parties may be involved in the decision, and the process of implementation may move through several hierarchical layers. It is amid this complexity that the fundamental need to implement the decision can get misdirected so easily.

*Some parts of this chapter were contained in my editor's introduction to the "Special Issue on Implementation," *Policy Analysis,* Vol. 1, No. 3, pp. 451–458 and are used with permission of The Board of Regents of the University of California.

The most pressing implementation problem is that of moving from a decision to operations in such a way that what is done bears a reasonable resemblance to the decision and functions adequately in its institutional environment. The past contains few clearer messages than that of the difficulty of bridging the gap between policy decisions and workable field operations. It is a general problem spanning most policy areas. Indeed, in the area of social policy from which the essays in this book are drawn, implementation looms as the major substantive—as opposed to monetary or political—hurdle to better programs. We simply do not know how to implement complex new social programs or major program modifications. This is not surprising, because implementation is an exceedingly difficult task. What is hard to fathom is why so little has been done to investigate the process of implementation,[1] since that activity is of crucial importance in program operations, policy analysis, and evaluative research, particularly social experiments.

More and more, the evidence drawn from direct observation of efforts to develop and operate social policies and programs in the field points to the saliency of implementation concerns. The Great Society

[1] It is not the purpose of this volume to present a critique or a detailed bibliography of the major pieces on implementation, but I am certain that no bibliographic effort, at least in the social policy areas, would refute the point that little research has been carried out either on the implementation of social policies, programs, or projects or on the implementation process in a social policy organization such as a federal agency. Actually, it is hard to find material with the term implementation in the title. Only a few recent books come to mind—for example, N. Gross, J. Giacquinta, and M. Bernstein, *Implementing Organizational Innovations: A Sociological Analysis of Planned Educational Change* (New York: Basic Books, 1971); and Geoffrey Pressman and Aaron Wildavsky, *Implementation* (Berkeley and Los Angeles: University of California Press, 1973). In *Social Policy Research and Analysis* (New York: American Elsevier, 1971), I have a chapter entitled "The Agency Implementation Process." Jerome Murphy's two studies of federal education legislation has produced a number of pieces on implementation, a good example of which is "Title I of ESEA: The Politics of Implementing Federal Education Reform," *Harvard Educational Review*, February 1971, pp. 35–63. As far as I can tell, there has been only one major empirical study of social implementation efforts that covers a large sample of projects—the Rand Corporation's "Change Agent Study" now reported on in several volumes. The study is summarized in Paul Berman and Milbrey McLaughlin, *Federal Programs Supporting Educational Change: The Findings in Review*, Vol. IV, R-1589/4-HEW, The Rand Corporation, April 1975, and discussed in this volume in the paper by McLaughlin. A few other works contain lengthy discussions of issues pertinent to the problem of social policy implementation. Examples that immediately occur to me are Robert A. Levine, *Public Planning: Failure and Redirection*, Basic Books, 1972; Martha Derthick, *New Towns In-Town*, The Urban Institute, 1972; parts of which are included in this volume; and Miriam Johnson, *Counterpoint: The Changing Employment Service*, Olympus, 1973, which does not discuss implementation *per se* but presents an extended case study of implementation difficulties in a social program. Others no doubt would cite different materials. However, the critical point is that only a small number of works discuss social program implementation in detail. Indeed, one purpose of the book is to stimulate additional work in this important area.

programs that were begun with such high hopes performed well below naive early expectations; frequently, they seemed to make little progress at all. It is becoming clear in retrospect that the architects of the new programs had many good ideas, but neglected their execution. As I observed about those Great Society programs writing from the perspective of the late 1960s: "Implementation was the Achilles' heel of the Johnson Administration's social policy."[2] What has occurred since then leads me to this conclusion: The greatest difficulty in devising better social programs is not in determining what appear to be reasonable policies on paper but in finding the means for converting these policies into viable field operations that correspond reasonably well to specifications.

A similar kind of frustration has followed in the area of policy analysis. Those of us who staffed the analytic offices located at the top of the agencies came to find that bright ideas accepted by key policymakers often began to flounder as policy moved toward the field. Again, implementation was the missing link. As Allison has observed so aptly:

> If one is primarily interested in what the government actually does, the unavoidable question is: What percentage of the work of achieving a desired governmental action is done when the preferred analytic alternative has been identified? My estimate is about 10 percent in the normal case, ranging as high as 50 percent for some problems. . . .
>
> If analysts and operators are to increase their ability to achieve desired policy outcomes, they will have to develop ways of thinking analytically about a larger chunk of the problem. It is not that we have too many good analytic solutions to problems. It is, rather, that we have more good solutions than we have appropriate actions.[3]

Implementation difficulties have plagued major social experiments to such a degree that it is often doubtful these studies will produce results in the short term directly useful in final decisionmaking. What is increasingly evident is that conventional methodological problems of sample design, outcome measurement reliability and validity, and the appropriateness of statistical tests—the topics generally covered in books or courses on statistics or experimental design—are not the main barriers to doing better experiments.[4] The primary obstacles are weaknesses in organization and personnel—in foreseeing the need for an experiment soon enough to meet decisionmaking demands, designing the experiment, getting it into the field, and determining if it is working well enough to provide a valid basis

[2]Williams, *Social Policy Research and Analysis,* p. 11.
[3]Graham T. Allison, *Essence of Decision,* Boston: Little, Brown & Co., 1971, p. 267.
[4]See: Garth N. Buchanan and Joseph S. Wholey, "Federal Evaluation Policy," *Evaluation,* Fall 1972, pp. 17–32; and John W. Evans, "Evaluating Education Programs—Are We Getting Anywhere?" (Address delivered to the American Educational Research Association, Chicago, April 18, 1974).

for testing the experimental hypothesis. The hard truth is that we did not know how to put an experiment into the field so that it corresponds reasonably well to the drawing board plans.

Déjà vu—here again, in the experimental efforts, were the problems that made implementing social programs so difficult. In fact, the problems in the experimental setting were even more vivid, for two reasons. First, because of the smaller scale of these efforts, many of the problems did not get masked, as they frequently are when inundated by the multilayered activities involved in carrying out a national program. Second, the experimental activities were cast in the framework of research, where proper specification of the treatment is a prominent requirement. Thus failed specification and failed implementation come through with special clarity—particularly in the case of recent experimental efforts in education that will be so prominent in this volume.

ORGANIZATION OF THE VOLUME

The book is divided into five major sections: An Overview of Implementation (in which the present introductory material is included); Education Programs; Community-Oriented Programs; Transfer Payment Programs; and Implementation Analysis and Assessment Efforts. The volume draws heavily upon recent experience with social programs and with social experiments undertaken by the federal government to test out new programmatic ideas. The following discussion of major sections and individual chapters in the volume provides brief descriptions of programs and experiments for the reader who is not familiar with them.

An Overview

In addition to this introductory essay, the section contains a chapter by Walter Williams discussing implementation problems in federally funded programs. The latter introduces the notion of policy and operations spheres and considers the linkages between the two from the perspective of a federal social agency. In the policy sphere, the president, congressmen, key agency officials, and others of high status interact to reach the major decisions that reflect "policy at the highest level." Below that is the operations sphere, in which a variety of actors (e.g., lower-echelon federal bureaucrats, officials of subnational governments, and project operators) become involved in implementing and carrying out programs. It often will be here that policy really gets made.

The chapter focuses upon a federal social agency because the agency illustrates implementation in all of its complexity, as policy made at the top travels a long route through many layers from subnational governments to operating entities. It introduces two themes that will occur again and again in the discussion of the case material. First, the weak linkages between the policy sphere and operations sphere, and to some extent within each sphere, cause much slippage in the passage from policy to operations. Second, in this long process, the question of responsibility is crucial. What we find from past experience is that responsibility—particularly implementation responsibility—is only assumed when it cannot be avoided. Implementation often seems to be viewed as someone else's task, and is passed to the next person down the line. No question will loom larger than that of responsibility as we proceed through the volume.

Education Programs

The opening chapter by John Pincus investigates the likelihood that innovations developed through federal research and development (R&D) will be adopted and implemented properly in a local school system that Pincus describes as a "self-perpetuating bureaucracy." The paper considers both federal (R&D) policy and local operations but is most concerned with the latter. It provides a good transition between Williams' treatment of federal agency issues and the specific educational programs discussed in the chapters that follow. At the local level, too, there are a great number of actors and a multiplicity of bureaucratic layers. Here also we find policy and operations spheres which, just as at the national level, seem to be connected poorly. In considering the disjointedness even at the local level, Pincus' distinctions between incentives to adopt and incentives to implement are important. For example, adopting an innovation that is gaining current vogue in educational circles may be very appealing to school superintendents. However, it may be quite satisfactory for the superintendent's purposes simply to take the name and the rhetoric and make a few superficial changes that will seem to indicate change to those who do not probe deeply, but not to make any of the hard and costly bureaucratic and organizational changes that implementation requires. Adoption in the sense of a local school district's taking funds for and the title of a federal program is not necessarily a decision to put it in place in the way the funders desire, a lesson that federal officials seem to forget repeatedly. The circumstances under which local people will take steps to implement is the crucial issue of this paper.

The Elementary and Secondary Education Act (ESEA) of 1965 was intended primarily to help State Education Agencies (SEAs) and local school systems better serve disadvantaged students. Jerome Murphy looks at Title V of ESEA, a title with special importance for the study of implementation because of the effort to increase the capacity of the SEAs to administer funds provided by the act. If state and local governments have limited capability in terms of organization and personnel, we must doubt their ability to implement and execute programs even if they mean well. Title V, in Murphy's terms, provided "virtually unrestricted aid" to SEAs to strengthen their capacity to administer educational programs. Although the SEAs receiving Title V funds did change, these changes were never of the magnitude, and sometimes not even in the directions hoped for by federal officials. What happened when the federal government gave SEAs money explicitly for capacity building provides crucial lessons for an understanding of the organizational and personnel problems of implementation.

The next three chapters in this section consider the two main experimental efforts to test new ideas in education. One, the Follow Through planned variation experiment—a project funded under the Economic Opportunity Act but administered by the Office of Education—was aimed at disadvantaged children from kindergarten through grade three. It came about after early efforts to assess the effectiveness of Head Start had found that for those treated there were usually learning gains during the Head Start summer, but that there were no differences between Head Start children and an untreated group after the first regular school year. A common explanation was that the regular schools dissipated the Head Start gains, and this led to the notion of a program to build on the Head Start experience. Follow Through was intended to begin without any initial testing, but when Congress provided only partial funding, administrators thought it would make sense to test the relative effectiveness of several different treatment packages, or models, in a number of schools—an exercise labeled "planned variation."

Apparently because of the expectation of early full funding, the effort was carried out hastily. Potential sponsors—organizations with models of teaching programs—were invited to submit proposals for participating in the venture; the sponsors and sites were quickly chosen, an evaluation contract let, and planned variation soon got under way. However, as Robert Egbert, the first head of the Follow Through program, has stated, "It was obvious that despite the growing interest in this field and despite extensive publicity given various new programs, no one was fully prepared to move into the primary grades with a completely developed, radically different program."[5]

[5]Robert L. Egbert, "Foilow Through" (unpublished manuscript, 1971).

The second major experiment, funded by the Office of Economic Opportunity (OEO), centered on performance contracting—an arrangement in which the level of payment to teaching agents (private companies or teachers themselves) depends upon how well their students do. The purpose of the performance-contracting experiment was to test the merits of such an arrangement by assessing the educational effectiveness of several learning-incentive models developed and operated by private companies.[6] To understand the lack of concern for implementation in this experiment, it is crucial to understand the controversy and sense of immediacy that surrounded the idea of performance contracting.

The Johnson administration closed with real doubts about the effectiveness of the many social programs begun during that period. One alternative being pushed hard in the analytic community was to use market-like incentives. The notion fit perfectly with the business-oriented philosophy of the Nixon administration. Also of importance was the fact that performance contracting had both strong support and strong opposition from different elements of the educational community. The main opposition was from teachers, who saw it as an economic threat or as a challenge to basic educational philosophy, or both. How much this opposition inhibited the experiment is not known. At the same time, performance-contracting firms already had emerged, and numerous school districts were considering signing contracts with these firms even though little or no evidence of their capabilities existed. There was, therefore, a real need for immediate testing to prevent school administrators from adopting large-scale performance contracting for their school systems if in fact the notion was a bad idea. In such a setting, it is small wonder that haste pushed implementation issues to the background.

The chapter by Richard Elmore might have been titled "The Politics of Experimentation (or Implementation)" or, perhaps more aptly, "How Politics Did in the Experiment." Elmore traces Follow Through from its inception through the implementation efforts, showing how political and bureaucratic factors compromised the validity of the experiment at every turn. First and foremost, the chapter is an account of the clash between experimental demands and political/bureaucratic demands, the former generally being overwhelmed by the latter. For example, the requirement that schools choose and hold to a design (the essence of planned variation) fell before political pressures; so it was with most of the other experimental requirements. In short, we have an extended treatment of the interaction between politics and technique.

[6]Late in the development of the performance-contracting experiment, some effort was made to have an arrangement run entirely through a public school (no private companies). However, the big concern was with contracts between a private company and a public school.

David Weikart and Bernard Banet report on the Follow Through implementation efforts of one sponsor, the High/Scope Educational Research Foundation. The detailed and rich account of implementation difficulties takes on special force because of the authors' past experience in the early childhood field. Previously Weikart, who headed High/Scope, had developed carefully and carried out an experimental treatment based on Piagetian theory with preschool children in Ypsilanti, Michigan. It had yielded significant classroom gains and provided much information on program development. Yet Weikart, one of the foremost names in the early childhood area, soon discovered how ill-prepared High/Scope was to move quickly from the highly controlled setting in Ypsilanti to several Follow Through sites. Indeed, he and his colleagues had expected to be able to take their tested methods into the field and, with a few training sessions, have teachers converted to the new approach. This was most naive, as Weikart and Banet observe: "There was a vast gulf between the smiles and nods of workshop sessions and actual classroom implementation of a model. . . . Apparently a teacher's repertoire and the constraints she perceives on her role . . . are not amenable to lightning-fast change." They note further that "it may seem strange that after five years we are just now at the threshold of what is possible with our model, but that is our position and probably that of most of the sponsors who have elected to follow a developmental approach."

Edward Gramlich and Patricia Koshel, both of whom were at OEO during the performance-contracting effort, trace the effect of extreme haste on the experiment. Implementation in this case appears to have been almost a caricature—everything in the implementation effort was done so poorly and hurriedly that simply recording it is quite sufficient to convince one of its ineptness. There was no lengthy development effort in this experiment, and hence no opportunity for the authors to delve, as Weikart and Banet do, into the nuances of implementation. However, performance contracting viewed from a somewhat different perspective does have a great deal to teach us, not only about implementation but also about experimentation. Surely the strongest lesson is that haste and lack of treatment specificity are incompatible with sound experimental outcome. Again, we have a vivid account of the interplay between political/bureaucratic forces and technical considerations that renders field experimentation so difficult.

The final chapter in this section, by Milbrey McLaughlin, draws on the Rand Corporation's change agent study (cited in a previous footnote), which included a sample survey of a large number of school programs and intensive field studies of a smaller number of them. From this base of information McLaughlin selected the material focusing on innovations that involved mainly organizational rather than technological changes—what she labels "classroom organization projects," of which the open classroom would be a prime example. In such projects, McLaughlin argues, *"successful implementation is characterized by a process of mutual adaptation. . . .* Implementation was a dynamic organizational process that was shaped over time by interactions between project goals and methods and the institutional setting."

The key point, and it is one which carries beyond the education area, is that a precise replica of a project design generally is not desirable in complex social projects. Rather, what appears to be needed for a viable project is a realistic development of the underlying design that takes into account the distinct features and needs of the local setting. The objective is performance, not conformance.[7] Adapting the underlying design has two main benefits. The most obvious is that the adaptation will be more responsive to the special aspects of the local setting. Less obvious is that the process of adaptation both increases the local people's stake in the project and provides a means of gaining confidence and competence (reinventing the wheel is not simply wasted motion). By looking in depth at the mutual adaptation process, McLaughlin summarizes many of the major findings of the change agent study and elaborates upon a crucial aspect of implementation.

Community-Oriented Programs

The Great Society years brought forth a host of programs aimed at improving communities' institutions and organizations, housing, and physical amenities. These programs are interesting for a number of reasons, including the fact that they contained many of the elements of Nixon's "new federalism." For example, the notion that local people know best, now so prominent in the ideology of the new federalism, was adopted with a vengeance in the Economic Opportunity Act of 1964 under the Community Action Program's (CAP) requirement of maximum feasible participation of the poor. In its earliest days, CAP provided funds to communities with almost no strings attached. However, unlike the grants of the new federalism, CAP grants usually did not go to local governments but rather to a specially established nonprofit corporation. CAP was often a device to bypass city hall, to get around the old power structure that had failed the poor in the past.

Model Cities, the program that will be considered in the case material in this volume, in some respects was an answer to the problems raised by

[7]This distinction is stated perceptively in Anthony's discussion, "The Conformance Fallacy" (pp. 28–30) in R. N. Anthony, *Planning and Control Systems,* Graduate School of Business Administration, Harvard University, 1965.

CAP. Many of the criticisms about individual community action agencies came from the local officials who complained that they had little or no control over these agencies and often found them fighting programs of the local government. Model Cities was to provide largely discretionary funds to mayors (or whatever the head of a city was called) to be used in a wide variety of ways to improve the Model City area.

Edward Banfield tells the story of the development of the Model Cities program, starting with the earlier Economic Opportunity Act, which established CAP, and continuing through the beginning years of Model Cities. There is an interesting similarity between Banfield's account and that of Elmore on Follow Through. Politics, before Model Cities ever got into the field, was to destroy President Johnson's grand design for putting large amounts of money into a few cities to show what could be done if massive funds were concentrated on urban problems. But Congress was not about to pass a bill that gave a few demonstration cities big grants and left most of the other cities with no new funds. The fuzzy compromise legislation that finally emerged presented a host of problems, and things went from bad to worse as the program moved into the field. Banfield provides a lively account of the interaction of political, bureaucratic, and technical problems that plagued Model Cities during the Johnson administration. However, his paper is much more than a good rendering of the history of a now-dead program. The problems that hindered Model Cities, including those of implementation, are still there to bedevil those who are trying now to implement its replacement, the Housing and Community Development Act.

The program to build new towns in-town presents an interesting contrast to Model Cities. As Martha Derthick observed in *New Towns In-Town* (sections of which are included in this volume):

> The program was President Johnson's idea. One morning in August 1967, as he was sitting in his bedroom at the White House and talking to Special Assistant Joseph A. Califano, Jr., it occurred to the President that federally owned land in the cities could be used for housing. Within hours, his staff had assembled a working group from the executive departments to figure how this could be done [p. 3].

Derthick tells the tale of a program that looked easy. In some cities there were both housing problems and federally owned surplus land. Moreover, the new program was small, with maximum presidential involvement to cut through red tape; since no new legislation was required, Congress could not thwart the President's will. To make things even easier, the first site chosen for a new town in-town was the federal city of Washington, D.C. Surely, early and quick success might be expected. Yet as Derthick shows in the case study of Fort Lincoln, just a few miles from the White House, everything imaginable that could go wrong, did, as HUD, the

D.C. government, and presidential staff tried to do the president's bidding. What no one could control was the local community: Fort Lincoln became embroiled in grass-roots politics and class conflicts, with middle-class citizens opposing housing for low-income people. Besides the Fort Lincoln case study, we include in the volume the final portion of Derthick's last chapter, in which she generalizes about why federal programs have so much trouble at the community level. Her insights concerning the federal government's tendency to be overambitious and unrealistic about programs and not to follow through at the local level are surely important to those who study implementation.

Transfer Payment Programs

The chapters in the previous two sections treat complex service delivery or community-oriented programs. Now we turn to a program simpler in terms of implementation and execution: the primary function is to deliver money through the monthly provision of a check. The classic example from the Old Age Survivors, Disability and Health Insurance (OASDHI) program is its retirement segment, usually referred to by the popular name of Social Security. A massive computer operation in Baltimore each month provides social security checks to millions of older Americans, apparently with very few errors and at a relatively low administrative cost. The Social Security Administration (SSA) that runs the entire OASDHI program has been viewed in the past as a model of federal efficiency.

The Supplementary Security Income (SSI) program federalized that segment of the public welfare system providing benefits to the aged, the blind, and the disabled. SSI was intended to remove the stigma of welfare for these three groups. Unlike social security, SSI did require a needs test to show deficient income, but the program was separated from the state-administered public welfare program and given to the Social Security Administration. Both the aura of Social Security and the efficiency of the SSA would make SSI a humane transfer payment program.

Beryl Radin's chapter investigates the Social Security Administration's effort to provide checks to several million poor aged, blind, and disabled, many of whom already were receiving regular social security checks. An interesting aspect of SSI is that the bill that passed in 1972 specified that the program would be initiated on January 1, 1974, leaving well over a year to prepare for the start of the program. However, as Radin points out, congressional changes between the 1972 enactment and the program's start made the detailed development of rules and regulations difficult. Other problems arose when SSA found that getting information about aged, blind, and disabled persons on the state welfare roles in order to establish their check-writing machinery was far more complicated than anyone expected.

Perhaps the largest problems, however, stemmed from the fact that SSA historically had dealt with people whose claims to a check were a matter of right, not of need (even though many were poor). Under these circumstances, local SSA offices took a "middle-class" approach to recipients. They were trusted—"they are like us"—and extended a high level of professional service. The people under SSI were supposed to be poor; SSA had to determine whether they were poor and whether they remained so over time. The simplicity of the rights-based social security program was gone. This critique of the early period of SSI shows the difficulties of implementing a needs-based transfer payment program. Here, too, as with service delivery and community programs, we find it is not easy to do what was intended by the legislation.

Implementation Analysis and Assessment Efforts

Walter Williams' chapter in this section discusses techniques and strategies for analyzing and assessing implementation. The paper provides definitions and a conceptual framework to be used in considering implementation analysis and assessment issues, touches on potential future research that might be undertaken in various disciplines, and evaluates some of the available techniques such as demonstration projects and monitoring that could *now* be applied to the analysis and assessment of implementation. In good part, the message of the paper is intended for policy analysts, because they will often be the ones applying the techniques or seeing that techniques are properly applied, and because analytic offices are seen as a key link between policy and operations. As Allison suggests, in words quoted earlier, the failure of policy analysts to push beyond a decision to implementation has flawed greatly the effectiveness of their efforts. The chapter is intended to develop a framework for determining what policy analysts should do to treat implementation issues more effectively, and to present some ideas on how to move in the desired directions.

One final comment: There is a Kafkaesque aspect to the implementation area, or at least to the implementation of social programs. As will be so apparent from the various chapters that follow, implementation is a crucial area, yet people act as if it does not exist. Implementation seems to slip between the cracks in social program organizations and has received scant attention by researchers and policy analysts. Why this is so is not obvious to me. What is obvious is that continuing in this way will certainly inhibit efforts to improve social programs and policies. It is my hope that this volume will help in overcoming this inattention.

2

IMPLEMENTATION PROBLEMS
IN FEDERALLY FUNDED PROGRAMS*

Walter Williams

Implementation presents major, unavoidable problems for federally funded programs, particularly for complex social service delivery and community-oriented programs. When federal social agencies have major implementation responsibilities, complex new programs must traverse a long route in moving from the policy sphere to the operations sphere, where ultimately clients will be served. Along the route, responsibilities within the agency and among the agency, subnational governments, and operators are often difficult to determine, and there can be many slips from original policy intent to actual practice. The new federalism that has ushered in general and special revenue sharing seeks to ameliorate these problems by placing more responsibility in the hands of subnational governments. But here, too, implementation problems loom large, and the precise nature of shared responsibility among the federal agencies and others continues to be vague. Nor is there any way of avoiding these implementation problems. Even when a program is supported solely by

*Work on this chapter was supported by a grant from the National Science Foundation. The views expressed, however, are solely those of the author.

15

local funds, there still will be multiple layers within government, dysfunc-
tional bureaucratic behavior, and the nagging question of responsibility for
implementation. Surely, no one who has dealt with a local school system or
city hall will doubt that local control, too, has many (most?) of the hard
implementation problems.

This paper will focus mainly on the social agency where the many
bureaucratic problems in a multilayered structure vividly illustrate crucial
implementation issues. Examined first is the long policy and operations
process that exists when major responsibilities for programs reside in a
federal agency. The next section considers in detail the construct of the
policy and operations sphere and the problems of linkages between them.
Next are treated the general issues of specification and implementation,
which are the crucial links between policy and operations. At basic issue is
the now familiar question of responsibility—who is to specify, who is to
implement? The main concern in this section is with the top policymakers
and the policy analysts in a federal agency. Finally, consideration will be
given to some of the key issues raised by the new federalism, which has
made so apparent the long-existent problems of intergovernmental relations and the critical issue of how the responsibilities should be shared at
different levels of government.

THE LONG PROCESS FROM POLICY TO
OPERATIONS

A vast distance in layers of bureaucracy stands between the major
decisions made at the top of the policy sphere and ultimate service delivery
at the bottom of the operations sphere. Consider a new piece of legislation.
In its development, the president, his principal aides, key members of
federal agency staffs, congressmen, their aides and the representatives of
various public and private interest groups will engage in a highly complex
advocacy and bargaining process. Although the legislation will no doubt
contain a number of compromises and much hazy language resulting in part
from attempts to hold together shaky compromises, it will still specify
objectives that speak generally to anticipated positive outcomes. In the
manpower area, for example, a newly legislated training program will be
expected to yield new jobs or promotions to jobs that are better paying,
more stable, of higher status, more likely to lead to career advancement,
and/or more personally satisfying. Generally speaking, the legislation setting out federal social policies and programs will indicate some economic,
social and/or psychological benefits (outcomes) for specified recipients.
Usually the law is not too precise on objectives and is likely to be silent or

vague about the means of achieving the objectives. Those details are seen as somebody else's problem.

The legislation then moves to a federal agency charged with the responsibility for implementing it. Top agency personnel, often working with persons and groups previously involved in the development of the legislation, will hammer out some broad directives, but eventually matters will be turned over to lower-level headquarters staff who develop (and subsequently extend and reinterpret) detailed regulations and guidelines. It is through these documents that the word passes to the field, first going to federal regional office staffs that serve as intermediaries between the headquarters offices and those who administer and operate projects. In serving this function, these staffs provide additional interpretations. All along the way, many minor and perhaps some major choices are made that in sum can alter substantially a policy's original intent. Moreover, in the long process of movement from the policy sphere to the operations sphere, people may lose sight of who is responsible for implementing and carrying out policies.

These issues are well illustrated by the Comprehensive Employment and Training Act (CETA) of 1973 which has often been billed as the first major special revenue-sharing package. Prior to the enactment of CETA there existed a large number of categorical manpower programs established over several years under the Manpower Training and Development Act and the Economic Opportunity Act. These categorical programs were administered by the Department of Labor in a process reflected in Figure 1. The major agency responsibility for these programs rested with the Manpower Administration, the Department of Labor's biggest bureau. A large headquarters staff carried out a number of tasks, including writing regulations. Then, both regional offices and separate area office staffs (more layers) gave further interpretations to those who ultimately ran the programs. Frequently the regional staffs dealt with a prime sponsor (often a Community Action Agency), which might contract with other entities for service delivery.

These many programs were open to charges of too much categorization, too many rules and regulations, too little coordination, and too little involvement by elected officials—the prime sponsors often were not governmental entities. The Nixon administration proposed to replace most of the categorical programs with a single block grant to prime sponsors who were to be elected officials of general governments. The final legislation provided generally that states, localities, or some combination of jurisdictions representing at least 100,000 people were eligible to be prime sponsors.

The original Nixon proposal might be labeled "pure" special revenue

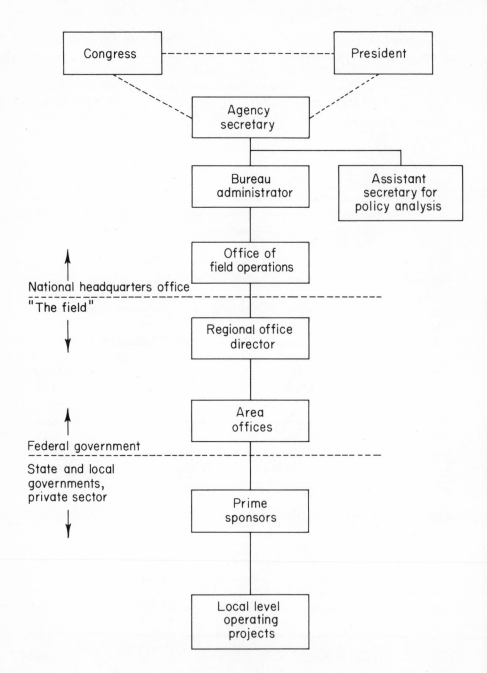

Figure 1. Illustrative policy and operations structure.

sharing. Much like general revenue sharing, pure special revenue sharing would set out some broad areas of activity (e.g., manpower or housing) and national priorities such as fair hiring standards to which subnational governments must adhere, but would leave the federal government with limited authority. The Department of Labor (or, as under general revenue sharing, the Office of Revenue Sharing in the Department of Treasury) would be mainly a fiscal auditor, with no substantive manpower policy responsibilities.

Congress did not accept fully the Nixon proposal but sought rather to require a federal presence and responsibility. The final CETA legislation gives the Secretary of Labor a number of responsibilities for seeing that prime sponsors act in a manner consonant with the CETA legislation. The legislation provides that the Manpower Administration must pass on the prime sponsor's plans and develop guidelines, and holds the Secretary of Labor responsible for ultimate performance (or, at least that is what many legislators thought, as will be discussed shortly). At the same time, there is an effort to decentralize power by requiring prime sponsors to be elected officials who have political clout. However, the prime sponsors may be relatively new to the manpower area and seldom will operate projects but rather will contract with local providers in the public and private sectors for the actual delivery of manpower services. Under CETA, even more than under the legislation it replaced, the Department of Labor deals with the prime sponsors, not directly with the local operators who ultimately provide manpower services.

CETA is supposed to be a compromise between pure special revenue sharing and block grants that decategorize programs yet retain a heavy federal involvement. Yet how much CETA has balanced power and responsibility between the federal government and subnational governments, or if it has simplified processes in the field, are issues that are far from settled. In the House of Representatives, during the floor discussion just before the final vote that passed the conference committee's version of CETA, Congressman Carl Perkins said:

> Finally, I have heard this bill described as "special revenue sharing" by some people downtown. Let me say flatly that it is not.

> This bill is a compromise between those who favored the so-called revenue sharing approach and those who believe in a strong Federal role and responsibility. . . . [The bill places] squarely with the Secretary of Labor the responsibility for seeing that the conditions and the special requirements of the law, as well as its general purposes, are in fact being carried out. The ultimate responsibility for success or failure rests with the Secretary and we will hold him strictly accountable.[1]

[1]*Congressional Record–House*, December 20, 1973, H11801.

However, in the next set of extended comments during that floor discussion, Congressman Lloyd Meeds observed:

> Some categorical programs will be eliminated. But when you multiply the number of new prime sponsors by the number of remaining programs, you have a multiplicity of bureaucratic growths. I believe that within 2 or 3 years of implementing this bill, the entire manpower program will be in such confusion that our problems now will seem like a Sunday School picnic. . . .

> The entire bill constitutes an abdication of responsibility by the Federal Government to try and shift national problems off on to local shoulders. . . .

> There are those who will contend this is not a revenue sharing bill. But it reads like a revenue sharing bill, it works like a revenue sharing bill, it comes from the same people who brought you general revenue sharing—the Nixon administration.[2]

The Department of Labor is now one and possibly two stages removed from the actual operation of manpower projects (local providers can subcontract with other local providers). Is the secretary really to be held responsible for whether or not the various manpower programs and projects yield positive outcomes to participants? Is it more reasonable to charge the Department of Labor with the mission of insuring that direct service providers have the capacity to help manpower project participants? Does the department itself have the capacity to carry out even this lesser set of responsibilities? What does Congress hold the Department of Labor responsible for? We should not think such questions are relevant only to special revenue sharing. Federal agencies generally do not provide social services directly in their categorical programs and often deal with an intermediary who receives funds and passes them to providers. For example, the Office of Education (OE) usually provides funds through State Education Agencies (SEAs) and sometimes through Local Education Agencies (LEAs). In a real sense the SEAs and the LEAs are OE's clients, just as general governments are the Department of Labor's clients, not schools or manpower projects, and certainly not participants whose improved outcomes are the principal theme in the rhetoric of legislation. It is hardly a seminal insight that HEW and other social agencies are some stages removed from the classroom or the training site or the welfare office where services are ultimately provided. But such obvious facts do raise basic questions about who is responsible for achieving the objectives of federal social policy and who really has the power in terms of reaching the desired outcomes.

THE POLICY AND OPERATIONS SPHERES

It is well to recognize that the notion of policy and operations spheres is a construct intended to aid us in investigating questions concerning

[2]*Ibid,* H11802.

responsibility and power that are basic to the study of implementation. A clear danger is that a user of a construct will forget that it is a simplification of reality and will try to stuff all of the untidiness of that reality into neat theoretical boxes. So we need to keep recalling that the policy and operations spheres are simply handles for getting at some very troublesome problems. At the same time, it will be a central argument of this paper that the failures to link these two spheres has tremendous implications for the appreciation of implementation problems.

Let us start the analysis by considering some key aspects of the policy and operations spheres. The primary actors in the policy sphere are those whose main functions include devising and establishing "major" policies. These people develop new agency or presidential initiatives, get legislation through Congress, etc. Those in the operations sphere mainly are concerned with operating programs, administering and servicing operations (e.g., regional offices), and implementation. The policy and operations spheres also might be conceptualized in geometric terms—perhaps as two ellipses; we might then ask the extent to which they overlap or the degree to which there are linkages between them. This provides a helpful visual image, but it may be more useful to think of a sociogram that shows who interacts with whom. In the policy sphere, some of the key actors are known—the president, agency heads, and congressmen—and the determination of the significant others with whom they interact would be one indication of who is a member of the sphere. This idea needs to be pursued before one other rather slippery conceptualization is suggested.

Important to understanding the policy sphere is the ongoing nature of the interactions among the individuals who occupy it. We should think not only in terms of key actors who come together to make one specific major decision but also of the circle of people who continue to interact and to be peers in the policy realm after decisions are made. If an agency head has close contacts on policy matters with a senator, an angry call from a mayor to that senator about a problem with the agency head's program—no matter how operational the issue may be—clearly becomes a concern in the policy sphere when the senator calls the agency head. The policy sphere also includes individuals who service the key actors actually responsible for policy. These could be members of an agency congressional liaison staff but well might include a regional director who sees as a main function interacting with key subnational government officials and members of the region's congressional delegation to field "hot" problems that could have repercussions in the policy sphere. So the policy sphere is not synonymous with the Washington, D.C. level, and the operations sphere is not synonymous with the field (see Figure 1: the dividing line is not the one between national headquarters office and the field). Lower-echelon headquarters' staff are—*or should be*—concerned with issues of implementation and operations. That is, they should look down toward operations, not up toward policymakers. At the same time, high-level officials in a region may be part of the policy sphere[3] or at least may interact with members of that sphere much more than with those in the operations sphere.

Thus far, the occupants in one or the other of the spheres have been distinguished by function (making policy or servicing those who make policy) and by interaction. Another means of separating spheres may be in terms of how people conceptualize their own position and role—what do they think is important, whom do they see themselves as serving, how are they trying to score points in the bureaucracy? A crucial question may be whether individuals, whatever their location, function, or interaction pattern, usually look up toward where policies are made or down toward the place of service delivery. One of the major problems of social programs appears to be that people look in the wrong direction and focus on the wrong issues, so this concept is a critical one. Let us pursue it by considering a seeming paradox in the policy sphere: top-level officials manifest all of the signs of real power and yet often seem powerless in the development and implementation of successful operating programs. Let us also consider how that paradox can be resolved.

The resolution starts with the realization that power often is seen in terms of policymakers' perceptions of what is important, what they want to affect. At the Washington level, the policy sphere customarily is viewed as all-important. For example, from the perception of a congressman, the passage of a bill is a power victory; he then moves to the problem of passing the next bill without really worrying about what happens as the first bill moves into the operations sphere.

Policy sphere decisions are also viewed as crucial because they determine the first big cut of resources. Agencies and organizations within agencies—with a good deal of justification—view the amount of money and personnel they will receive as a most critical aspect of their power status in the policy sphere. In the same way, members of Congress see as crucial the basic decisions concerning allocation formulas that determine in gross terms how much goes to their constituencies, the subnational governments. These concerns are hardly surprising. Even in the business sector, share of the market and company size are considered reasonable goals, though often obtained at the expense of profits. Since government has nothing analogous to profits, share and size stand as measures of organizational health far more than performance, especially in the field.

Another way of looking at the phenomenon of power is to recognize

---

[3]For example, mayors either individually or through organizations such as the National Conference of Mayors or National League of Cities may influence legislation concerning cities.

that power is a personal thing. An individual has power. The high status of an agency head carries with it a number of accouterments which demonstrate quite clearly that the person has command over people and other resources. Even though we can see power of this type, we still do not know whether it works to further the agency objectives of benefiting the clients served by its programs. Does power in the policy sphere imply a power—a degree of control—over outcomes? Clearly "power" in the last sentence has two meanings, yet it seldom carries the second connotation of "outcome impact." Rather, power is usually conceived of as control over resources and as the breadth of personal prerogatives of individuals exercising it. In this sense, major policymakers have real power (observable, amenable to a feature story in the *Washington Post* or cocktail party discussion in the right places); but it is power in their sphere of interaction. These men (and an occasional woman) of power almost never formulate their actions or think in depth about the agency's mission of trying to help people. This is hardly surprising, given the great distance in layers of bureaucracy between their spheres of interaction and the point at which people participate in programs. In short, high-level agency policymakers act in terms of policy-sphere power, not agency mission.

When a program moves toward the field, these policymakers tend to lose interest. More accurately, they are interested if events occur which push program issues back into the policy sphere. If something happens in the field that raises the ire of an important congressman, agency policymakers are immediately concerned. However, their concern is not with the often tedious activities that carry the program from level to level, and finally to an operating entity, which may have the greatest power to affect participants in the program. Yet it is in this mundane world that power in the sense of effect may be found. At some point far down in the process, away from the policy sphere, people can bungle things badly, and their mistakes probably will go relatively unnoticed by those concerned with "big" policy issues. Of course, the consequence is that things do not work out as policymakers planned. This is why power and powerlessness can exist together.

RESPONSIBILITY FOR IMPLEMENTATION IN A
FEDERAL SOCIAL AGENCY[4]

In a large social agency, the multitude of layers and actors involved in the process of implementing a major program is striking, perhaps even

[4]This section was previously published as a section (pp. 549–554) of my paper "Implementation Analysis and Assessment," *Policy Analysis,* Vol. 1, No. 3, pp. 531–566, and is included here with the permission of The Regents of the University of California.

appalling. With so many complex layers of power and authority, it is easy to lose the sense of direction that should steer people toward the basic goals of the organization. What could be more obvious and fundamental than the fact that decisions need to be implemented, and that inattention to implementation almost certainly will be fatal? Yet bureaucratic foliage so obscures the way that social agencies can lose sight of this. *Responsibility for implementation tends to slip between the cracks.* Almost everyone assumes that specification and implementation are somebody else's task. Higher-ups see implementation as being a lower-level responsibility; but the lower levels look to higher echelons for specification and guidance.

Another reason why implementation slips between the cracks is that social agencies rarely deal directly with the building of implementation capability or see it as a separate activity. The agency's program offices are concerned with operating existing programs, not with future large-scale implementation questions. There is no separate staff charged with *direct responsibility* for improving the capability to mount complex new programs. Instead, activities that may increase implementation capacity primarily *derive* from ongoing attempts to improve present operations.

No one denies the importance of implementation, yet everyone has reasons why their office cannot or should not be responsible for it. When implementation responsibilities finally are picked up, it is usually by a lower-echelon unit which cannot avoid them. Without an emphasis on implementation in general or a specific concern for capacity building, programs still get into the field, but through a process that is usually sloppy and poorly planned.

The Process of Implementation and Top Management

Weaknesses in the agency process of implementation appear to stem from basic causes that relate to the fundamental issue of management responsibility. Recent work by the Urban Institute's program evaluation studies group highlights this point. On the basis of its earlier findings that the results of federal evaluation in the social areas have had a most limited impact on policy,[5] the group asks: "Why have those in charge of programs and those who evaluate them not been able to join their efforts in a way that leads more frequently to significant improvements in program performance?"[6] The group argues that the failure of evaluations to have a material impact on policy derives from three prime causes:

[5]See: Joseph S. Wholey, et al., *Federal Evaluation Policy,* The Urban Institute, 1970; and Garth M. Buchanan and Joseph S. Wholey, "Federal Level Evaluation," *Evaluation,* Fall 1972, pp. 17–22.

[6]Pamela Horst, et al., "Program Management and the Federal Evaluator," *Public Administration Review,* July/August 1974, p. 300.

Lack of Definition: The problem addressed, the program intervention being made, the expected direct outcome of that intervention, or the expected impact on the overall society or on the problem addressed are not sufficiently well defined to be measurable.

Lack of Clear Logic: The logic of assumptions linking expenditure of resources, the implementation of a program intervention, the immediate outcome to be caused by that intervention, and the resulting impact are not specified or understood clearly enough to permit testing them.

Lack of Management: Those in charge of the program lack the motivation, understanding, ability, or authority to act on evaluation measurements and comparisons of *actual* intervention activity, *actual* outcomes, and *actual* impact.[7]

The first two causes flow from the basic failure to specify in terms that have clear operational meaning either the program objectives or the treatment and its relationship to the objectives. The Urban Institute group points to the vagueness of language in federal legislation and guidelines, where so much of what is said is cast in terms of "vaporous wishes" and almost meaningless phrases of guidance such as "improved local capacity" or "accessibility of services."[8] Just as with implementation, the process of evaluation runs into trouble because of failures to specify programs properly. The parallel is hardly surprising. Both activities require a degree of concreteness or they may become meaningless, futile exercises. Without a reasonable specification of objectives or of the treatment package, evaluators not surprisingly flounder, struggling to create hard objectives out of vaporous wishes, and implementers have developed massive regulations addressing mainly financial and administrative concerns.

Finding that clear specification is a necessary condition for sound outcome-oriented evaluation is hardly startling. What is less obvious is that the responsibility for determining definitions and the logic of treatment is not the responsibility of evaluators, but of program management. The fundamental point, of course, is not that evaluators should be absolved of all blame for the shoddy work of the past. Rather it is that evaluators can do little if program management either does not want evaluation or is not willing to exercise its responsibilities in developing specifications. Precisely the same thing is true for implementers. The attitude of management is the first and by far the most important factor in improving implementation. *Wanting better implementation will go a long way toward achieving it.* But "wanting it" does not mean that top-level management can mouth platitudes about the need for good implementation. Rhetoric is not enough. Management must make the hard choices required to institutionalize implementation as a critical part of programmatic activity.

[7]*Ibid.,* p. 301.

[8]I note only a few terms; the reader may have other favorites. For additional Urban Institute choices, see *ibid.,* p. 303.

Earlier experience with the Planning, Programming, Budgeting (PPB) System well illustrates the management issues involved. Separate surveys by the General Accounting Office and the Bureau of the Budget (now the Office of Management and Budget) were conducted 3 years after the start of the 1965 effort to implement PPB throughout the federal government. Using the criterion of policy analysis having become an important part of agency decisionmaking, the surveys found that only three of sixteen domestic agencies had implemented PPB successfully. In a summary article based on the findings of the two surveys, Marvin and Rouse observed: "The attitude of the agency head has been the single most important factor in the development of a PPB system and its integration with the agency decisionmaking system."[9] Agency heads who had relatively sound analysis accorded their central analytic offices (1) high status (generally assistant secretary rank or the equivalent), (2) direct responsibility and authority for carrying out analysis, and (3) sufficient personnel positions, in terms of both numbers and high civil service grades, to allow for the development of a viable analytic staff. The agency head was willing to make the basic changes in structure and status needed to get good analysis.

The changes needed for improved implementation may be even more difficult to make than those for policy analysis because the implementation process moves so widely and deeply in an organization. However, if management has a hard task, it also has the power to start in the right direction. If it is willing to make basic structural changes, the biggest hurdle will have been passed. To say this does not deny that techniques are important or that developing technical capability in the implementation area is also a critical need. Rather, the point is that the management commitment is more important. Not only that, but management's unwillingness to face up to the problems of implementation will so hinder implementation efforts that technical improvements probably will have little or no effect. Finally, techniques are available for making real improvements in implementation, but again, only in the presence of a strong commitment on the part of management. In the chapter "Implementation Analysis and Assessment" presented later, we will look in some detail at implementation techniques that should be used by policy analysts in their information search and synthesis. These techniques are important, yet it must be recognized that a change in management's perception, not a change in techniques, is the big first step.

[9]Keith E. Marvin and Andrew M. Rouse, "The Status of PPB in Federal Agencies: A Comparative Perspective," U.S. Congress, Joint Economic Committee, *The Analysis and Evaluation of Public Expenditures: PPB System,* vol. 3, Government Printing Office (1969), p. 808.

Policy Analysts and Implementation

An analytic office with responsibility for implementation analysis and assessment could be a key link between policy and operations.[10] A choice by top management to emphasize implementation is itself a decision that requires implementation. Someone in the agency must press for including implementation issues in the policy process and for keeping such concerns prominent as policy moves down. A strong analytic office could be pivotal in the process. If so, many changes are needed.

In the past, the relatively good social agency analytic offices have both improved the basis of decisionmaking and had a significant influence on agency decisions. However, the influence has generally been on people at the top of the Washington policy structure—the agency head and the staffs of the Office of Management and Budget (OMB) or the White House. The analyst's modus operandi has been to produce a document, a policy analysis report, and to see that it moves up through the policy sphere. In this milieu, what is valued are good ideas and sound reasoning *without* a great deal of detail. Indeed, those at the top of the policy sphere do not have time for programmatic detail, and they might not be comfortable with it even if they did. However, approval by the agency head and OMB does not convert magically a document's decisions into effective action. Dollars and slot levels, of course, impel action, but action does not necessarily flow from a document's words, however much lauded by the agency head and OMB. Implementation stands in the way. This simple truth has been very hard for analysts to comprehend.

To see how far removed policy analysts have been from implementation—both the agency's process itself and their own problems of getting action on approved decisions—let us speculate about some of the issues they would need to face in order to move toward a meaningful concern with implementation problems. It seems fair to generalize that analytic staffs in the past have been naive about the complexity of converting fairly abstract social policy concepts into terms useful for field operations. Policy analysis can include a step in which a decision document's relatively brief recommendations (e.g., more remedial education) are converted into detailed, operational-like instructions. However, this detail is not a necessary condition for the high-level decisionmaking phase, so the step is best viewed as a separate activity beyond decisionmaking.

Reasonable specification is only one of the problems that an analytic office must face if it is to have a marked effect on implementation. The

[10]The focus here is mainly on bureaucratic and political issues. In the chapter just mentioned above, more technical issues concerning the policy analyst and implementation will be addressed.

analyst also may need to address such questions as: How capable is the national office of developing guidelines and regulations for operating units and assisting the regional or local offices in carrying out these instructions? How capable are regional staffs of aiding in the implementation of a new policy? Is there clear responsibility for transmitting implementation information, and are there established lines of communication for such transmission? Basically, these are questions about the linkages between the policy and operations spheres and within the latter that require an analysis of organizational capability and responsibility.

What about the analyst's ties to the implementation process? Certainly a senior analyst needs to be concerned with the analytic office's specific involvement in the process of preparing guidelines by headquarters' staff. It is through the guidelines, not through the formal policy analysis report, that the field staff finds out about decisions. But what role should the analyst take? One possibility is that the analyst should be responsible for judging whether what has been written in the guidelines is reasonable in terms of what was decided earlier. Such a determination is a straightforward matter, it would seem, until one confronts the reality of a large federal agency. Agency guidelines and regulations are often set out in massive documents or sets of documents prepared by many authors. A new program—especially if it has an established date set by law—may be in the field long before the final guidelines and regulations are issued. Does it really make sense to give an analyst the responsibility for passing judgment on these documents? If so, what is to be the process for changing those documents with poor specifications, and who is to be responsible for getting the new words translated into action?

It may seem reasonable to argue that the analysis of implementation capability should be carried out by an independent office that (1) is separate from both the program bureaus *and* the senior policy analyst and (2) reports directly to the agency head. *Yet the assessment of implementation capability seems to be so integral to any policy analysis underlying a decision that removing the responsibility from the analyst would create a severe problem.* In making a set of programmatic recommendations, analysts ought to answer for their implications, including the prospects for success of the implementation strategy. It seems almost frivolous to specify a set of complex programmatic actions without also considering in some detail the requirements for the implementation of those actions.[11]

---

[11]As mentioned earlier, the specifics of implementation analysis and assessment and the development of an implementation strategy by an analytic office will be discussed in a subsequent paper.

THE IMPLICATIONS OF THE NEW FEDERALISM
FOR IMPLEMENTATION

The federal programs started in the 1960s, generally speaking, specified rather narrow funding areas, for example, a particular manpower training approach for disadvantaged youth. The image of these "categorical" programs is of massive, tightly drawn federal regulations and much federal involvement stretching down to the local level of operations. In many cases, this imagery is pure myth. Some of the categorical programs such as the Community Action Program and Title I of the Elementary and Secondary Education Act were precursors of the new federalism in a rather pure form with most limited federal involvement. However, it is true that the Great Society period that preceded the new federalism did spawn too many programs. Each had slightly different rules; *even if none were individually oppressive*, in total they came to present a maze of rules and regulations that summed up to too much centralized federal direction or misdirection.

General revenue sharing and special revenue sharing were intended to usher in a new era. The key elements of decategorization (broad block grants) and decentralization aimed at less federal control and more responsibility at the subnational government level.[12] Although the new federalism may reduce categories and shift responsibilities, it would be a grave mistake to assume that the emerging "postcategorical" programs will escape the problems of the past that made implementation and execution so difficult in categorical programs. Names may have changed but the bureaucratic/political setting and the organizations and the people involved have not. As Murphy observed after discussing the monumental problems with the Elementary and Secondary Education Act enacted at the height of the period of strong federal intervention:

The nature of the bureaucratic problem in implementing governmental programs has been obscured. Blame has been placed on the inefficiencies of the federal aid delivery system, when in fact major faults associated with categorical aid appear to be general features of public bureaucracies. As long as the investigation of the problem of governmental paralysis is reduced to a search for scapegoats, at the expense of attempting to understand organizational behavior, we can expect only limited improvement in the way educational bureaucracies work.[13]

[12]This section will discuss the concept of the new federalism, taking it at face value as a real effort to change the locus of responsibility. I will not explore the extent to which the new federalism as practiced in the Nixon administration was a disguised attempt to cut back certain social programs or an effort of the federal government to flee from responsibilities.

[13]Jerome T. Murphy, "Title V of ESEA: The Impact of Discretionary Funds on State Education Bureaucracies," in this volume, p. 100.

Responsibility as the Core Issue

The new federalism has brought to the surface a number of complex relational issues in federally funded programs between federal, state, and local governments, and ultimately between these governments and their citizens—issues finally leading back to the fundamental questions of federal responsibility and power versus that of states and localities. For our purposes, it is not necessary to make recommendations concerning the resolution of these basic issues, but rather to consider how different determinations or different perceptions of responsibility and the related execution of power affect policy as it moves down the policy and operations spheres.

In approaching the basic dilemma of how responsibility should be shared among government and citizens, it is helpful to consider three possible models of federally funded social service delivery and community-oriented programs. The first model, full federal control, almost always has been rejected because, with only a few exceptions, the federal government simply does not serve as the final deliverer of complex services such as education or manpower training (as opposed to straight transfer payments). The second *pure* model would provide federal funds to general governments headed by elected officials *without federal specification* of either (1) the particular priorities and objectives beyond designating the broad special revenue sharing area or (2) the process procedures to be employed in arriving at priorities and objectives (e.g., mandating citizen participation). That is, there would be a political determination of the acceptability of priorities and outcomes at state and local levels rather than by politicians and their appointees at the federal level or by federal bureaucrats.[14]

The original general revenue sharing legislation basically followed this model in that it had a few bland spending priorities so general that almost anything could qualify, and some requirements about process and nondiscrimination without any real teeth in them. However, even the general revenue sharing legislation envisioned activities (e.g., citizen involvement in local planning) beyond those of the regular political elective process. Furthermore, as general revenue sharing is being considered for renewal in Congress, questions are being raised concerning whether or not state and local governments either provided sufficient funds for particular services (mainly social ones) or complied with such requirements as nondiscrimination or citizen involvement in the decision process.[15] It is in-

[14]Providing funds directly to citizens or nonprofit organizations without strings is a theoretical pure alternative but so unlikely now as not to merit discussion.

[15]See, for example, Patricia W. Blair, "General Revenue Sharing in American Cities: First Impressions," National Clearing House on Revenue Sharing, December 1974.

teresting to observe that the disquiet is not only with noncompliance but also with choices that are legal, but do not accord with national preferences. The key point is not that general revenue sharing necessarily has failed, but that the pure model of local checks through the political process will be hard to maintain for very long in federally funded programs.

It seems much more likely that federally funded programs will be administered under a third alternative, the "mixed" model, in which the federal government will be involved in varying degrees in the specification of priorities and objectives, the determination of the nature of the process through which decisions are made at the local and state levels, and/or the monitoring and evaluation of projects and programs. This model covers a lot of ground. We might think of a continuum stretching from the pure model of complete federal control to that of complete local autonomy with the mixed model lying in between. In terms of preferences over time, the pendulum will swing between the two end points. For example, since the late 1960s it has been moving toward the local autonomy end. But the question remains as to the degree of real movement—in the present setting, will subnational governments gain markedly more responsibility and power? In good part the answer will depend on the implementation process.

The mixed model presents a complex set of interrelationships among governments and among governments and their citizens for which there are unlikely to be clear answers or simple approaches because of the multiplicity of actors and activities in the process. Moreover, the situation is confounded by the distrust going both ways between federal and subnational governments. Much of the impetus for the Great Society programs, especially the Economic Opportunity Act, was the belief that recalcitrant subnational governments would block programs for the disadvantaged. Even though Congress has moved far from these programs, it remains reluctant to trust subnational government in the setting of priorities and objectives and the execution of programs. Nor is this necessarily unwarranted since there is strong past evidence indicating that state and local governments have not been trustworthy in some areas such as education. However, neither have the federal bureaucrats. Part of the rationale for trying to reduce the federal role in providing services is a distrust of the federal bureaucracy and its propensity to create more and more rules.

The problem is further compounded by the fact that it is hard to tell how much the distrust arises from the belief that people and/or organizations will act badly *purposely* and how much from a recognition of various technical and organizational weaknesses. Even if we trust state and local governments to try to do the right thing, we may still agree with the statement by Ginsberg and Solow: "The sorry fact is that most state and local governments—with some notable exceptions—are poorly structured and poorly staffed to carry out new and innovative tasks. They have a hard time even meeting their routine commitments.''[16] Others would debate the extent to which state and local governments are capable of running programs, but I think it is fair to say that many do feel that these governments are sadly deficient in their capabilities. So, too, is the federal government. A key point that must be recognized if we are to make any progress in the future is that *neither the Federal nor the local governments know very much.*

New Federalism and the Old Constraints

Past weaknesses and problems of personnel, organizations, and techniques that marked the categorical period of federal funding will continue to plague the so-called postcategorical programs. This is not to say that the new federalism is meaningless—simply old wine in new bottles. There can be quite significant changes in the distribution of responsibility and power among governments and among governments and citizens. A new approach could reduce drastically the role of the federal government. However, and this is a key point, legislative language alone is unlikely to be enough. If a strong federal statement about local autonomy leaves in place the federal bureaucracy at both the headquarters and the regional office levels, the end result may be far different from what Congress and top executive branch policymakers desire.

The Model Cities program is a good case in point. It started as a program of broad block grants to urban governments. Here was the fundamental new federalism concept of the elected official as the responsible decisionmaker. But the Department of Housing and Urban Development (HUD) never could bring itself to let the local people have much autonomy. As Marshall Kaplan observed in commenting on Model Cities just prior to the passage of the Housing and Community Development Act:

> Application-review processes, some seven years after Model Cities, continue to seem to reflect at times the invention of visitors from outer space rather than the product of earthlings desiring to identify reasonable local behavior, capacity, and commitment in advance of releasing federal beneficence. To put it bluntly, Model City-initiated or -supported efforts at simplification and consolidation were by and large unsuccessful. They came up against traditional agency and program manager-resistance to change, resistance premised at times on apocryphal visions of a loss of program control and at times, on the legitimacy of competing interest groups' claim on the federal dollar. . . .

[16]Eli Ginsberg, and Robert M. Solow, "Some Lessons of the 1960's," *The Public Interest,* Winter 1974, p. 217. Another good paper on state and local capability is Leigh E. Grosenick, "Institutional Change to Improve State and Local Competencies," in Leigh Grosenick (editor), *The Administration of the New Federalism: Objectives and Issues,* American Society for Public Administration, September 1973, pp. 91–110.

In effect, even in such an ostensibly home-rule-oriented program as Model Cities, the requirement that the Secretary approve local plans was converted initially into weighty, often obtuse, guidelines; irrelevant administrative prescriptions concerning local planning processes (understandable only to Ph.D. students and clearly out of sorts with the planning state of the arts); and, often, extended, torturous handbooks.[17]

Let us dwell briefly upon the role of these bureaucrats. As policy moves down toward operations, the actions of a number of lower- and middle-echelon bureaucrats both in headquarters and in the regions become critical. It is not necessary to conjure either an evil or a slothful bureaucrat to recognize that these people can cause trouble in the shift from an old to a new system. Organizations and bureaucrats have limited repertoires.[18] They tend to do things as they did before and to operate by earlier established practices even when the rules suggest new practices. Take the two new special revenue sharing acts as examples. Under the previous legislation that mandated various categorical programs, detailed regulations poured forth, and the writers and the interpreters tended to build up the importance of guideline writing and interpretation. We can think either of the typical bureaucrat who goes strictly by the book— chapter, verse, and line; or we simply might recognize that everyone tries to make his job seem important. Although special revenue sharing implies far less in the way of detailed guidelines and interpretations from above, the regulation writers and the interpreters generally stay in similar jobs, no doubt with some revision in their job descriptions. And one would guess many of them keep doing very much what they did before because, after all, developing detailed regulations and interpretations is what they have learned to do reasonably well in the past.

Local officials also can contribute to federal control. These officials may be quite leery of autonomy, in part because they do not know very much about programs and in part because they know that in the past those above attached much importance to rules and regulations. So even under special revenue sharing some local officials, just to be safe, will ask for clarification of any action that may seem out of the ordinary. Although that request comes from only one of the ten federal regions, the regulation writers may send the interpretation to all ten of them. In the course of this process, administrative rulings may rebuild the kind of categorical structure that ostensibly had been undone by the legislation.

After a major change in responsibility in the mixed model, there may be movement back toward the old equilibrium relationship point (in special

---

[17]Marshall Kaplan, "Model Cities and the New Inventory," in Joseph D. Sneed and Steven A. Waldhorn (editors), *Restructuring the Federal System,* Crane, Russak, 1975, pp. 76, 81.

[18]See Graham T. Allison, *Essence of Decision,* Little, Brown, 1971, p. 83.

revenue sharing, toward more federal rules and control) as bureaucrats interact in terms of a past history and succumb to the well-recognized bureaucratic tendencies to make rules. *Unfortunately, with the new federalism we can be left with the worst of both worlds: federal officials regain some control over details without reasserting responsibility; local people are thus confused about where responsibility really resides and fail to exert initiative and control.*

This tendency to draw strict rules and regulations is a widespread sickness of the bureaucracy. The ever-perceptive Meg Greenfield has put the case well:

> When I try to imagine how HEW or any other government agency would deal with Solomon's most familiar administrative challenge, I come up with two different conclusions that have one thing in common. Either they would invoke federal regulation CR (03X-14) and actually cut the baby in half, or his contending mothers, under regulation DL-9B (15), would still be filing documents before an interagency proceeding when he had reached the age of 43. But either way, the government officials in question would have avoided judgment, responsibility, the burden of using their wits and a particular kind of trouble. By formulating endless rules, we put the problem on "automatic," and there are very few officials in this town who are willing to take the heat that goes with trying to make commonsense rulings—instead of just more rules.

> And why do the rest of us go along? Probably because we have an abiding fear of discretionary government and a misplaced belief in the capacity of written regulations to ensure fairness and to prevent our officeholders from treating us in capricious or tyrannical ways. Now the regulations themselves have become tyrannical, but this comes at a moment when government officials are feeling anything but audacious and when the public is awash in suspicions concerning both their competence and good faith.[19]

Alas, even if we eliminate middle- and lower-level federal bureaucrats by the score, state and local bureaucracies persist in doing things as they were done before or in creating new rules—Greenfield's "law" does not pertain *only* to the federal bureaucracy.

Although the picture painted is grim, it does not mean that major changes will be impossible, but they will come about only if we are realistic about the continuation of old constraints and old ways after the euphoria of new legislation and new directions. Those who are really concerned about policies' being effective will have to worry about the numerous details that stretch from regulations to results. It will be necessary to search for new techniques of doing things and for realistic implementation strategies that take into account the various constraints imposed by personnel and organizations.

[19]Meg Greenfield, "Can Mr. Ford Break the Rules?" *Washington Post,* August 30, 1975.

SOME FUTURE DIRECTIONS FOR FEDERAL
FUNDING POLICY

Determining Responsibilities and Functions

The first major hurdle in resolving some of the problems of federally funded programs is a realistic determination by policymakers of the division of responsibilities and functions among governments and citizens. We should be clear that defining responsibilities and functions in a mixed model in which there is both distrust and deficient capabilities will be difficult and certainly will leave overlapping gray areas of conflict between governments. Yet a more clear determination of responsibilities and functions is a crucial first step, without which little real progress can be expected.

In trying to get at the issues involved, let us pose the questions of who knows what best and who can do what best in complex social programs. A distinction needs to be made between generalized and localized knowledge. The former is based on broad sets of experiences and information that address national needs in specific policy areas, the programs available including the intent and meaning of the legislation and regulations relevant to them, the various treatment elements that might be used in programs, the bureaucratic and political variables that generally impinge on the development and operation of programs in the field, and the various methods available for analysis and assessment of programs. Localized knowledge includes programmatic needs in a specific community, the past experience in that community in terms of the application of various techniques, and the peculiarities of the local political and bureaucratic structure in which programs operate. Generalized knowledge increases from a breadth of experiences. For example, information gathered from a number of communities may indicate that an approach which works reasonably well under one set of conditions will not work under others, or that a problem in a specific community has occurred in other places and there are some feasible approaches to it. Localized knowledge, on the other hand, increases from a depth of investigation concerning the specifics of one locality. An approach may make sense in some communities, but a particular locality may not be able to use it until it increases capability or overcomes certain bureaucratic blockages.

Cast in these simple and straightforward terms, the division of labor between federal and local governments seems clearcut. The R&D and dissemination functions—the latter including information both on new R&D results and techniques already in use in operational programs—would be federal activities. So would the provision of technical assistance about the process and substance of programs based on a summation of national experience and information. Local people would develop information to facilitate adjusting general findings to meet the specific needs of their situations.

In the discussion thus far, we might assume that federal advice based on generalized knowledge would be there to be used or ignored depending upon the judgment of the local officials. The world, however, is not so simple—other functions such as checking (monitoring), approval, and evaluation are difficult to parcel out. National legislation or the regulations and guidelines written to interpret it will specify spending priorities, objectives, or restrictions (e.g., the Housing and Community Development Act bars expenditures that increase concentrations of minority housing). Who is to determine whether or not local activities are in compliance, or assess whether or not objectives are reached? Manpower and housing and community development special revenue sharing packages require that the federal government approve local plans. Is this an appropriate federal function? Recall Kaplan's warning from Model Cities that plan approval is the federal handle on reestablishing control. But should there be no scrutiny of local plans? Can the federal government trust local administrators?

So we enter vast gray areas that complicate not only the approval, checking, and evaluation functions, but also advisory activities. Consider a simple example that illustrates these problems. Suppose a federal monitoring team looks at a local manpower project and finds (1) that the project is out of compliance in some areas and (2) that it is engaged in practices that are not circumscribed but that the monitoring team believes should be improved. In the former case, a monitoring team statement indicating how the project could be brought into compliance would appear to be a directive to undertake or desist from certain activities or suffer the consequences at the time of refunding (or even lose current funds). The second set of recommendations would seem to be advice offered on a take-it-or-leave-it basis. But it is not clear that a monitoring team can offer such advice without that advice being seen as a directive to act or suffer the consequences. If there is a past history of strong federal intervention under categorical programs, it well may be that local people simply will not believe in a hands-off policy even when contained explicitly in new legislation.

A clear delineation of responsibilities and functions is a basic requirement. In some areas there will be clear comparative advantages, so the sorting out may be easy. Usually, it will not be. Hard decisions will be required about who does what, decisions that may mean bruised feelings and lost jobs, and that certainly will leave residual areas of overlap. But without a realistic determination of responsibilities and functions, the muddle we are in seems certain to continue.

Improving the Implementation Process

The whole process of implementation including the linkages between the policy and operations spheres must be improved. Power is the central issue. The anomaly of power and powerlessness in the policy sphere has already been discussed. The point to emphasize now is that those in the policy sphere granted the accouterments of power bear some responsibilities for the effectiveness of social service programs; yet there is no real loss of power or status if programs are ineffective. Neither high status nor incentives specifically reward making programs more effective. For example, those who implement, those who bear responsibilities in the federal bureaucracy for getting programs into the field, have relatively low status; the incentives in the system seem to reward looking up toward policy and policymakers rather than down toward operations and recipients. Over time, it may be necessary to restructure both pay and status in the policy and operations spheres, so those who concern themselves with linkage issues or produce better programs and projects receive greater benefits.

Then, there is the question of power redistribution. A relatively pure model of local determination of the effectiveness of social programs might be much more palatable *if* program participants or their representatives have a strong voice in the judgments rendered. One of the major criticisms of revenue sharing is that decentralization to local officials allows a local majority to impede programs for disadvantaged groups. Under such circumstances there may need to be a one-time federal effort to redistribute power toward these groups. Both Levine in his discussion of the Community Action Program and King in an account of his personal experiences in one city suggest how the power redistribution might work in practice.[20] With a real local power redistribution, one might be tempted to join King in opting "against highly specialized professional bureaucrats [to determine or assess objectives] and in favor of political accountability exercised by citizens and elected officials."[21] We professionals tend to place far too much faith in standards set by fellow "experts" and to be suspicious of the political process, a judgment that may not stand up very well if a careful look is given to past results.

[20]See Robert A. Levine, *Public Planning,* Basic Books, 1972, pp. 95–102, and James R. King, "The Big OEO-MC-Annual Arrangement–Planned Variation-IGA-PNRS-Allied Services-MRS-BCA-Revenue-Sharing Power Trip," in Sneed and Waldhorn (eds.), *Restructuring the Federal System,* pp. 122–128.

[21]*Ibid.,* p. 121.

Even if we downgrade professional expertise—especially that of distant federal bureaucrats—we should not swing the other way to deify local political control. Shifting to a pure local autonomy model would still leave us with most of the current implementation problems. This is not to deny that fixing responsibilities and eliminating bureaucratic layers could have a beneficial impact. However, the local residents will not know how suddenly to solve programmatic problems that have heretofore baffled us. It will still be necessary to seek better techniques. And bureaucratic blockages will continue at any level of government. Further, specification and implementation will still be necessary. The new federalism may shift the location of implementation problems, it may even reduce them somewhat; but anyone who fears that we "implementation specialists" will be out of business should be reassured.

A Broader Perspective

There remain some broader questions. In social service delivery and community-oriented programs, it is quite likely that both responsibility and power will move down toward subnational governments. Such a decrease in federal power in some cases may increase program effectiveness. However, it is vital that special revenue sharing, or in a broader sense the new federalism, not become a federal flight from power and responsibilities. The goal should be a proper balancing of power in government, not a federal retreat from legitimate responsibilities. What is sought is the restriction of federal intervention where it seems deleterious (and we seem to be finding more and more cases where it is), not the dumping of problems on local government and walking away.

I certainly do not feel the recent evidence proves a general federal incapacity for involvement in complex social programs, at least compared to the capacity of subnational governments. The mixed model is a frustrating one that lacks the comforts of claiming absolutely that either the federal or the local government always knows best. Instead, there is a need to blend strengths and offset weaknesses. However frustrating, this seems to be what we must do.

Nor does the past evidence indicate that there should be a withering away of federal responsibilities for social problems. Mr. Nixon's new federalism appeared at times to be a cover for making severe cuts in social programs for the disadvantaged.[22] To question this is not to imply no reasonable person can come to the conclusion that there should be a shift in

[22]It is not fruitful to assess the motives of the Nixon administration, but it seems only fair to the reader to record my longstanding distaste for Mr. Nixon and my view that the new federalism of the Nixon administration was often less a political philosophy than a subterfuge

federal spending priorities including an absolute or relative decline in total social program expenditures or in certain types of social programs. However, such issues do need to be addressed explicitly. Warren's remarks on revenue sharing are worth heeding:

> Finally, although the issues that federal special revenue sharing addresses are important and understanding and choosing wisely among the many possible trade-offs involved in these issues are important, one cannot escape the disquieting notion that special revenue sharing constitutes a passing of the coordination buck to the localities, after unsuccessful attempts to deal with it in Washington. More importantly, preoccupation with special revenue sharing to localities has the side effect of distracting us from measures which in my opinion can be taken only at the federal level, measures without which much of the talk of funding this or that program at the local level assumes the proportions of Tweedledee versus Tweedledum. Questions of income distribution, income maintenance, power distribution, national economic policy and employment levels, and provision of work opportunities for all those ready and willing to work are questions which cannot be dealt with adequately at the local level. They call for strong federal policies and programs, not the abdication of the federal government from responsibility for social problems.

> Although community-level phenomena are important, I am convinced that many of the basic problems that confront the American people are products not so much of local community forces as they are of the national institutional structure. To expect that they will be solved community by community is to ignore their roots in national institutions which can be gotten at only at the level of national policies and programs. It would be unfair to ask special revenue sharing, or any other bundle of components, to accomplish tasks that can only be accomplished at the national level, at which level we refuse to face them.[23]

What many of us dealing with social problems over the years have learned is that the questions concerning the level of economic activity and the distribution of resources are crucial to a viable social policy. A strong economy (low unemployment, reasonable inflation), better transfer payment programs that redistribute resources, and a renewed effort to reduce discrimination seem to me to be necessary if social service delivery and community-oriented programs are to make much headway. In terms of implementation, this statement simply reminds us that sound implementation will not substitute either for more funds or for a more just distribution of resources. Carrying this notion one step further, implementation may be (and I think it is) the single most important blockage to improving the *quality* of social programs and projects. Quantity, however, also is impor-

---

for cutting back on social commitments. Given the circumstances of Mr. Nixon's fall, it hardly seems total paranoia to suspect that some of the malaise of the late 1960s and early 1970s, including the seeming inability of the federal government to do much of anything, was the result of the Nixon years and may not be a full indication of lasting federal incapacity.

[23]Roland L. Warren, "Competing Objectives in Special Revenue Sharing" in Sneed and Waldhorn (eds.), *Restructuring the Federal System*, pp. 58–59.

tant. A few well-implemented manpower programs will not be enough. Neither are many well-implemented manpower programs likely to thrive in stagnant economy. The point, of course, is not to downplay the importance of implementation but rather to remind ourselves as we become immersed in these issues that they are only one part of social policy.

II

EDUCATION PROGRAMS

3

INCENTIVES FOR INNOVATION
IN THE PUBLIC SCHOOLS*

John Pincus[1]

INTRODUCTION: THE INSTITUTIONAL SETTING

This chapter sets out some propositions about the structure and incentive systems of public schools as they relate (1) to the *adoption* of innovations and (2) to their *implementation* in the schools. These propositions may have certain systematic implications for educational research and development (R&D) policy as well as for such broader questions as how to implement planned change in bureaucracies. The propositions are not based on careful testing of hypotheses, but on a blend of evidence and speculation, and are aimed at influencing how we might think about educa-

*Pincus, John, "Incentives for Innovation in the Public Schools," *Review of Educational Research*, Volume 44, 1974, pp. 113–114. Copyright 1974, American Educational Research Association, Washington, D.C., reprinted with their permission.

[1]I have benefited in writing this paper from discussions with George R. Hall. Several people, including David K. Cohen, T. K. Glennan, Jr., Gordon Hoke, Herbert Kiesling, Robert Klitgaard, Milbrey McLaughlin, David Mundel, and Daniel Weiler offered useful suggestions and comments on an earlier draft. A referee for the *Review of Educational Research* pointed out flaws in the original manuscript. None of these persons bears responsibility for any shortcomings herein.

tional R&D policy. Furthermore, implicit herein is the notion that society will be better off if schools could offer more diverse alternatives in respect to both organization of schools and curriculum. It also implies that such changes are possible—that is, that society is neither so rigid nor so well satisfied with its schools as to veto increased diversity. The second section discusses incentives to adopt innovation. Section three discusses the problems of implementation. The fourth section suggests some implications for R&D policy. The general thesis of this paper is that the *market structure* of the public school "industry" has a major effect on schools' decisions to adopt innovations, and the *bureaucratic structure and incentives* of schools shape in specific ways the transition from adopting innovations to implementing them. This distinction is somewhat artificial. The ultimate objective should be a testable theory which integrates the incentive effects of both market structure and bureaucratic structure. This paper is therefore a halfway house toward that goal, and not a fully specified model of how school systems behave in response to opportunities for change.

Public elementary and secondary school systems in the United States are, like many governmental functions, a form of public utility. The public schools are given by state government action a virtual local monopoly of schooling services. The monopoly is not complete because there are four alternatives open to parents who do not choose to send their children to the local public schools: (1) private schools; (2) another public school in the district; (3) another public school in another district; (4) religious schools. The first and third options, private schools and moving to a "better" school district, are open primarily to the wealthy or to those who are both upwardly mobile and who also attach primary importance to schools as a determinant of residential location. The second option, another school in the same district, is generally limited by such factors as transportation constraints, school capacity limits, school district regulations limiting transfer, and the relative homogeneousness of neighboring schools. The fourth option, parochial schools, is open primarily to Catholics, and is the most important single alternative to public schools. However, with the progressive reduction in numbers of Catholic parish schools in recent years, most Catholics' alternatives also are being narrowed, a trend which could be reversed only by significant and unlikely changes in church policies toward racial integration or by government subsidy.

For the great majority of clients, the public schools are a *de facto* local monopoly, which is different from many other local public utilities in several respects. First, unlike most telephone, gas, and electric service, and so on, the quality of school service can vary substantially within a district, which often creates serious perceived issues of equity along income, race, and neighborhood lines.

Second, in contradistinction to many other local public utilities, the aims of schooling are unclear, or at least there is no consensus about what priority should be given to the various aims.

Third, the technology of schooling is unclear, unlike that of most public utilities. In economists' language, we don't know what the educational production function is, or even if there is one, except perhaps in some nonoperational sense.[2] More generally, we are often unsure whether one method of providing school services is consistently better in terms of output effects, however defined, than any other method.

Fourth, school districts may have very little incentive to be economically "competitive"—to increase their registration at the expense of other districts. The perceived financial gain or loss from interdistrict shifts in public school registration depends on several factors, including the ratio of state and federal aid to local taxes, effects on the local tax base, possiblities of adding or dropping staff or facilities, socioeconomic characteristics of shifting students, and so on.

Fifth, although the schools are educational institutions, they apparently provide only a small part of the student's educational resources. Other influences—heredity, family and peer-group environment, communications media, and so on—appear to be the prime determinants of how much people learn, how they learn, and how they respond to contacts with other people and social institutions. This situation makes it very difficult to gauge the effects of schooling on people's lives and learning.

The public schools, of course, do share a number of common characteristics with other nonmarket-oriented public utilities. They are self-perpetuating bureaucracies, thanks to tax-supported status, certification practices for teachers and administrators, and the custom of promotion from within. In these respects, the schools resemble many civil service agencies, notably public health, welfare, and criminal justice systems. They also share with these systems a characteristic which profoundly affects their institutional response to innovation: They cannot select their clients, and the client must, as a practical matter, accept the service, whether or not he is satisfied with its quality (Carlson, 1965b).

Like the systems cited above, school districts operate under a highly

---

[2]It is nonoperational because we now have no satisfactory way of measuring many of the multiple outcomes of schooling, nor of adjusting for differences in teacher and student quality, nor for taking account of the interaction among students, teachers, and curricula, which introduces systematic bias into empirical estimates of educational production functions.

decentralized system of governance, but a highly complex structure of influences. There are nearly 18,000 school districts in the United States, each subject to a range of local community influences, as well as to the influence and legal authority of state and federal governments.

Finally, like certain other self-perpetuating bureaucracies (police, fire, public health services), the schools are a labor-intensive craft industry whose managers often present to the outside world the impression that their craft is highly specialized, that its functions cannot be carried out by replacements whether in the form of uncertified labor or machines.[3]

CONSEQUENCES FOR DISSEMINATION OF INNOVATIONS IN THE PUBLIC SCHOOLS

How would we expect a self-perpetuating bureaucracy to respond to R&D findings if (1) it is not market-oriented; (2) it is widely considered to be socially necessary and therefore deserving of public protection—is, in fact, the captive servant of a captive clientele; (3) it is open to a good deal of public scrutiny on issues having to do with perceived equity, quality, and goals; (4) it cannot unambiguously define its aims or clearly identify technologies that are dominant in light of aims that might be specified; (5) its contribution to its clientele's life and learning is uncertain and also modest as compared to other societal influences; (6) its governance is highly decentralized, yet subject to a wide variety of influences, so that each unit perceives itself as facing a unique configuration of clients and masters?

Before discussing the consequences of this market situation, it is important to start out by defining innovations. People associated with the schools often appear to define as innovation any new policy, process, or organizational change. In one sense this is valid, even when the innovation is new only to the particular class, school, or district and is very well established for the educational system as a whole. However, this definition is of little value when the aim of innovation is taken to be the improvement of educational processes, educational outcomes, or the economic efficiency of education. In this sense, an innovation is a technology which improves educational outcomes, improves working relationships or processes within the school system (or between the school system and the pub-

---

[3]The recent widespread introduction of teacher aides may represent some potential competition for the teacher guild. This threat is presumably offset in teachers' minds by the value of having assistance in routine and menial chores. It is predictable that teacher aides will themselves "professionalize" before long.

lic), or reduces the costs of education without significantly reducing the quantity or quality of desired outcomes or processes. In a competitive economic system, we would expect, as discussed below, that these results would come about primarily through market forces. Therefore, innovations that are adopted tend to work toward economic and social improvement, as marked by the decisions or choices actually made by consumers and producers.

But because schools do have the six characteristics discussed above, we cannot expect their institutional "marketplace" to produce the same results as the marketplace of the competitive industry. Nor can we realistically expect the school system to judge innovations by the same criteria of profitability as private firms. Schools use their own definitions and their own criteria. Although these criteria often are not specified publicly, they are—given the institutional setting—no less rational than those of competitive firms. For example, in schools and many other bureaucracies, it is important to attract more resources into the system to meet the demands of various constituencies (teachers, administrators, school boards, parents, and so on). It is also important not to introduce changes that appear to harm the interests of any major constituency. At the same time society, including the various constituencies of the schools, puts a positive value on "progress," as measured by new technologies and improved outcomes.

Because society looks on the schools as an important element in the preservation and transmission of its values and priorities (and because of the absence of market forces or clear goals), we might expect them to face fewer incentives for change than competitive firms. This is probably true, if we define innovation by standard economic criteria. But under the broader and looser definition adopted by the educational community, in which innovation is viewed partly as a lubricant of social and bureaucratic pressures, the conclusion is less clear.

As has been pointed out often (Carlson, 1965b; Miles, 1964; Havelock, R. G., Frohman, M., Guskin, A., Havelock, M., Hill, M., & Huber, J., 1969(a); Rogers & Shoemaker, 1971), the schools have tried out and adopted a large number of innovations. Certain innovations (the new mathematics, language laboratories) have spread very rapidly; others (junior high school, kindergarten, driver training) more slowly; still others (ungraded classes, open schools, decentralization of decision-making from district level to school level) very slowly. Then there are some educational innovations (voucher systems, abolition of teacher tenure, abolition of formal schooling, parent evaluation of school staff as a basis for retention and promotion) which have not spread at all yet. Finally, there have been many innovations that have been adopted but often are not successfully implemented. (A great many applications of new technologies, such as audiovisual equipment and computer assisted instruction, appear to fall into this category, as well as, in all probability, such new management techniques as Planning, Programming, Budgeting System (PPBS), accountability, administrative decentralization of large districts, etc.) The impedimenta of these innovations—in the form of equipment, or a new set of management structures, or the vestiges of "bold, new" curricula—remain beached by the wake of ephemeral educational revolutions while the system continues to operate as before.

The responses of schools to opportunities for innovation appear therefore to be complex; and between the adoption and the implementation, innovations routinely disappear or suffer sea-changes (Gross, Giaquinta, & Bernstein, 1971; Havelock et al., 1969a; Goodlad, 1969).

The Schools' Response to Innovation:
A Market Analogy

In order to understand under what circumstances schools will or will not be likely to adopt and implement innovations, it is instructive to compare the responses one might expect from the public schools with those one might expect from a competitive private firm (say a private vocational school, such as a computer programming school or a secretarial school).

Educational innovations can affect the schools' operations in diverse ways: increasing the level of resource use only ("more of the same"—e.g., a smaller class size); changing the resource mix (a higher proportion of teacher aides, relative increase in capital equipment); changing instructional processes or methods without significantly changing resource level or mix (new math, new reading curriculum); affecting administrative management, without significant effects on organizational power structures (computerizing data management, new accounting systems); changing either the organizational structure of the schools or their relation to external authority (community control, open schools, voucher systems).

Compared to a competitive firm, we would expect the public schools to:

1. *Be more likely than the competitive firm to adopt cost-raising innovations,* since there is no marketplace to test the value of the innovation (e.g., smaller class size) in relation to its cost. Therefore, any cost-raising innovation that is congenial to the public school authorities and acceptable to local taxpayers or state and federal funding sources will be adopted.

2. *Be less likely than the competitive firm to adopt cost-reducing innovations,* unless the funds so saved become available for other purposes within the district.

3. *Be less likely than the competitive firm to adopt innovations that significantly change the resource mix* (e.g., a higher ratio of teacher aides to teachers, sharply increased use of capital-intensive technologies), because any consequent productivity increases are not necessarily matched by greater "profits" to the district, and because any replacement of labor by capital may threaten the guild structure of the schools.

4. *Be more likely than the competitive firm to adopt new instructional processes or new wrinkles in administrative management* that do not significantly change institutional structure, because such innovations help to satisfy the demands of the public, of state and federal governments, and of teachers and principals themselves for change and progress without exacting heavy costs to the district in the form of organizational stress.

5. *Be less likely than the competitive firm to adopt innovations that change the accustomed authority roles* and established ways of doing business, because changes in these relations represent the heaviest kind of real cost to bureaucracies.

6. *Be equally unwilling as competitive firms to face large-scale encroachments* on protected markets (voucher systems, metropolitan-areawide open enrollment), although for somewhat different reasons.

In other words, schools are less likely than a competitive firm to adopt innovations as defined by a market economy—those that contribute to the economic efficiency of the system—and more likely to adopt innovations that respond to system demands for more resources, for evidence of progressive management, or for evidence of system responsiveness to client problems. From this perspective, the public schools can be seen as more likely than private firms to adopt innovations that do not require complex changes in management structure or organizational relations. Such innovations help to satisfy staff and client demands for change without requiring from the organization the difficult task of self-renewal, which many of the organization's clients, as well as the organization itself, might resist. Such innovations are also safe, in that it is nearly impossible, given the present state of educational information systems, to document whether a new curriculum, or new physical plant, or an audiovisual system helps or hurts children's learning or attitudes. Therefore, the innovating district, if it uses reasonable sense, is unlikely to get in trouble as a consequence of adopting or abandoning such innovations. Private vocational schools, whose policies are closely tied to student success in job placement, are quite conservative about adopting the latest thing in curriculum, because the risks are excessive in the absence of evidence (Belitsky, 1969).

Although there are probably significant differences in the kinds of innovations that schools and competitive firms are likely to adopt, it is impossible to generalize about whether public schools will adopt more or fewer innovations than competitive firms, except to say that private firms are more likely to adopt innovations that promote economic efficiency, whereas schools are more likely to adopt innovations that promote bureaucratic and social stability. It is often pointed out (e.g., Mansfield, 1963) that competitive industries characterized by relatively small firms (e.g., farming,[4] apparel, hardware) are likely to innovate less than large firms in less competitive industries (e.g., pharmaceuticals, electric equipment, computers), but in this context that is somewhat beside the point, as is the presumably correct argument that no firm, public or private, likes to make uncongenial changes. The point is that differences in market structure and social roles tend to lead to different patterns of innovation, through differences in the nature of incentives, whether positive (higher profits, larger Federal grants) or negative (impending bankruptcy, threatened teacher strikes).

From the viewpoint of a market economy, it might be argued that many of the innovations adopted by the schools are not innovations at all, but only fads, since there is little or no serious attempt to validate them in terms of productivity or effectiveness criteria, nor is there any market-like mechanism that automatically separates wheat from chaff. The validation process for educational innovation is ultimately measured by bureaucratic and social acceptability—criteria that are far more tenuous than those of a competitive market, but no less important for the actors in the bureaucratic marketplace.

Bureaucratic Factors Supporting Innovation

The considerations given above are quite general, of course. What are some of the more specific bureaucratic conditioning factors that lead school districts to adopt innovations? For years a dominant view was that the primary determinant of willingness to innovate was the level of per capita school spending (Mort & Cornell, 1941; Carlson, 1965b). This view was based on extensive studies of school district administration conducted by the Institute of Administrative Research at Columbia Teachers College. These findings, which were widely disseminated, buttressed the school superintendent's natural desire to maximize his per-pupil budget, providing thereby a happy coincidence of organizational self-interest and socially endorsed "progressive" behavior.

More recent research (Mansfield, 1963; Carlson, 1965a; Havelock et

[4]Farming is actually an innovative industry in the United States, but, as in the case of education, the research and development bill is almost entirely paid by the federal government and oligopolistic farm supply industries. Competitive industries that are less powerful politically than agriculture receive little or no subsidized research and development, while individual firms are too small to finance internally significant levels of R&D.

al., 1969a; Gross et al., 1971) casts doubt on this contention with respect to schools as well as to industrial firms, without denying the usefulness of command over resources. A more complex view of the determinants of innovation in the school emerges. Three factors seem favorable to innovation in the schools.

1. *Bureaucratic Safety:* When the innovation is perceived as favorable with respect to the current status and organization of the bureaucracy (because in a self-perpetuating nonmarket system, these bureaucratic values become socialized and tend to dominate other criteria; or in other words, the bureaucratic costs are the real costs of the system).

2. *Response to External Pressure:* When external pressures for innovation are perceived as irresistible (because school systems cannot be entirely unresponsive to external pressures and financial constraints).

3. *Approval of Peer Elites:* When key figures in the bureaucracy and their colleagues in other educational bureaucracies can agree about the acceptability of the innovation (because in the absence of clearly defined output criteria, consensus among the elite is often the primary decision-making criterion).

These elements are interrelated. For example, external pressures can lower the school district's perception of bureaucratic safety, thereby providing negative incentives to innovate; or if a particular innovation is neutral with respect to bureaucratic safety, then peer approval may act as a positive incentive. They are also complex. For example, approval of peer elite can be used by individual administrators as a justification for pursuing deeply held beliefs, but it can be ignored when it endorses policies that the same administrators are opposed to. Finally, they are relative. In each organization, depending on the circumstances, a constraint may be more or less elastic, and one object of R&D policy may be to make these constraints more elastic, thereby creating greater willingness to change (see following pages).

In addition to these factors, which apply particularly to the public school setting, there may be elements present in any organization, whether or not educational, that encourage innovation. These have been discussed widely in the literature on innovation (Lippitt, Watson, & Westley, 1958; Marcum, 1968; Bennis, Benne, & Chin, 1969; Havelock, Huber, & Zimmerman, 1969b; Rogers & Shoemaker, 1971). These elements, although clearly important in many instances, will not be discussed in detail here. The kinds of factors that students of planned change have identified as generally supporting innovation in organizations include, after the outline of Glaser (1971): organizational attitudes that support change (such as free communication, support from administration and colleagues, high staff morale); clarity of goal structures; organizational structures that favor innovation (sufficient decentralization of authority, existence of a large number of occupational specializations, existence of structures for self-renewal); professionalism of staff; organizational autonomy (not excessively dependent on public opinion or tests of political feasibility to validate planned change); and few strong vested interests in preserving the status quo in methods of operation.

Some of these elements (e.g., lack of clear goal structures or organizational autonomy) are implicit in the three factors described above (Bureaucratic Safety, Response to External Pressure, Approval of Peer Elites). Those that are not implicit obviously can affect the propensity to adopt innovations in schools, as elsewhere, and we would expect different school systems to exhibit these qualities in varying degrees.

But if we accept the proposition that the unique elements in the schools' response to opportunities for innovation stem from their special institutional role, market structure, and the systematic set of economic and bureaucratic incentives so created, then there emerges a somewhat different perspective from that usually set forth in the literature on innovation. The three factors described above can, in this perspective, be considered as reflections of institutions, markets, and consequent behavioral incentives facing the public schools.

Therefore, if we can identify the kinds of innovations that are likely to be adopted by school districts that follow such behavioral styles, we may be able to identify ways that R&D products can be oriented in order to gain acceptance. As soon becomes apparent, the three conditions favorable to adoption of innovations in the present setting are themselves rather restrictive. Advocates of substantial innovation in the public schools aren't likely to be very satisfied by a R&D dissemination strategy that takes these conditions as operative constraints. Therefore, it is useful to examine the ways in which R&D dissemination policy could take advantage of the existing structure of market and bureaucratic incentives, and also to examine the ways in which these incentives could be modified by conscious R&D policy.

The *bureaucratic safety constraint* means that schools are unlikely to accept radical changes in educational institutions, such as taking instruction out of the classroom, introducing capital-intensive instructional technologies, or new forms of educational market organizations, because such changes might be expected to affect the organization of the system substantially.

The fear of *external social and political pressures on the school system* means that schools will be reluctant to enter into genuine collaboration with other social groups at the policymaking level, such as community or student participation in control of school district policy, or providing the public with educational information systems that could be used as a step towards "accountability." Extra-system knowledge of school affairs is perceived as leading to greater extra-system pressures for reform, thereby creating unwanted problems for the school system.

The *elite consensus constraint* tends to prevent any but marginal changes from current practice. School districts are of necessity unclear about educational goals, and educational research and development has failed to enlighten them substantially about the relationship between various educational technologies and any specified instructional aim. Therefore, faced by such enormous uncertainties, a rational bureaucratic elite would be unlikely to experiment voluntarily with major changes in structure or method. Social and political consequences would be incalculable while benefits would necessarily be uncertain.

Given these constraints, and the market structure of the public school "industry," schools tend voluntarily to adopt innovations which promote the schools' self-image by demonstrating that the schools are:

1. *"Up-to-date"*: introducing modern physical plant, new curricula not requiring changes in bureaucratic organization or staff rules, reduction of class size, use of teacher aides, team teaching.

2. *"Efficient"*: adoption of electronic data processing, new budgeting and accounting systems, portable classrooms.

3. *"Professional"*: adoption of curricula that are espoused by the educational leadership, hiring well-trained teachers, subsidizing in-service training and workshops, consulting with faculty of leading schools of education.

4. *"Responsive"*: establishing formalized links to parents, using blue-ribbon advisory committees to submit reports on policy issues, establishing counseling and guidance functions, establishing special programs for handicapped, gifted, slow learners, and so on, providing vocational programs that respond to needs of local industry, offering a variety of adult extension courses.

Because the 18,000 school districts have a great deal of autonomy in deciding whether and how to innovate, we would expect adoption of innovations often to be a selective and idiosyncratic process varying according to administrators' tastes and their perceptions of school and community needs. The empirical evidence shows that small districts adopt fewer innovations than large ones (Lindeman, Bailey, Berke, & Naum, 1968), presumably because large districts are more able to keep informed of new methods, and face a wider variety of both external and system-generated pressures for change.

Those innovations that are widely adopted generally share common characteristics of substantial consensus in their favor among the elite and present no major bureaucratic or social problems. The most widely adopted (adopted by half or more of the largest school districts) instructional innovations, as of 1969, were: teacher aides, ability groupings, team teaching, elementary resource teachers, movable partitions, TV instruction, and nongraded sequencing. Curriculum innovations were introduced widely by large districts over the period 1965–69 in science, math, and reading (Lindeman et al., 1968). The curriculum innovations were influenced by the National Science Foundation (NSF) science and math curricula and by the sales efforts of new commercially marketed curricula (e.g., the EDL reading labs and SRA reading program).

These findings indicate that large-scale, carefully planned R&D efforts are, in curriculum change, likely to be more effective in gaining adoption than more modest efforts (the current success of the Southwest Regional Laboratory prereading program is another case in point). It should also be noted that the NSF and SWRL programs were worked out in close collaboration with practitioners, which helped encourage adoption. Finally, these programs were widely publicized and praised by professional education groups, so that there were social pressures for adoption.

This last characteristic has significant general implications for acceptance of R&D products. Since the incentives for a school superintendent or principal to adopt or reject an innovation are so diffuse and so closely related to administrators' preferences and to their perceptions of internal and external constraints, R&D organizations should clearly do their best to work closely with school administrators and those who influence them (county and state school officials). In part, this is a question of co-optation. But considering the characteristic remoteness from the client of educational R&D organizations, which traditionally have been university-centered, it also can serve as a form of reality therapy for the researcher. Of course, the opposite problem can arise, as witness the rather poor record in innovation of school districts' internal research staffs, probably because they share too closely the bureaucracy's perspectives and priorities.

Adoption also can be catalyzed by pressure, subsidy, or other incentives from external jurisdictions or interest groups (e.g., federally mandated or subsidized innovations, such as Head Start or Follow Through; state mandating of kindergarten programs or programs for education of the handicapped; court decisions on desegregation or finance; influence of industry or interest groups on obtaining special programs, such as vocational education or driver education; minority community influences in achieving black or Chicano study programs, or varying degrees of decentralization).

School districts face a certain set of incentives that systematically affect their preferences for different kinds of innovations. A rational state and federal R&D policy, to the extent that it aims at encouraging innovations that schools would normally be reluctant to adopt, should presumably devote most of its funds to innovations that are uncongenial to the schools, with payments based on evidence that reforms actually are undertaken. If reformers seek to affect the ways that districts respond to internal and external institutional pressures, they will have to pay for it. Therefore, some federal and state subsidy for R&D and for innovation (both directly to schools and indirectly to R&D agencies) should go not for things that schools want to do, but rather for things that they would otherwise be reluctant to do.

Large-scale, well-planned support for innovative efforts aimed in part at rectifying the existing institutional biases, and a conscious policy of collaboration with school administrators (and increasingly with leaders of teachers' organizations) are therefore two potential catalysts for adopting policies which rank high in reformers' preferences—the first aims at reducing existing barriers to innovation, whereas the second aims at achieving more innovation within the existing constraints.

A school district, whatever its critics may aver, is a going concern, one whose "survival" is under existing laws, threatened only to the extent that school boards can replace superintendents and that the public can replace school boards. Other employees are relatively invulnerable to these possibilities. Therefore, given the risk-avoiding mentality that we normally might expect in such a bureaucracy, real costs of innovations that affect internal or external relations of the system are likely to be magnified. At the same time, gains from such innovations are likely to be discounted, because institutions' operational focus is necessarily short-range, tending to stress immediate costs to the system, whereas the benefits of such changes are typically uncertain and remote. This creates a built-in conflict between practitioners and those researchers who seek innovation through methods that require reform of structures (which incidentally provides further argument in support of external subsidy for uncongenial innovations, such as vouchers, ungraded schools, or alternative schools). The research community typically complains that practitioners and politicians are unrealistic in their desires for immediate results. One method that researchers can use to appear responsive to this desire is to promise more performance from an innovation than the evidence warrants. This response, which is the more understandable if the R&D organization stands to benefit in prestige or money from the adoption, tends to heighten the district bureaucracy's skepticism about the merits of any R&D initiative that engenders significant organizational stress.

Because so many factors, not the least of which are the uncertainty of benefits and the certainty of resistance, tend to operate against any substantial voluntary change in the structure of the schools, desires for progress and reform therefore tend to be channeled into "safer" areas—those that involve spending more money on the existing resource mix (more teachers, more administrators), or those that involve the kinds of changes in curriculum or administration that don't seem to threaten organized groups in or out of the bureaucracy. This is a collateral reason for the oft-noted prevalence of faddism in school reform. If structural changes are prohibitively costly in real (institutional) terms, then the attractiveness of less costly reforms, or even of chasing after will-o'-the-wisp, is heightened.

FROM INNOVATION TO IMPLEMENTATION

Frequently change may be made still less costly in terms of the system's values by not implementing innovations along the lines proposed by their developers. Perhaps the most common complaint of the R&D community about adoptions is that the innovations are not actually implemented as prescribed, so that they never get a fair trial. This clearly has been the fate of most audiovisual developments, for example. Goodlad and Klein (1970) have pointed out that, despite years of discussion and professional support leading to widespread adoption of such innovations as ungraded classes and team teaching, these innovations are rarely implemented. A school district will adopt ungraded classes and then implement by teaching essentially a graded curriculum in the "ungraded" class.

There are several reasons for this failure to implement innovations effectively:

1. R&D organizations frequently do not provide sufficient implementation guidance, in light of the variety of school situations where adoption is tried.

2. Teachers, administrators, and students may not accept the obligation to change their behavior patterns in ways consistent with implementation.

3. The schools may simply not know how to implement the innovation. As Smith and Keith (1971) have said, describing one such effort: "In spite of prodigious effort, common guidelines that guided did not exist; the language of school organization, teaching and goals for pupils remains metaphorical and literary but neither practical nor scientific [pp. 52–53]."

4. As a sort of corollary, if the language of the schools is "neither practical nor scientific" but metaphorical and literary, it often may be the

case that school personnel will be more interested in the language of innovation than in the complexities of translating that language into innovative practice. This style of operations referred to as the "alternative of grandeur" [Smith & Keith, 1971] may well be entirely reasonable in the absence of evidence that conclusively supports the advantages of innovation. For the schools' purposes, verbal adoption of innovations may be entirely sufficient, and a preference for the verbiage of magnificent vistas has been noted by various observers.

The problems associated with implementing major innovations in public schools are too substantial to discuss in detail here. Suffice it to say that, even when motivations to implement are strong, innovations that are perceived as radical by the schools and their clients are exceedingly difficult to implement (Smith & Keith, 1971; Gross et al., 1971). Frequently cited barriers in cases where there is widespread support for the innovation include unclear objectives or methods, and too little time allotted for planning change and informing people of what is planned and why. In instances where there is not widespread support, there may come into play such factors as the need for stability, personal or institutional perceptions of threat or vulnerability, inertia, perceptions of client response, and so on. An important causal factor seems to be a lack of communication between sponsors of innovations and the ultimate users—students, parents, and teachers—which tends to work against significant change at the user level (Fullan, 1972).

The Institutional Setting for Innovation

The principal funding sources that support innovations in the schools are federal and state governments, either directly through grants to school districts or indirectly through funding educational research and development. Cases in point are Head Start, Titles I and III of ESEA, the Emergency School Aid Program, Career Education funds, Miller-Unruh reading programs in California, urban aid in New York State, federal support of regional labs and R&D centers, and so on.

In practice the only real control that the federal government has over district use of funds is the relatively unlikely option of withdrawing support. As the history of efforts to obtain Title I "comparability" indicates, use of this weapon is largely symbolic, as an adjunct to moral suasion (Wirt & Kirst, 1972).[5]

---

[5]If, in the future, federal aid to schools is offered by automatic revenue sharing formulas, even this symbolic weapon will disappear.

Local school authorities know that, once they receive a grant, they have much more freedom to use it in accord with their own priorities than the granter might wish.

School districts are characteristically hard-pressed, squeezed between voter reluctance to raise property taxes and employee wage demands. This squeeze tends to buttress whatever preference the school authorities have for system maintenance over innovation, and the actual flow of funds is likely to reflect those preferences (Coleman, 1972).

Some attributes of federal aid enhance these tendencies and act to discourage incorporation of innovations into school systems.

1. There is a tendency to subsidize educational research and development without particular reference to the effects of the developments on various outcomes of schooling.

2. There is a tendency to ignore in setting policy the evidence of evaluation reports on innovative programs, allowing districts to introduce or perpetuate pet projects without regard to the alleged aims of innovation. (This does not imply that all evaluations are worth heeding, a fact which buttresses the policymaker's natural tendency to support whichever innovations his personal or bureaucratic preferences may dictate.)

3. There are too frequent changes in program priorities and too short a life for educational experiments. Many federally funded innovative programs are based on trials of one to three years, with two major consequent disadvantages: (1) not enough time is allowed to separate effects of the innovation from effects of the frictions arising from the effort to implement; (2) because the districts know that the programs cannot get a fair test in such a short time, they are unlikely to take much interest in the programs as exemplars.

4. A related difficulty is the tendency of federal and state agencies to view their contributions as seed money to be replaced by district funds if the program is a success. But school districts know that the typical cost of such programs ($100-$500 or more per student per year) is beyond their ability to finance for the student body at large, and the use of district funds for applying the innovation to only a small number of students raises serious ethical questions for a regulated public utility.

5. The school districts do not perceive the federal government as demonstrating clear or consistent policies toward innovation. There is no clear long-term benefit or penalty to a district if it adopts or fails to adopt one set of innovations in preference to another. This tends to reduce the schools' respect for federal policies toward innovation, and to breed a certain cynicism as to the merits of serious efforts at innovation. Furthermore, since federal aid fails to support systematically the hard alternatives

and to scamp easy ones, it in effect encourages a strategy of "grantsman-ship."

6. The schools interpret these peculiarities of federal aid policies as meaning that federal aid is unreliable—"soft money" that will disappear as suddenly as it arrived. Therefore, school districts characteristically refuse to use federal money as the basis for any substantial long-run changes in ways of doing business.

7. Furthermore, the federal government's support of innovation is relatively small-scale compared to other programs, such as impact aid and compensatory education. Therefore, funds for innovation, although help-ful to a school district on the hunt for federal largesse, are a second order quest. This is rather ambiguous, though. If federal support of innovations were larger than it is, the institutional pressures to call almost anything by the name of innovation would be irresistible. Apparently, under the exist-ing set of institutional relations, no federal investment in innovation is optimal—low levels of funding are insufficient to call forth substantial efforts of organizational reform, whereas large-scale funding would clearly lead down the path already blazed by impact aid and Title I—compensating the schools for following the path of least resistance.

IMPLICATIONS FOR EDUCATIONAL R&D

The schools are a unique social institution, molding the clients who, in ways reflecting reverence and resentment, also control it. From a certain point of view, the schools are primarily the agents of socialization, teaching successive generations how to accommodate to social and economic in-stitutions in the interests of the existing social order (Dreeben, 1968; Bowles & Gintis, 1972). To accept such a view is, in effect, to deny the possibility of significant innovations in schooling, except as dictated by changing interests of ruling social and economic forces. But this view is far more optimistic about the merits and possibilities of innovation than some current empirically based analyses (Averch, Carroll, Donaldson, Kiesling, & Pincus, 1972; Jencks, Smith, Acland, Bane, Cohen, & Gintis, 1972). It posits the inevitability of effective innovation under the influences of changing social regimes, whereas Averch et al. and Jencks et al. seem to cast strong doubts about the ability of the schools to affect learning and attitudes in any systematic and significant way, perhaps under any social regime.

If we are to believe Bowles and Gintis, the only way to change the schools is to reform or revolutionize society, because the schools today are in effect performing the role that the majority influences in society want them to, and not the way that reformers want them to. If we are to draw reasonable inferences from Jencks et al. and Averch et al., it makes more sense to invest in innovations in the nonschool environment than in the schools themselves, because environmental factors account for far more of the variation in achievement tests, college attendance rates, lifetime earnings, and so forth, than school factors do or can.

If these researchers are correct in their conclusions, much of the money spent on educational innovation, however carefully allocated it may be, is wasted by social policy criteria. Whether or not they are right is debatable. After all, society does not choose to affect heredity systematically; the outcomes of its attempts to influence the broad social environment are characteristically far from the mark; in practice this leaves the educational system as the principal vehicle for policy reform. The fact that the schools are not omnipotent in shaping educational outcomes is partly irrelevant. In current circumstances, the market structure of the schools, the uncertainty about their goals and technology, and the particular set of institutional incentives that school districts face lead to systematic preference for certain kinds of innovations over others. This paper aims at suggesting ways for the schools to become more open to a variety of innovations, particularly those that the schools have not yet adopted. Measurement of the consequences can appropriately come later. As long as the schools can become more open to certain kinds of innovations, their prospects for performing better will be enhanced in the long run. It is probably true that many attempts at innovation will fail, not for technical reasons, but because the demand is not there—society prefers the status quo. But if we believe that society's perceptions are subject to change, and that research and development can expand the variety of useful alternatives, then such failures can be seen as an inevitable adjunct of the innovation process. That process itself may best be viewed both as a stimulus to social change and as a socially approved process of testing society's readiness for change.

The discussion of sections one and two previously leads to an important conclusion for R&D policy. *If goals are in some sense undefinable, it is inappropriate to adopt the standard rationalist approach of first defining goals, then seeking means appropriate to achieve them efficiently. Instead, R&D strategy should be based at least in part on the converse approach.* If the present situation is unsatisfactory, then it may be wiser to try out systematic innovations and assess their consequences than to continue to pursue uncertain goals with unclear technologies. (For a similar view, see March, 1972.) Adopting this strategy means finding ways to do three things:

1. Adopt R&D policies that appeal more effectively to the existing set of bureaucratic incentives, and policies that attempt to modify those incentives.

2. Adopt policies that permit the public, acting through a variety of institutional means, to assess more accurately what the schools are doing and how well they are performing.

3. Introduce changes in the market structure of the schools that will facilitate innovation.

This suggests five broad emphases for R&D policy in encouraging adoption of innovation: (1) large-scale experimentation; (2) collaboration between R&D agencies and educational leadership networks; (3) case studies of successful and unsuccessful innovation; (4) research that will improve the R&D community's understanding of the existing pattern of incentives in the schools; (5) trying out methods of restructuring system incentives. Most of these approaches have been tried to greater or lesser degrees. The following discussion attempts to link them to the discussion of incentives.

Large-Scale Experimentation

Most educational innovations are tried out on a small scale in one school or in one district. They tend, whether considered successful or not, to disappear from view. The National Center for Educational Communications, through ERIC and other devices, tries to disseminate information about innovations, but the results to date in terms of adoptions so generated have not been impressive. Large-scale experiments, either planned or emerging as offshoots of other programs, include Head Start, Follow Through, Titles I, III, VII, and VIII of ESEA, the NIE experimental schools program, Higher Horizons, More Effective Schools, Sesame Street, The Electric Company, NIE career education models, and performance contracting. There has been wide variation in the perceived success of these efforts, both between and within programs (Averch et al., 1972). But the experiments in general have not been designed or evaluated in ways that would allow anyone to assess the reasons for their success and failure in the real-life setting of the schools. This kind of assessment is difficult, both because education is a complex phenomenon and because innovations that impinge on bureaucratic values make headway slowly. There is not only the obvious point—experimenting with a major educational innovation for one year or a few years is unlikely to reveal much about its merits even in its own terms—but also a less obvious and far more general one—any substantial intervention in an existing social system is very likely to have important unintended effects, reflecting the system's effort to respond and accommodate to the new stimulus. For example, one of the unintended effects of New Deal agricultural price support programs was to subsidize large commercial farmers heavily without significantly halting the decline of family farming. This effect reflected both changes in agricultural technology and the strong influence of commercial farmers in the structure of agricultural politics, which in turn was able to exert its influence on the broader structure of national politics. By the time these unintended effects became apparent, it was too late to rectify them, had experimentation been possible, the eventual outcome might have been avoided through different policies.

In education, suppose that an unintended effect of ESEA Title III were that Title III schools or districts behaved no differently from others three years after federal support expired. This result would provide strong evidence that system behavior is extremely stable with respect to perturbations introduced by temporary funding in support of innovation. This might, in turn, argue either for longer term support of effective innovations or for abandonment of the present Title III program.

As noted above, some experimentation has already been undertaken and offers a substantial opportunity for seeing how R&D initiatives have actually affected the schools as institutions, offering thereby guidelines for future R&D policy. But two kinds of new, large-scale natural or planned experiments are also needed. The first kind of experiment involves finding out more about the effects of new methods on educational outcomes, given the current institutional structure. Examples include: (1) long-term analysis of cohorts that, through chance or design, receive different educational treatments (the Progressive Education Association's Eight-Year Study, 1934–1941, is the only major example of such an approach); (2) highly capital-intensive forms of education; (3) curricular that make sharp changes in existing pupil–teacher, pupil–method, and teacher–method interactions.

The second kind of experiment is more deliberately aimed at modifying the current structure of institutional or market incentives. Examples, discussed in more detail below, include: (1) educational vouchers; (2) youth endowment plans; (3) alternative schools within a district; (4) decentralized governance; (5) merit pay; (6) compensating R&D agencies and school personnel for both the development and the implementation of innovations.

But all such research and experimentation should focus not simply on the effectiveness of meeting stated goals but also on the system-wide effects of the experiment, in particular the institutional response of the schools to the new stimulus. This approach will help create a corpus of knowledge about the response mechanisms of schools to innovation in different fields, as advanced in different ways; in particular it will show which innovations, if any, are most effective under current incentives, and which ones effectively modify those incentives.

Large-scale, appropriately publicized experiments are important to demonstrate to schools and the public that a particular innovation can succeed in a variety of settings. They are also important in some cases to provide convincing demonstrations of failure. Educational research and development organizations espouse a wide variety of innovations. Some large-scale experiments, even if carefully chosen, are likely, after a reasonable test, to fail of their objectives. It is appropriate that knowledge of unpromising innovations be as widely disseminated as promising ones.

Collaboration with Educational Leadership

There is strong evidence that school district administrators rely primarily for research and development information on personal contact with researchers and with other administrators, through informal channels, workshops, and professional meetings (Carlson, 1965a; Havelock et al., 1969a; Greenwood & Weiler, 1972). It also seems clear that most educational research and development has been oriented to academic peer approval rather than to adopting innovations in the schools (Havelock et al., 1969a; Glaser & Taylor, 1969). It has been said, for example:

Many academic scientists value the prestige that their contributions to basic research and theory give them in the eyes of their peers more than whatever rewards might be obtained from clients who would find their work useful. . . . Much of the applied work in disciplinary departments is done by those who for one reason or another do not compete for the highest prizes of their disciplines. [National Academy of Sciences, 1969, p. 93]

Policymakers who come to social scientists for advice often go away empty-handed. A local school superintendent in California addressed exactly this charge to the staff of one research and development center. "They're always chasing theoretical rainbows, and frankly I doubt that there's a pot of educational gold at the end." [Baldridge and Johnson, 1972, p. 33]

It is clear that these misunderstandings (between researchers and practitioners) develop because there has not been a meeting of the minds between the research and the organization. The atmosphere, during early stages, of cordiality, implicit mutual assurances, and reciprocally unrealistic expectations compounds an already precarious balance. . . . The "loser" is not just the agency or a disappointed researcher; it is the field, the clients, and all participants as well as future research endeavors. [Glaser and Taylor, 1969, p. 91]

We have here a vicious circle: (a) many educators do not conceive of the scientific method and research as being of primary significance to their work; (b) this state of mind creates an atmosphere in which low priority is given to the conduct or utilization of research; (c) because of low evaluation or neglect, research continues to be a dubious enterprise; and (d) because condition (c) exists, condition (a) is perpetuated. [Carlson, 1965b, pp. 71–72]

The present situation tends to combine several disadvantages:

1. Researchers are interested in disciplinary prestige more than in problem-solving in the schools.

2. Even when, as in the case of regional labs, there is considerable incentive to produce R&D results that can be applied in the schools, the gulf between innovation and implementation remains all too often unbridged.

3. Researchers disseminate results through journal articles and reports; practitioners learn through briefings, meetings, and informal discussion.

4. Research and development agencies follow an R&D change model that views the schools as passive adopters of new products, but the schools themselves decide to adopt and implement innovations in light of a host of organizational considerations that are not incorporated in the R&D model of change.

5. Researchers and practitioners often don't talk the same language because their operating styles, perceptions of issues, and professional priorities are so different.

The policy implications appear evident, although the remedy is likely to be slow.

First, educational R&D organizations should be interdisciplinary and problem-oriented rather than disciplinary and methodology-oriented. This is not a criticism of either basic research or focusing on discipline or methodology. But in the context of this paper, which focuses on how to increase the adoption of R&D products in the schools, they are evidently of little proximate value.

Second, R&D organizations should work more closely with principals, district administrators, and teacher representatives during the development period. Several such organizations regularly employ school administrators, on leave from their districts, in R&D planning. This practice should be extended. There is a delicate balance, of course, between systematically improving researchers' and school staffs' mutual understanding and allowing research and development to be dominated by the institutional perceptions of the schools.

Third, R&D organizations should conduct regular seminars, workshops, and institutes for school district and state education agency staff designed to communicate both R&D results and schoolmen's perceptions of appropriate priorities, implementation problems, and technical assistance requirements.

Fourth, it is important for R&D agencies to understand the nature of regional and national influence networks and to identify potential innovators. In the public schools, as elsewhere, there are organizations and individuals who are more disposed to innovate, and who feel less threatened than others by the prospects of change. For example, USOE in its experimental schools program and OEO in its voucher and performance-contracting demonstrations in effect have identified a few such districts. R&D organizations can work with such innovators to demonstrate the new methods and find out how they work in practice, meanwhile collaborating with broader leadership networks to disseminate the findings.

Fifth, and most important in the transition from innovation to implementation, is the need for R&D personnel to work closely with school staff during the implementation period. Otherwise, it is clear from the evidence (Goodlad, 1970; Gross et al., 1971) that the R&D task is cut off before its fulfillment. The view taken here is that incentives to adopt and incentives to implement are largely different from each other. Innovation and implementation work through different agents in the institutional setting. The federal or state agencies propose; school superintendents or principals dispose; the teachers and students transform.

Therefore, the R&D job does not end at the school district line or the schoolhouse door, and close collaboration with the schools is probably a necessary condition of implementing any innovations that depart from the established pattern of innovations that, as we have seen, the schools customarily accept. This approach means that R&D agencies will have to assure the training and recruitment of people who work well with both researchers and people in the schools. This form of technical assistance for implementing innovations will be expensive.

For the major innovations that proponents of school reform are seeking, it often may be a matter of years, not months, to build up the kind of orientations and mutual understanding that will be required, and, through a process of successive approximation, to create new institutional structures and values. It will in effect require R&D institutions to turn much more to a clinical model of change (one which adapts general findings or processes to the specific circumstances of the client) and away from the engineering model, which offers a standardized product to the clients at large (Weiler, 1973; House, Kerins, & Steele, 1972).

Case Studies of Innovation

There is a sizable literature on education innovation (see bibliography), including some interesting analyses of the success and failure of particular innovations (Carlson, 1965a; Smith & Keith, 1971; Gross et al., 1971). However, the literature, with a few exceptions, does not describe the implementation process. As Goodlad (1970) and Gross et al. have pointed out, it is impossible to judge the merits of an innovation unless we have substantial information about how, and even *if*, it was implemented. If some innovations are, as Goodlad claims, implemented in name only, then the innovation remains untested. At the same time, such evidence clearly indicates a failure in the R&D process. Innovations that consistently remain unimplemented hardly can be regarded as arguments in favor of perpetuating existing R&D styles. Either the innovations or the implementation arrangements, or both, are inappropriate.

The discussion of the previous sections indicates a number of reasons why innovations might not be adopted or implemented. These arguments, based on unsystematic observation supplemented by a few case studies, need to be rejected or confirmed by more systematic case studies. Such studies can point the way to more effective strategies for development and implementation. Some R&D agencies have shown an ability to work with schools to implement innovations, and others have not; yet there is surprisingly little documentation of the record.

Analysis of Incentive Patterns

What are the institutional incentives that motivate school districts, administrators, school boards, teachers, and state and federal educational agencies? Are the respective sets of incentives consistent with each other? If not, how are inconsistencies typically resolved?

In general, we would expect school districts' values to dominate in the resolution of interjurisdictional differences, since they are closer to operations than other jurisdictions, and exercise de facto control over funds, no matter how they are nominally earmarked.

But the relationships are complex. The federal government has clearly forced state school agencies and local districts to pay more attention to disadvantaged students and to innovation than they would have otherwise. Changes in state education codes and in financial support regulations systematically affect local school districts' incentives and responses. The emergence of strong teacher unions has reduced school boards' and administrators' freedom of action, as has the emergence of a number of vocal and conflicting community interest groups.

In general, groups and institutions involved in the multi-bureaucratic structure of educational governance do not appear to gauge each other's motivations and responses well. Evidence for this lies in: (1) the frequently voiced disappointment of federal and state agencies in local districts' failure to do a good job in carrying out mandated programs; (2) local community groups' perception of school authorities as unresponsive; (3) district administrators' frequent impatience or contempt for state and federal agencies' inability to understand the local perspective; (4) R&D

agencies' frequent ignorance of or disrespect for district administration; (5) teacher groups' increasing militance, reflecting impatience with the perspective of school boards and administrators; (6) the public's increasing unwillingness to vote more funds for schooling.

There is no accepted theory of interbureaucratic organizational behavior. Organization theory has concerned itself mostly with the internal structure and incentives of individual or representative bureaucracies, and first steps toward a more realistic description of how bureaucracies interact are barely under way (see Levine, 1972).

There have been formal treatments of interbureaucratic financial behavior (Barro, 1972) and descriptive treatments of individual bureaucratic levels—federal, state, local, R&D agencies (see bibliography). But it seems safe to say that most external efforts to promote innovation in the schools have foundered in part through their ignorance of the tunes to which school districts must dance. Federal programs, for example, often seem to assume that, because schools want to prevent high school dropouts, federal funding of dropout prevention programs will therefore result in a coincidence of federal and local interest. The reality is far more complex. School districts have a number of priorities, and dropout prevention ranks much higher in the verbal agenda than in the hidden one. For good reasons, the schools feel that some people should be encouraged to drop out and others discouraged from doing so. But dominating those perceptions is the need to prevent any important client groups from creating crises, to keep them at least relatively satisfied. Therefore, dropout prevention funds—like compensatory education funds, driver education funds, or any other largesse—will be spent as much as possible to keep parents, teachers, students, school boards, and "external" bureaucracies in some kind of equilibrium. The nominal purposes of the funds are regarded at the district level as constraints on the objective function, and one measure of an administrator's success is his ability to make the constraints nonoperative, to allocate external funds so that they do double duty.

Therefore, if externally encouraged innovative efforts are to avoid a great deal of waste motion, they must be based on a far more detailed appraisal of the reality of the schools as institutions than is now the case. For this reason, studies of the operative behavior of school districts, in their relation to their own clients and to the state and federal bureaucracies they must deal with, should be of high priority in R&D funding.

Restructuring System Incentives

A theme of this paper is that the schools, as a peculiar form of regulated public utility, have a different set of incentives to innovate than do competitive firms. It is undesirable to take the private market model as

a general exemplar for school district behavior (most people would be reluctant to allow only those who can afford schooling to obtain it), but it seems
well worthwhile to experiment with changing the incentive system of the
schools in a variety of ways. There is no guarantee that new system incentives will result in performance that satisfies society more than the present
systems, but, given the great expense of schooling and widespread dissatis-
faction with current performance, the social costs of experimental restructuring of incentives cannot be very great.

Experimentation with restructuring incentives should take four
forms:

Changes in Market Structure. These experiments would cover:

1. A range of voucher alternatives from the public school open
enrollment version currently under way in Alum Rock to those that would
include establishing new schools and allowing participation of existing
private and public schools.

2. Youth endowment plans under which each young person would
have a lifetime entitlement of money to be spent on supplemental schooling
or other beneficial use at the recipient's discretion—for example, supplemental educational or extracurricular experiences during the elementary
and secondary school years; college expenses, cost of private vocational
schools as a substitute for high school; costs of going into business, and so
on. One version of this proposal, the educational bank, has been described
by Killingsworth (1967).

3. Permitting open enrollment across district lines among the public
schools of a metropolitan area, with public funds following the student.

Changes in Locus of Control. Both greater centralization of control
and greater decentralization of control are likely to lead to their own sets of
systematic biases in incentives to adopt innovations and incentives to implement them. The object of experimentation and analysis should be to
discern the nature of these effects. Obvious candidates for initial analysis are
responses to innovation in New York City schools, as an example of decentralization to the neighborhood level; private schools, free schools, and
alternative schools, as an example of decentralization to the school level; and
jurisdictions such as the French and Swedish schools or Los Angeles and
Chicago districts, as examples of centralized decision-making.

It should also be possible, with assurances of long-term funding, to
mount new experiments such as paying school districts to decentralize
decision-making to principals or to community boards or to teacher–
student governance, or subsidizing a state government to centralize and
implement innovative policies.

Changes in Individual Incentives. The schools have long resisted any moves to "deprofessionalize" the system, whether by paying people on the basis of performance or by allowing the schools to hire anyone they want to as teachers or administrators. Certification and the unified salary schedule are the shibboleths of professional educators. Some of the reasons are obvious: (1) certification offers the advantages of a sort of tariff barrier; (2) it also offers status—certification enhances the esteem of lawyers, doctors of philosophy or medicine, licensed plumbers and morticians. Why should schoolmen not garner the same psychic benefits?

Some of the reasons are less obvious. Many teachers and administrators believe that both the ends and the means of their work are uncertain. Others believe that the ends and the means are certain, but unrevealed to those in position of authority. In either case, where does merit lie, and who should decide it? If salary differences are desirable as incentives and as recognition of increased social responsibilities associated with aging, then why not condition salary rewards on objectively measurable signs—years of experience in teaching and in learning—rather than on unverifiable judgments about individual merit? Stated differently, productivity criteria are one thing where some form of market appraisal or a generally approved surrogate exists (batting averages, journal articles, or shorthand speed); the criteria may be resisted, but they are hard to gainsay entirely. Matters are quite different when each observer is free to assert his own criteria, or when centrally imposed criteria are regarded widely as arbitrary.

This leads to some conclusions for experimentation. Dispensing with certification requirements for recruitment and promotion should be tried out, under subsidy, in school districts. Merit pay experiments should preferably be implemented in association with reasonable evidence that certain kinds of teacher characteristics or behavior lead to better student outcomes than others. There has been a good deal of research on teaching, but rather little of it has been associated with student outcomes (Hanushek, 1970; Averch et al., 1972). Beyond that, research is fragmentary and not conclusive.

In light of uncertainties about what merits should be compensated, it seems advisable to study through natural experiments (longitudinal studies of teachers and students) and planned experiments (assigning teachers with certain characteristics randomly to students) whether the objective correlates of merit can be determined. For both teachers and administrators, one dimension of merit to be compensated might be the successful implementation of specified innovations. Compensation could take the form of salary, or perhaps more acceptably, some agreed-upon level of "free" funding for innovating schools or districts.

Clearer Standards for Accountability and Better Information Systems. Accountability and information systems for the schools have been discussed carefully (Barro, 1970; Dyer, 1970; Coleman & Karweit, 1972), but they remain in public discussion largely catchwords, two more footnotes for the historian of educational rhetoric.

Nonetheless, such catchwords, in this case as in others, represent a recognition of issues which, though dimly perceived, are fundamental to social choice. Why do such vague concepts as "accountability" and "information systems" represent something fundamental, and what can planned experiments do about them? The phrases are important probably because they recognize implicitly a search for consensus; and one task of experimentation can be to give that search some content. If the objectives of schooling are multiple and unclear, if there are no market tests of efficiency, if there are generally only weak performance criteria for R&D product adoption, and if, at the same time, the public is dissatisfied with its youth, and therefore with its schools, where should reforms begin? Why should the public endorse or the schools adopt, at considerable travail, new methods that will create political and institutional problems, when the resulting prospects for school improvement are so uncertain? In some sense, then, the call for accountability and for information is more than a blending of old nostrums—searching for scapegoats—and new ones—appealing to technology. It is a recognition of a disturbing situation. Unless the things the schools do can be tested in light of well-established and widely disseminated criteria, there is not much rational basis for preferring one policy over another. Even the obvious ones, like spending less money to put the same number of children through school at some average achievement levels, are unreliable. Saving money may be less important not only to the schools but also to the public than continuing to do things as before.

This chapter contends that the search for accountability cannot be based on agreed-upon objectives starting from first principles, because there will never be agreement about the nature or priority of social objectives. Who is to decide ex ante what is the right combination of basic knowledge, vocational skills, child care, socialization, or motor development for the schools to produce? Instead, as suggested above, the present uncertainties should lead R&D planners to a strategy in which the process of experimentation is consciously used as the mechanism that helps define social values.

Market-oriented innovations, such as vouchers or the educational bank, are more or less consciously aimed in that direction. Many of the experiments suggested in this section are directed toward the same general goal, within the present public utility framework, primarily by trying to compensate for the innovative biases created by the local monopoly status, and by trying to assure that educational R&D is carried through to the implementation stage—the analogue in a competitive market would be production engineering—a function which does not emerge automatically from the dynamics of the educational marketplace, because there is no necessary payoff for implementing planned change in ways that mirror the developers' intent.

Once planned experimentation and analysis of existing natural experiments offer some idea of what different people in and out of the schools value, and what costs in money, in bureaucratic upheaval, and in alternative outcomes forsaken they are prepared to pay, we are at the threshold of genuine accountability, of systems that could allow assessment of the progress of a teacher, an administrator, a school district toward specified goals. But it is only a threshold in the absence of widely disseminated information about the outcomes of schooling in achievement, attitudes, career paths, in social integration, and perhaps ultimately in people's conceptions of education. Without comprehensive information flow to policymakers and the public, any new era of experimentation is likely to end where past experiments have—in the research libraries. The widespread dissemination of information will give the public, as individuals and in various institutional roles, opportunities to campaign or to be inert, on the basis of some more realistic appraisal of cause and effect than has yet been possible. If this is no guarantee of more effective schooling, it at least comes closer to an uncertain ideal—public participation in an informal decision-making process. The devising of such comprehensive information systems in support of accountability has been discussed elsewhere (Farquhar & Boehm, 1971; Coleman & Karweit, 1972).

In conclusion, it should be pointed out that accountability in the sense of standards of accomplishment for school staff would require constant revisions. This would not reflect an effort by society to speed up the assembly line once initial norms were achieved; but society's tastes change, and therefore the ordering of its preferences as expressed through experimental results would perennially impose new standards on the schools.

But in a diverse society, perennial change in standards implies that at any one time there will be a variety of standards—including, as pointed out above, the coexistence of incompatible standards. In private markets when consumers want different things, the response is to provide a variety of alternatives, allowing each consumer to choose the particular kind of housing, insurance, or toothbrush that comes closest to meeting his preferences in light of his means. Given a somewhat analogous set of competing demands in the public utility market of the schools, diversity will have to take place primarily in a public marketplace, which, as we have seen, behaves differently from a private one. In light of the standards implicit in this chapter, a major focus of R&D policy should be—through experimentation and through incentives that encourage new patterns of institutional behavior—to encourage a long-overdue diversity of approaches to schooling. Even with more sophisticated approaches to R&D management and to the realities of implementation, the task will be long, costly, difficult. In the current state of knowledge, this process must be justified primarily on the grounds that an educational system which develops effective mechanisms for innovation is more likely to respond to changing social needs than one which is primarily centered on preserving the existing institutional order. This viewpoint implies that diversity in organizational response itself should be a prime target of policy.

REFERENCES

A model for innovation adoption in public school districts: Research on the characteristics of selected school systems as they relate the need for appraisal, acceptance, and use of innovations. 1968. Boston: Arthur D. Little, Inc.

Agger, R. E., & Goldstein, M. N. 1965. *Educational innovations in the community.* Eugene, Oregon: University of Oregon.

Averch, H., Carroll, S. J., Donaldson, T. S., Kiesling, H. J., & Pincus, J. 1972. *How effective is schooling?* Santa Monica, California: The Rand Corporation, R-956.

Baldridge, J. V., & Johnson, R. 1972. *The impact of educational R&D centers and laboratories: An analysis of effective organizational strategies.* Stanford: Stanford University. (mimeo.)

Barro, S. M. 1970. *An approach to developing accountability measures for the public schools.* Santa Monica, Calif.: The Rand Corporation, P-4464.

Barro, S. M. 1972. *Theoretical models of school district expenditure determination and the impact of grants in aid.* Santa Monica, Calif.: The Rand Corporation, R-805.

Becker, M. H. 1970. Factors affecting diffusion of innovations among health professionals. *American Journal of Public Health*, 60, 294–304.

Beckhard, R. 1959. Helping a group with planned change: A case study. *Journal of Social Issues*, 15, 13–19.

Belitsky, A. H. 1969. *Private vocational schools and their students.* Cambridge, Mass.: Schenkman Publishing Co.

Bennis, W. G., Benne, K. D., & Chin, R. 1969. *The planning of change.* New York: Holt, Rinehart, and Winston.

Blum, R. H., & Downing, J. J. 1964. Staff response to innovation in a mental health service. *American Journal of Public Health*, 54, 1230–1240.

Boulding, K. E. 1972. The schooling industry as a possibly pathological section of the American economy. *Review of Educational Research*, 42, 1, 129–143.

Bowles, S., & Gintis, H. 1972. *IQ in the U.S. class structure.* Cambridge: Harvard University, July. (mimeo.)

Brickell, H. M. 1961. *Organizing New York State for educational change.* Albany: New York State Department of Education.

Buchanan, P. C. 1967. *Change in school systems.* Washington, D. C.: National Training Laboratories.

Bushnell, D. D., Freeman, R. A., & Richland, M. 1964. *Proceedings of the conference on the implementation of educational innovation.* Santa Monica, California: System Development Corporation, 1–318.

Bushnell, D. S., & Rappaport, D. (eds.). 1971. *Planned change in education: A systems approach*. New York: Harcourt Brace Jovanovich, Inc.

Caffery, J. G. 1965. *The innovational matrix*, Paper prepared for Institute of Government and Public Affairs Conference on Educational Innovations, UCLA Lake Arrowhead Conference Center, 17–20 December.

Carlson, R. D. 1965(a). *Adoption of educational innovations*. Eugene, Oregon: The Center for the Advanced Study of Educational Administration.

Carlson, R. D. 1965(b). *Change processes in the public schools*. Eugene, Oregon: University of Oregon.

Cartwright, D. 1962. Achieving change in people. In W. G. Bennis, et al. (Eds.), *The planning of change: Readings in the applied behavioral sciences*. New York: Holt, Rinehart, and Winston, 698–710.

Chesler, M., & Flanders, M. 1967. Resistance to research and research utilization: The death and life of a feedback attempt. *Journal of Applied Behavioral Science*, 3, 469–487.

Chorness, M. H., & Rittenhouse, C. H. 1968. *Decision processes and information needs in education: A field survey*. Berkeley, Calif.: Far West Laboratory for Educational Research and Development.

Chorness, M. H., Rittenhouse, C. H., & Heald, R. C. 1969. *Use of resource material and decision processes associated with educational innovation*. Berkeley, Calif.: Far West Laboratory for Educational Research and Development.

Coleman, J. S. 1972. Incentives in education, existing and proposed. Unpublished manuscript.

Coleman, J. S., & Karweit, N. L. 1972. *Information systems and performance measures in schools*. Englewood Cliffs, N. J.: Educational Technology Press.

Coleman, J. S., Katz, E., & Menzel, H. 1966. *Medical innovation: A diffusion study*. New York: Bobbs-Merrill.

Cooper, C. R., & Archambault, B. (eds.). 1968. *Communication, dissemination, and utilization of research information in rehabilitation counseling*. Proceedings of a regional conference sponsored by the Department of Guidance and Psychological Services, Springfield, Massachusetts.

Croker, G. W. 1961. Some principles regarding the utilization of social science research within the military. In *Case studies in bringing behavioral science into use. Studies in the Utilization of Behavioral Science*, Vol. 1. Stanford, Calif.: Institute for Communication Research, Stanford University, 112–125.

Dreeben, R. 1968. *On what is learned in school*. Reading, Massachusetts: Addison–Wesley Publishing Co.

Dyer, H. S. 1970. Toward objective criteria of professional accountability in the schools of New York City. *Phi Delta Kappan*, 52, 212–216.

Eidell, T. L., & Kitchel, J. M. (Eds.). 1968. *Knowledge production and utilization in educational administration*. Eugene, Oregon: Center for the Advanced Study of Education Administration, University of Oregon.

Evans, R. I., & Leppmann, R. I. 1968. *Resistance to innovation in higher education: A social psychological exploration focused on television and the establishment*. San Francisco: Jossey–Bass.

Fairweather, G. W. 1967. *Methods for experimental social innovation*. New York: John Wiley & Sons, Inc.

Falton, B. J. (ed.). 1966. *Educational innovation in the United States*. Bloomington, Indiana: Phi Delta Kappan.

Farquhar, J. A., & Boehm, B. W. 1971. *An information system for educational management: Vol. I. Design considerations*. Santa Monica, Calif.: The Rand Corporation, R-930.

Flanagan, J. C. 1961. Case studies on the utilization of behavioral science research. In *Case studies in bringing behavioral science into use. Studies in the Utilization of Behavioral*

Science. Vol. 1. Stanford, Calif.: Institute for Communication Research, Stanford University, 36–46.

Fleigal, F. C., & Kivlin, J. E. 1966. Attributes of innovations as factors in diffusion. *American Journal of Sociology*, 72, 235–248.

Foshay, A. W. 1970. *Curriculum for the 70's: An agenda for invention.* Washington, D. C.: National Education Association Center for the Study of Instruction.

Fullan, M. Overview of the innovative process and the user. *Interchange*, 1972, 3, 1–46.

Gideonese, H. D. 1968. Research, development and the improvement of education. *Science*, November 1.

Glaser, E. M., & Ross, H. L. 1971. *Increasing the utilization of applied research results.* Los Angeles: Human Interaction Research Institute.

Glaser, E. M., & Taylor, S. 1969. *Factors influencing the success of applied research.* Washington, D. C.: Institute of Mental Health, Department of Health, Education, and Welfare, final report on Contract No. 43–67–1365.

Glaser, E. M., & Wrenn, C. G. 1966. *Putting research, experimental and demonstration findings to use.* Washington, D. C.: Office of Manpower Policy, Evaluation, and Research, U. S. Department of Labor.

Glaser, E. M., Coffey, H. S., Marks, J. B., Sarason, I. B., Anderson, F. W., Dorcus, R. M., Gordon, B. R., Greening, T. C., & Ruja, D. H. 1967. *Utilization of applicable research and demonstration results.* Final report to Vocational Rehabilitation Administration. Washington, D.C.: Department of Health, Education, and Welfare, Project RD–1263–G.

Goodlad, J. I. 1969. Thought, invention and research in the advancement of education. In Committee for Economic Development *The schools and the challenge of innovations.* New York: McGraw-Hill Book Company.

Goodlad, J. I., & Klein, M. F. 1970. *Behind the classroom door.* New York: Charles A. Jones Publishing Co.

Greenwood, P., & Weiler, D. 1972. *Alternative models for the ERIC Clearinghouse network.* Santa Monica, Calif.: The Rand Corporation.

Gross, N., Giaquinta, J., & Bernstein, M. 1971. *Implementing organizational innovations: A sociological analysis of planned educational change.* New York: Basic Books, Inc.

Guba, E. 1965. *Methodological strategies for educational change.* Washington, D. C.: ERIC Document Reproduction Service, November 8–10.

Guetzkow, H. 1959. Conversion barriers in using the social sciences. *Administrative Science Quarterly*, 4, 68–81.

Hanushek, E. A. 1970. *The value of teachers in teaching.* Santa Monica, Calif.: The Rand Corporation, RM–6362.

Havelock, R. G. 1970. *A guide to innovation in education.* Ann Arbor: Center for Research on the Utilization of Scientific Knowledge, Institute for Social Research, University of Michigan.

Havelock, R. G., Guskin, A., Frohman, M., Havelock, M., Hill, M., & Huber, J. 1969 (a). *Planning for innovation through dissemination and utilization of knowledge.* Ann Arbor: Institute for Social Research, Center for Research on Utilization of Scientific Knowledge, University of Michigan.

Havelock, R. G., Huber, J. C., & Zimmerman, S. 1969 (b). *Major works on change in education.* Ann Arbor: Center for Research on Utilization of Scientific Knowledge, University of Michigan.

House, R. E., Kerins, T., & Steele, J. M. 1972. A test of the research and development model of change. *Educational Administration Quarterly*, January, 1–14.

Husén, T., & Boalt, G. 1967. *Educational research and educational change: The case of Sweden.* New York: John Wiley & Sons, Inc.

Jackson, K. 1971. *The politics of school community relations.* Eugene, Oregon: The ERIC Clearinghouse on Educational Management, University of Oregon.

Janowitz, M. 1969. *Institute building in urban education.* New York: Russell Sage Foundation.

Jencks, C., Smith, M., Acland, H., Bane, M. J., Cohen, D., & Gintis, H. 1972. *Inequality.* New York: Basic Books, Inc.

Joly, J. 1967. Research and innovation: Two solitudes? *Canadian Education and Research Digest,* 2, 184–194.

Katz, E. 1961. The social itinerary of technical change: Two studies on the diffusion of innovation. *Human Organization,* 20, 70–82.

Kiesling, H. J. 1971. *Input and output in California compensatory education projects.* Santa Monica, Calif.: The Rand Corporation, R–781.

Killingsworth, C. C. 1967. How to pay for higher education. Address to Economic Society of Michigan. (mimeo.)

Klitgaard, R. E., & Hall, G. R. 1973. *A statistical search for unusually effective schools.* Santa Monica, Calif.: The Rand Corporation, R–1210.

La Pure, R. T. 1965. *Social change.* New York: McGraw-Hill.

Levine, R. A. 1972. *Public planning: Failure and redirection.* New York: Basic Books.

Lindeman, J., Bailey, S. K., Berke, J. S., & Naum, L. H. 1968. *Some aspects of educational research and development in the United States—Report for the OECD review.* Syracuse, N. Y.: Syracuse University Research Corp.

Lippitt, R., Watson, J., & Westley, B. 1958. *The dynamics of planned change.* New York: Harcourt Brace & Company.

Mackie, R. R., & Christensen, P. R. 1967. *Translation and application of psychological research.* Goleta, California: Human Factors Research, Inc., Technical Report 716–1.

Maguire, L. M. 1970. *Observations and analysis of the literature on change.* Philadelphia: Research for Better Schools, Inc.

Maguire, L. M., Temkin, S., & Cummings, C. P. 1971. *An annotated bibliography on administering for change.* Philadelphia: Research for Better Schools, Inc.

Mann, F. C., & Neff, F. W. 1961. *Managing major change in organizations.* Ann Arbor: Foundation for Research on Human Behavior.

Mansfield, E. 1963. Speed of response of firms in new techniques. *Quarterly Journal of Economics,* 77, 290–311.

March, J. 1972. *The technology of foolishness.* Unpublished manuscript, Stanford University.

Marcum, R. L. 1968. *Organizational climate and the adoption of educational innovations.* Logan, Utah: Utah State University.

Miles, M. B. 1964. *Innovation in education.* New York: Bureau of Publications, Teachers College, Columbia University.

Miller, D. R. 1968. *Planned change in education.* Report of Operation PEP: A Statewide Project to Prepare Educational Planners for California.

Mort, P. R., & Cornell, F. G. 1941. *American schools in transition.* New York: Bureau of Publications, Teachers College, Columbia University.

Nasatir, D. 1965. Resistance to innovation in American education. Paper prepared for Institute of Government and Public Affairs Conference on Educational Innovations, UCLA Lake Arrowhead Conference Center, December 17–20.

National Academy of Sciences and Social Science Research Council. 1969. *The behavioral and social sciences: Outlook and needs.* Englewood Cliffs, N. J.: Prentice–Hall.

National Institute of Mental Health. 1971. *Planning for creative change in mental health services: A manual on research utilization.* Rockville, Maryland: National Institute of Mental Health, Report No. (HSM) 71–9059.

National Institute of Mental Health. 1971. *Planning for creative change in mental health services: Information sources and how to use them.* Rockville, Maryland: National Institute of Mental Health, Report No. (HSM) 71–9058.

National Institute of Mental Health. 1971. *Planning for creative change in mental health services: Use of program evaluation.* Rockville, Maryland: National Institute of Mental Health, Report No. (HSM) 71–9057.

Oettinger, A. G. 1969. *Run, computer, run—The mythology of educational innovation.* Cambridge: Harvard University Press.

President's Science Advisory Committee. 1964. *Innovation and experiment in education.* A progress report of the Panel on Educational Research and Development. Washington, D. C.: Government Printing Office.

Rickland, M. 1965. *Traveling seminar and conference for the implementation of educational innovations.* Santa Monica, Calif.: System Development Corporation, Technical Memorandum Series 2691.

Rittenhouse, C. H. 1970. Innovation problems and information needs of education practitioners. *ERIC Report, Vol. 1.* Washington, D. C.: Department of Health, Education, and Welfare, Education Resources Information Center.

Rogers, E. M. 1962. *Diffusion of innovations.* New York: The Free Press.

Rogers, E. M., & Shoemaker, F. F. 1971. *Communication of innovations.* New York: The Free Press.

Rogers, E. M., & Svenning, L. 1969. *Managing change.* Operation PEP: A statewide project to prepare educational planners for California. Washington, D. C.: U. S. Office of Education, Department of Health, Education, and Welfare.

Rosenau, L. H., & Hemphill, J. 1972. *Utilization of NIE output.* Berkeley, Calif.: Far West Laboratory for Educational Research and Development.

Smith, L. M., & Keith, P. M. 1971. *Anatomy of educational innovation.* New York: John Wiley & Sons.

Stufflebeam, D. L. 1970. *Proposal to design new patterns for training research, development, demonstration/dissemination and evaluation personnel in education.* Washington, D. C.: U. S. Department of Health, Education, and Welfare.

Taylor, J. B. 1968. Introducing social innovation. Paper presented at meeting of American Psychological Association, San Francisco, California, September.

U. S. Congress, House of Representatives, Committee on Education and Labor. 1972. *Educational research: Prospects and priorities.* Washington, D. C.: Government Printing Office.

U. S. Congress, House of Representatives, Committee on Education and Labor. 1972. *Purpose and process: Readings in educational research and development.* Washington, D. C.: Government Printing Office.

Watson, G. (ed.). 1967. *Concepts for social change.* Washington, D. C.: National Training Laboratories.

Watson, G., & Glaser, E. M. 1965. What we have learned about planning for change. *Management Review*, 54, 34–46.

Weiler, D. 1973. *The dissemination of educational R&D products: Research and policy issues for the Federal Government.* Santa Monica, Calif.: The Rand Corporation, P–4984.

Wirt, E. W., & Kirst, M. W. 1972. *The political web of American schools.* Boston: Little, Brown.

York, L. J. 1968. *Arrangements and training for effective use of educational R&D information.* Berkeley, Calif.: Far West Laboratory for Educational Research and Development.

4

TITLE V OF ESEA:
THE IMPACT OF DISCRETIONARY FUNDS
ON STATE EDUCATION BUREAUCRACIES*

Jerome T. Murphy

Heading for Capitol Hill in March 1973 to defend the Nixon Administration's plans for education reform, HEW Secretary Caspar W. Weinberger and his aides were weighed down by the usual paraphernalia for a congressional hearing—briefing books, charts, distribution tables, and a hundred copies of printed testimony. But this time the load was heavier than usual. The secretary's lieutenants also carried a two-foot stack of federally required paperwork, the state plans for federal education aid for Kentucky and Minnesota.[1] Carefully placed on the witness table in full

*Jerome T. Murphy, "Title V of ESEA: The Impact of Discretionary Funds on State Education Bureaucracies," *Harvard Educational Review,* **43,** August 1973, 362–385. Copyright © 1973 by President and Fellows of Harvard College. Reprinted with their permission. This article is a substantially reduced version of a longer report conducted under contract HEW–os–71–132 with the U.S. Department of Health, Education, and Welfare, and with the partial support of the Carnegie Corporation. The full report has been published as: *State Education Agencies and Discretionary Funds* (Lexington, Mass.: Lexington Books, 1974).

[1]It was no coincidence that the Chairman of the General Education Subcommittee, Rep. Carl Perkins, is from Kentucky and the ranking Republican, Rep. Albert Quie, is from Minnesota.

view of the congressmen, this massive sheaf of paper sat there throughout the hearing as a reminder of the ensnarling red tape and governmental paralysis wrought by the federal reformers during the 1960s.

The administration exhibited these state plans to dramatize its case, reflecting a widespread concern that education bureaucracies are not working as they should. Indeed, the hope and exuberance which marked the passage of the 1965 Elementary and Secondary Education Act (ESEA) has given way in some quarters to disillusionment about the capacity of government to cope with social problems.

The pile of paperwork symbolized what current executive branch reformers consider the chief obstacle. Narrow categorical programs, overlapping guidelines, and the ensuing red tape have created an administrative nightmare. As Secretary Weinberger said in his testimony, "Comprehensive, coordinated educational planning is made difficult," and the "inflexibility of federal programs means that money is spent on programs that have outlived their usefulness."[2] What is needed, the reformers say, is to revitalize the structure of government by removal of federal bureaucratic stumbling blocks and by greater use of financial aid with few strings attached. This would promote comprehensive and flexible programs, it is thought, while strengthening the capacity of state and local institutions themselves to respond to state and local needs.

Even diehard liberals have been shaken by the apparent ineffectiveness of bureaucratic action in education. But the current analysis of the cause and cures for governmental ineptitude raises several basic questions. When organizations are free to terminate outdated programs, do they in fact take such action? Does unrestricted aid actually foster comprehensive and coordinated planning? And, at bottom, are the root causes underlying the current bureaucracy problem really the staggering red tape and the narrow categorical programs which typically have been blamed?

This chapter explores these questions by examining a specific program—Title V of ESEA—which since its inception has provided virtually unrestricted aid to state education agencies (SEAs).[3] Experience with Title V is important because it illustrates the way bureaucracies work

---

[2]Statement of the Honorable Caspar W. Weinberger, Secretary of Health, Education, and Welfare, before the General Education Subcommittee, Committee on Education and Labor, U.S. House of Representatives, March 19, 1973, p. 5.

[3]Title V actually authorized three separate programs. One called for personnel interchanges between the states and the U.S. Office of Education (USOE). Another program authorized the U.S. Commissioner of Education to make special project grants to the states for solving problems or testing new ideas common to two or more SEAs. The third program apportioned 85% (changed to 95% in 1968) of the funds among the state and outlying territories for use as so-called basic grants. This article focuses exclusively on the basic grant section of Title V (Section 503).

and the way they change, particularly when they are provided with discretionary funds. Money under Title V also is important simply because it has supplemented state educational funds. The initial appropriation of $14.5 million resulted in an average SEA budget increase of 11%, and during the first 7 years of the program some $175 million was apportioned to SEAs.[4]

To begin, some important Title V background factors are presented—the conditions leading to passage of the legislation, its intent, and the findings of some earlier investigations. After that there is a discussion of the impact of Title V, concentrating for the most part on findings about three SEAs. Next, in the longest section of the chapter, I explore why the program was implemented as it was. This is particularly important because Title V, although it strengthened SEAs in several ways, did not promote the basic changes hoped for by some of its legislative designers. In a concluding section I examine the implications of these findings for further strengthening SEAs and for informing the current debate about improved bureaucratic action.

It should be emphasized that this article is mainly descriptive, not normative. My purpose is *not* to say what SEAs should have done with Title V or to suggest the proper educational priorities of SEAs or to indicate that SEAs should necessarily be strengthened at all. On these basically political and philosophical issues, reasonable men differ. Furthermore, I do not mean to imply that Title V was a failure. The article only suggests that the hopes for Title V outstripped what reasonably could have been expected.

TITLE V BACKGROUND

SEAs were engaged in a wide variety of activities at the time ESEA was developed. They collected statistics, distributed state education funds, certified teachers, accredited schools, administered federal programs, and provided certain supplementary services to schools, such as instructional assistance for classroom teachers. Despite these diverse responsibilities, many SEAs were reputed to be weak and conservative,[5] and most were lacking the personnel "for adequate leadership, direction, and service of existing State educational programs."[6] The number of profes-

---

[4]Data supplied by USOE Division of State Agency Cooperation.

[5]Stephen K. Bailey and Edith K. Mosher, *ESEA: The Office of Education Administers a Law*, Syracuse, N.Y.: Syracuse University Press, 1968, p. 140.

[6]Statement of U.S. Commissioner of Education Francis Keppel, before the General Subcommittee on Education of the House Committee on Education and Labor, on H.R. 2361 and HR 2362, 89th Congress, 1st Session, January 22, 1965, p. 105.

sional employees in 1965 ranged from 613 in New York to 15 in North Dakota, with 75 professionals on the average SEA staff.[7]

The staffing problem involved not only the number, but the overall quality of SEA personnel. Some SEAs were bureaucratic jungles, politically dominated. Many were characterized by staff homogeneity, with their personnel coming mainly from rural school districts. First-rate superintendents of education were rare. Personnel problems were made worse by lopsided staffing patterns created by federal categorical programs. Subsidized areas, such as vocational education and certain subject matter disciplines, had disproportionately large staffs. Other areas thought vital, like planning and research, were staffed sparsely if at all.[8]

Not surprisingly, the authors of Title V felt that SEAs needed substantial improvement, especially in light of their new responsibilities in the administration of ESEA. The result was Title V, which in effect provided each SEA with funds to be expended for anything related to the program's broad purpose, which was to "stimulate and assist States in strengthening the leadership resources of their State educational agencies, and to assist those agencies in the establishment and improvement of programs to identify and meet the educational needs of States."[9] While the law contained a laundry list of suggested projects as a guide, each SEA could expend its Title V apportionment as it wished. The only counterweight to this delegation of discretion to the states was USOE's authority to disapprove projects not making a significant contribution. For political and other reasons, USOE never exercised this legal power. As a result, in administrative practice if not in legislative intent, the program became a source of discretionary funds for SEAs, with virtually no federal accountability.

The money was to be used in part to fill important gaps in management and services, thus improving SEA administration of state and federal programs. But in addition some educational reformers, notably U.S. Commissioner of Education Francis Keppel and John Gardner, then President of the Carnegie Corporation and Chairman of a Presidential Task Force on Education, believed that it was essential to enhance the leadership of SEAs, especially with the expanded role of federal programs in education. These reformers hoped that Title V would stimulate SEAs to undergo a "thorough overhaul,"[10] to develop certain entirely new activities (e.g., planning), and to hire more qualified staffers including some with careers initially outside education. In this process, it was hoped that Title V

[7]Data supplied by USOE Division of State Agency Cooperation.
[8]Keppel, pp. 104–105.
[9]Section 501(a) of P.L. 89–10, April 11, 1965.
[10]Francis Keppel, *The Necessary Revolution in American Education,* New York, Harper and Row, 1966, p. 81.

would revitalize SEAs by building the kind of "balanced, professional, high-quality staff that would be needed" for educational leadership.[11] Ultimately, Title V was viewed as a vehicle for maintaining and strengthening the nation's decentralized system of education.[12]

How has Title V worked in practice? The only full-scale extragovernmental investigation of the program, conducted by Roald F. Campbell and his colleagues, concluded in 1967 that Title V was being used "chiefly to provide more of the traditional services," with "overmuch attention" on consultation to local school districts. They found virtually no evidence that SEAs were "considering procedures which might develop new sources, new career programs, or new inducements to attract top educators" to SEAs.[13] These findings, buttressed by those in several other reports, indicate that SEA staffs and budgets roughly doubled between 1965 and 1970. But expansion took place largely in traditional areas.[14] While this growth did allow SEAs to provide more services and to be more visible than in the past, the hoped-for thorough overhaul of SEAs through Title V apparently did not take place.

EXPLORING TITLE V: ASSESSMENT OF THE PROGRAM'S IMPACT

My investigation addressed the same basic question as previous studies: How has Title V worked in practice? Rather than collecting data to categorize Title V-funded activities for all the states, however, I examined Title V at work in selected states. This was done mainly through interviews, which made it possible to explore in detail the program's cumulative effect over the years and its differing impact from state to state, as well as

---

[11]Keppel, Hearings Before the General Subcommittee on Education, p. 134.

[12]Aside from these Title V purposes, the program also played an important political role in 1965. Title V was widely viewed in Washington political circles as a way to persuade the Council of Chief State School Officers to support passage of the entire ESEA legislation.

[13]Roald F. Campbell, Gerald E. Sroufe, and Donald H. Layton, ed., *Strengthening State Departments of Education*, Chicago: Midwest Administration Center, The University of Chicago, 1967, pp. 74–75.

[14]See Ewald B. Nyquist, "State Organization and Responsibilities for Education," in *Emerging Designs for Education*, ed. Edgar L. Morphet and David L. Jesser, Denver, Designing Education for the Future, 1968, p. 148; Advisory Council on State Departments of Education, *Focus on the Future: Education in the States*, Third Annual Report, Washington, D.C., U.S. Government Printing Office, 1968, pp. 5–6; U.S. Senate Committee on Labor and Public Welfare, *"Elementary and Secondary Education Amendments of 1969,"* Report No. 91–634 on H.R. 514, 91st Congress, 2nd Session, 1970, p. 50. The data on staff and budget doubling were supplied by the USOE Division of State Agency Cooperation.

decision-making processes on the state level and the influence of various factors such as state politics and traditions on the program's implementation.

Questions were designed in part to discover how well Title V lived up to its intent "to strengthen state departments of education." Aside from budget increases and staff growth, "strengthening" was assessed by focusing on Title V's impact on the SEA's existing roles or traditional activities. I looked at specific projects in the areas supported by Title V to compare past and present performance. I also focused on the total impact of Title V projects on the SEA. If the Title V projects were considered together, did they result in more effective services and management throughout the department? Recalling the hopes of Commissioner Keppel and other reformers, I also sought evidence that Title V had stimulated SEAs to pursue new roles such as planning and research, to recruit new kinds of staff, and generally to institute basic structural changes. Finally, as a measure of enhanced political strength, I explored the past and present capacity of SEAs to influence their state legislatures.

It is important to point out that other measures of how Title V strengthened SEAs were not systematically examined. First, it would have been possible to gauge the past and present influence of SEAs with local school districts. Limited time and resources did not permit me to select appropriate samples of school districts and then collect the necessary data to draw conclusions. Second, I could have attempted to measure systematically the effect of Title V on the influence of USOE with SEAs. Although federal–state relations in the administration of Title V were explored and discussed in the full report on this research, I did not examine changes in the overall balance of power between USOE and the states. My decision was determined by limited resources, and the existence of other research which concluded that the 1965 fear of federal dominance by USOE was a misperception of power relationships in education. If anything, research suggests that the states' problem is not federal control, but rather local autonomy.[15]

It also should be emphasized that Title V was not the only new federal program in 1965 designed to strengthen SEAs. During that year, state departments also received some $6.5 million for the administration of Title I of ESEA (aid to the disadvantaged) and $2.4 million for the administration of Title II (textbooks and school library resources). Indeed, in 1970, 40% of SEA administrative expenditures came from federal sources, with only

[15]David K. Cohen *et al.*, "The Effects of Revenue Sharing and Block Grants on Education," Cambridge, Mass.: Harvard Graduate School of Education, October 31, 1970, p. 157.

one-fifth of these federal funds provided through Title V.[16] Unlike Title V, however, these other funds are nominally tied to special projects or to the administration of specific federal categorical programs.

Nine states were studied: Colorado, Kansas, Kentucky, Maryland, Massachusetts, New York, South Carolina, Tennessee, and Texas. They were chosen according to objective background variables that could be expected to differentiate SEAs and their experiences with Title V. The variables included size of SEA, geographical region, SEA budget increase from Title V, percentage of school aid from the state level, urbanization, and method of selecting the chief state school officer. States were chosen according to these variables to avoid a biased sample. Among the states studied three were selected for intensive study—Massachusetts, New York, and South Carolina—because they seemed to be exceptions to the overall conclusions of previous Title V reports. Title V apparently had caused these SEAs to reconsider their priorities and to initiate basic changes.

Even among these three states, Title V's impact varied widely. The Massachusetts SEA in 1965 was underfinanced, fragmented, and already undergoing major reorganization. It operated within a political setting dominated by localism, personal politics, and weak state agencies. Title V money was mainly allocated to meet the two most pressing problems of the education department—the need to generate research and statistics, and the need to regionalize its services. Improvements were made, but progress was slow, with the agency making only marginal changes. These Title V-funded activities had limited visible impact on the overall management and policy positions of the Massachusetts Department. The agency was poorly managed in 1965, and in 1971 it was still plagued by outmoded procedures, abnormal internal conflicts, the absence of a clear sense of direction, and limited influence with the state legislature.

The New York SEA, in contrast, was considered a pacesetter in 1965. It was large, well financed, highly professional, and concerned with all facets of education. The SEA was part of a political culture fostering disciplined, nonpartisan public administration. Title V money supported a variety of small projects throughout the agency, with most of the money, 69% in 1970, supporting additional staff.[17] These efforts usually strengthened the discrete SEA subunits that the money was earmarked to help, but many of the projects were little more than "add-ons" to the

[16]Data supplied by USOE Division of State Agency Cooperation.
[17]U.S. Department of Health, Education, and Welfare, *State Departments of Education and Federal Programs: Annual Report, Fiscal Year 1970*, Washington, D.C., U.S. Government Printing Office, 1972, p. 8.

existing structure, with limited impact on the overall effectiveness of the agency. Title V did not affect the SEA in any fundamental way, and in fact the department's influence with the legislature seemed to be on the wane in 1971.

The South Carolina SEA, like its counterpart in Massachusetts, was a weak agency when ESEA was enacted. It was small, politically dominated, fragmented, and had little visibility in the state. The state's political ethos placed a high premium on avoiding open conflict, maintaining stability, and moving forward slowly and cautiously. Between 1965 and 1971, however, the SEA was significantly strengthened. The quality of its staff was improved, and the department nearly tripled in size. In addition, Title V enabled the SEA to build the basic organizational infrastructure necessary to shift from a traditional passive role to a new planning orientation. For the first time, the agency was doing research and information analysis and was developing specific objectives and plans. The SEA's influence with the state legislature also had increased, and although the department had somewhat oversold to the public the importance of its planning activities, Title V had nevertheless played a central role in the agency's development. The South Carolina SEA, weak in 1965, was stronger in 1971.

In brief, significant change took place over the years in the South Carolina SEA, but in Massachusetts and New York Title V did not result in marked changes in procedures, activities, or roles. Similarly, the patterns of SEA influence with state legislatures varied. The Massachusetts SEA was weak in 1965 and remained weak in 1971; New York was among the most influential SEAs in 1965 but seemed to have grown weaker by 1971; and South Carolina was weak in 1965 and appeared to have grown stronger. The relationship between Title V and the strengthening of SEAs was at best inconsistent.

TITLE V OUTCOMES: AN EXPLANATION

What accounts for the diversity of Title V outcomes? Was South Carolina an exception to the general pattern? And why did the unrestricted aid not uniformly promote the hoped-for overhaul of SEAs?

For Title V's shortcomings, individuals familiar with the program tended to blame someone, some organization, or some circumstance. Many chose to blame the Congress. Appropriations were usually tardy, preventing preplanning and making it almost impossible to hire SEA staff in the middle of the school year. In addition, Title V appropriations did not grow as rapidly as anticipated.

Others placed the blame on the states. SEA salaries were not competitive, because state legislatures refused to appropriate funds to raise them. Also, bureaucratic requirements often prevented the hiring of the best job applicants if they lacked the standard credentials.

A third group placed the blame on the weak condition of the SEAs. They were badly understaffed in 1965 and needed Title V funds to enable them to fill "critical gaps in service" rather than to develop long-range strategies.[18]

Some also attributed Title V problems to resistant attitudes toward any new federal program. SEAs were described as unimaginative and conservative, backing into the future reluctantly. Chief state school officers were characterized as "damned ornery."[19] Finally, planning was viewed negatively by some state officials because the idea was associated with communist countries.[20]

These conventional explanations are sometimes helpful in understanding Title V's implementation. For example, late congressional appropriations definitely did create problems in finding staff and implementing the initial Title V projects. But such interpretations do not tell the whole story. There is another view of Title V's implementation which is more fundamental, having to do with the way people typically conceptualize the process of organizational change.

Many assume that competently led, properly functioning organizations act like individual, goal-directed decision makers. They assume that organizations proceed sequentially from establishing general objectives, to weighing alternative strategies toward these objectives, to choosing specific activities that maximize the chances of achieving the objectives. If they do not act this way, it is assumed that *someone* or *something* can be found to explain the distortion of normal procedures.[21] This assumption was clearly evident with the Title V blame-sayers, who thought that if the obstacles to the program had been removed and if those "damned ornery" chiefs had not been in charge, then SEAs would have worked properly and the reformers' hopes would have been met. Similarly, the Title V reformers seemed to assume that Title V decisions would grow out of a rational planning process, and SEAs, in turn, would change in a flexible fashion. Such a process was anticipated in Commissioner Keppel's 1965 congres-

[18]Interview with USOE official, 1972. (Interviewees were usually promised anonymity to assure candid replies. Hence they are not identified by name.)

[19]Interview with USOE official, 1972.

[20]The "blame" explanations presented here come from interviews with current and former state and federal officials, and others knowledgeable about Title V. Also, publications about Title V and other federal programs have pointed to these problems.

[21]For a clear discussion of this, see Graham T. Allison, *Essence of Decision: Exploring the Cuban Missile Crisis,* Boston, Little, Brown, 1971.

sional testimony which said, "Title V has been written to *encourage* each department to determine its own significant needs and to develop *plans* for meeting them."[22] Also, after the bill was passed, USOE asked the states to conduct an extensive needs assessment before making their Title V decisions.

The assumption of unitary, purposive organizational behavior is widespread, but it has been challenged by recent theories of organizational decision-making.[23] These theories contend that properly functioning organizations typically change slowly, settling for solutions that produce the least disorder. In this view, to suggest that SEAs should have acted in a substantially different manner when provided with unrestricted aid is to substitute utopian hope for the reality of organizational behavior. Furthermore, if this view is substantiated it suggests that problems underlying Title V involve more than individual culpability, institutional idiosyncrasy, or unique historical circumstance.[24]

Although this is not the place to review extensively the literature on organizational decision-making, it seems wise to outline briefly certain basic concepts. First, theorists maintain that agency decision-making has less to do with calculated choices to meet agreed-upon goals than with intra-agency competition and bargaining, with goals growing out of the bargaining process. This view rests on the notion that every organization is a coalition of participants and subunits with conflicting demands, changing foci of attention, and only limited ability to deal with all problems simul-

[22]Francis Keppel, Hearings before the General Subcommittee on Education, p. 104 (emphasis added), I do not mean to imply that Keppel and others had carefully thought in advance about how decisions would be made in the states once Title V became law. Problems were being met a step at a time, and prior to ESEA's passage virtually all of Keppel's attention was understandably directed toward securing passage of ESEA. Still, the evidence does suggest that Title V was based in part on the assumption, whether implicit or explicit, that the stimulus of the legislation and, later, the needs assessment to help choose projects would produce a "rational" process for selecting the initial Title V activities. Presumably, the program would then be used flexibly to meet higher priority needs as new problems developed.

[23]Herbert A. Simon, *Administrative Behavior,* 2nd ed., New York, The Free Press, 1957; James G. March and Herbert A. Simon, *Organizations,* New York, John Wiley and Sons, 1958; Richard M. Cyert and James G. March, *A Behavioral Theory of the Firm,* Englewood Cliffs, N.J.: Prentice-Hall, 1963; Aaron Wildavsky, *The Politics of the Budgetary Process,* Boston, Little, Brown, 1964; Daniel Katz and Robert L. Kahn, *The Social Psychology of Organizations,* New York, John Wiley and Sons, 1966; Seymour B. Sarason, *The Culture of the School and the Problem of Change,* Boston, Allyn and Bacon, 1971; Allison, *Essence of Decision;* and John Steinbruner, *The Cybernetic Theory of Decision: New Dimensions of Political Analysis*, Princeton, N.J., Princeton University Press, 1974.

[24]This does not mean, of course, that individuals are free from responsibility for their actions, but rather that the conventional explanations are incomplete.

taneously.[25] For example, all subunits of an SEA may be staffed by educators interested in strengthening the department, but different educators and subunits will interpret "strengthening" differently; the kindergarten unit will have different views from those of the secondary education unit.

The availability of unrestricted resources would likely result in intra-agency competition for funds, with the various subunits expecting their fair share. The allocation of funds is apt to take place in an informal bargaining process characterized by give and take, and mutual adjustment among the SEA's highest officials. The needs of the SEA are defined not by any formal assessment, but by the desires of those with access to the bargaining game. If a need does not have an advocate, it usually is not considered.

The action advocated by a particular official depends on his interests and experience, his perception of internal and external crises, his sense of the maintenance needs of his sector of the department, his own desire for promotion, and his understanding of acceptable practices. The results of the bargaining process depend in large part on the skill and power of the bargainers and the reasonableness of their demands. But negotiations are sophisticated. In the process different subunits control different information, and they tend to provide officials with incomplete or selective information about their needs and successes. Decisions therefore depend in part on what is known and in part on what is overlooked or withheld. In addition, one prime concern of higher officials works against any strong choice for funding some programs and ignoring others: Organizational well-being requires that current employees in *all* sectors of the department be reasonably happy. In demonstrating the necessity of any unprecedented or disproportionate funding of certain programs, the burden of proof is on the high officials themselves and not on lower employees.

This bargaining for funds, of course, does not occur in a vacuum. Decisions are also affected by the department's unique cultural characteristics, such as its traditions, norms, accepted programs, and standard operating procedures.[26] In every state there is a different organizational culture, according to the background and expectations of SEA staffers, the structure and the reward system of the organization, and the agency's political constituencies. In my research it was difficult to avoid caricaturing the dominant bureaucratic modes of certain state education agencies: the pre-bureaucratic orientation in Tennessee, personal politics in Massachusetts, pedestrian efficiency in Kansas, clubbish mentality in South

---

[25]See particularly Cyert and March for a discussion of this concept.
[26]See particularly Sarason for a discussion of organizational culture.

Carolina, and technocratic professionalism in New York. The organizational culture of the SEA helped determine both how Title V funds would be spent and how much the resources would affect the SEAs.

Aside from these cultural constraints on flexible organizational change, theorists maintain that organizations and individuals do not constantly search for better, or the best, way of doing their job. Instead, procedures good enough to get by are kept, and any new departures take place only when existing practices are found completely unsatisfactory. Organizations and individuals act this way because, in Herbert A. Simon's words, "they have not the wits to *maximize*."[27] That is, too much confusion and uncertainty exists in a complex world for organizations to make a comprehensive search for all available information sources and to consider all possible alternatives in order to come up with the best solution to a problem. To maximize would put impossible demands on human capacity for thought.

This organizational tendency helps to explain the "overmuch attention" concentrated on hiring additional subject matter consultants with Title V money. School visitations were an accepted practice in 1965 and were taken for granted in discussions about additional services for the schools. Failure to explore alternatives was exemplified clearly in Massachusetts, where the rationale for Title V decision-making about instructional services was portrayed by one SEA staff member in a candid interview:

> What do we have now? Where are the gaps? What kind of people do we need? . . . The conscious determination was made to add subject matter specialists in those areas where we didn't have them. I don't think we ever said should we or shouldn't we have them. [There was] acceptance of the fact that we should.[28]

Since the existing practices were not found unsatisfactory, alternative procedures were rarely, if ever, considered.

A final concept drawn from decision-making theory holds that organizations avoid uncertainty in allocating their resources.[29] In the case of SEAs, uncertainties arise over the behavior of schools, the demands of citizens, the actions of the federal government, and the proclamations of the legislature. Moreover, there is usually insufficient information about complex problems, and only limited knowledge of appropriate solutions. Thinking about all possible outcomes of anticipated actions is painful and puts an impossible load on organizational officials. To function at all,

---

[27]Simon, p. xxiv, emphasis in original.
[28]Interview with Massachusetts SEA official, 1972.
[29]See Cyert and March for an extended discussion of this concept.

though, they must learn to cope with choices under uncertainty. One way is to sidestep the multiple uncertainties associated with future events by concentrating organizational energy on pressing, short-term problems. A pressing problem or crisis is relatively well defined. Hence there is little uncertainty in dealing with it. It is not surprising that organizations tend to behave like fire companies, moving from crisis to crisis extinguishing brush fires, rather than developing long-range plans.

SOME WORKING HYPOTHESES

Based on these concepts, I have developed a series of propositions about the way SEAs could have been expected to respond to Title V aid. They are working hypotheses used to explain why the program's impact fell short of the hopes of some reformers. Because these hypotheses grow out of the decision-making branch of organizational theory, they do not cover all the facets of SEA processes that could be explored. But this orientation seems to hold out the promise of fresh insights into the varied outcomes of Title V.

First, one would expect competition for the funds, with the money distributed to satisfy the interests of important elements in the organization. Funds would not be allocated according to a set of abstractly determined priorities agreed upon in advance.

SEA practice was basically consistent with this hypothesis. In New York, the advent of Title V resulted in an invitation to the professional staff, including those concerned with higher education, to offer suggestions on how to spend the money. "In almost any bureaucracy when money becomes available," one staffer noted, "it is put up for competition, as was done here."[30] Rough proposals made their way through channels with little review to the desk of the newly designated Title V coordinator. Meanwhile, a more informal process of proposal review was also taking place. One Title V project director stated, for instance, that he took his proposal directly to the commissioner. In all, 30 to 40 ideas reached the Title V coordinator. Decisions were made by a group of top administrators. Criteria were developed *during* this process that gave priority to "immediate needs," activities "for which it would be difficult or impossible to secure State funds," and "innovative changes."[31] Twenty-four projects from across the agency were chosen initially with little evidence of conflict. Most of the other projects were simply postponed. *After* the ideas were agreed upon,

[30]Interview with New York SEA official, 1971.
[31]Ewald B. Nyquist, "Proposals for Using Funds Under Title V-ESEA" (Typewritten). September 20, 1965, p. 1.

general priorities were formally stated which rationalized the areas covered by the proposed activities.

The working hypothesis was similarly borne out in South Carolina, but competition among proposals was more vigorous than in New York because of the relative poverty of the state agency. There was a scramble for the money, with the competition extending even to education units outside the SEA, such as the Educational Television Commission. An SEA official explained that "there was an almost overwhelming pressure to add personnel. Almost nobody is ever convinced that he has enough manpower to do the job as he thinks it ought to be done."[32]

The final decisions evolved from a bargaining process extending over several months, with three major projects emerging. The champion of the research proposal wanted a unit to meet the growing requests for SEA information. Meanwhile, the superintendent wanted to conduct additional comprehensive surveys of schools. The outcome—the new Division of Research, Experimentation and Surveys—reflected both ideas. When asked about his success, the research director responded, "I never was bashful about asking for more money."[33] The decision to fund the Director of Instruction's project apparently was a foregone conclusion. He was a respected educator, and as one official said, "You had to satisfy the basic requests of the division heads. Each had his concern for his own area."[34] Finally, the Director of Teacher Education and Certification bypassed the superintendent and approached friends on the State Board of Education, thus helping to assure his project's final approval. Those subunits and individuals seeking their fair share of the newly available money were usually successful in obtaining it.

In Massachusetts, the money was not distributed evenly across the agency. There was no general invitation to the staff to offer ideas about how the money should be allocated. Instead, competition for resources took place at one remove, as different subunits routinely informed the departmental management of their needs for additional resources. Decisions were made by the commissioner, with some input from a small group of advisors. The process was to a large extent preordained, since the major needs—regionalization and research—were known prior to the passage of ESEA. As one official put it, "We had things thought through before Title V about where the Department ought to be going. When money [Title V] came along, we had to fit the ideas to the available funds."[35] This fitting, according to one 1965 staff member involved in the process, depended largely on

[32]Interview with South Carolina SEA official, 1971.
[33]Interview with South Carolina SEA official, 1971.
[34]Interview with South Carolina SEA official, 1971.
[35]Interview with Massachusetts SEA official, 1972.

who "yelled the loudest" and "who was championing what particular cause."[36]

Although the process differed somewhat from state to state, three characteristics were common to each. First, discussions of Title V allocations proceeded from specific needs, such as an additional specialist or a new curriculum guide, to general goals, such as enhancement of SEA leadership in instruction. Abstract goals were established only after project decisions were made. Second, Title V may have been viewed by some reformers in Washington as a vehicle to stimulate SEAs to rethink their priorities, but within these agencies the program was mainly viewed as a supplemental resource to be tapped to meet pre-existing priorities. Third, it was important that a need have an advocate. One must wonder, for example, whether the New York SEA would have allocated part of its Title V resources to set up an Office of Science and Technology if there had not been a highly regarded employee arguing for it.

Needs must be articulated if action is to follow. In the normal situation where there are more needs than the available resources to meet them, a persuasive and persistent advocate can play an important role. Referring to Title V, a Rhode Island SEA staffer made this point succinctly: "It's the old adage of the squeaky wheel."[37]

A second working hypothesis is that Title V would be expended mainly to meet pressing problems, through the simple expansion of existing modes of operation. Entirely new priorities, like planning, rarely would be established.

Despite the wide diversity among SEAs and their Title V projects, the data were consistent with this working hypothesis. The initial Title V projects were budgeted mainly to meet short-term problems, rather than to finance the development of long-range strategies. The major emphasis of the SEA projects was on the expansion and marginal adaptation of ongoing activities. The program resulted in few basic structural changes. For example, only two states used Title V the first year to establish planning offices. In at least one of these states, this came as the result of external pressure rather than any agency initiative. Moreover, even the new research office in South Carolina and the new regional offices in Massachusetts were designed mainly to provide additional staff for activities already in progress prior to ESEA.

Interestingly, this hypothesis was borne out most clearly in the amply staffed and competently led New York SEA. There was a backlog of teacher certificates to be typed and sent to applicants; Title V funded a

[36]Interview with Massachusetts SEA official, 1972.
[37]Letter to the author, April 4, 1972.

project called ATTAKCERT to hire office staff for twelve weeks. The supply of state-supported in-service education resources exceeded teacher demand; Title V was used for a multimedia presentation to promote the departmental activity. The Fiscal Crisis Task Force, formed because of state aid cutbacks, needed to "build the case for additional funds";[38] Title V was used for a comparative study of the cost of education in New York and six other states. The Cooperative Review Service, started in 1961, had a large backlog of unfinished reports; Title V funded a unit.

At least half the initial projects funded in fiscal 1966 and still supported in fiscal 1972 fell into this "pressing problem" category. These examples support the notion that the department did not weigh alternatives which might maximize long-term organizational goals, but rather moved from crisis to crisis.

Clearly, such organizational myopia was not limited to New York. It existed in varying degrees in all the states studied. A memorable notice posted in the office of a prominent Colorado SEA staffer made the point well.

NOTICE

THE OBJECTIVE OF ALL DEDICATED DEPARTMENT EMPLOYEES SHOULD BE TO THOROUGHLY ANALYZE ALL SITUATIONS, ANTICIPATE ALL PROBLEMS PRIOR TO THEIR OCCURRENCE, HAVE ANSWERS FOR THESE PROBLEMS, AND MOVE SWIFTLY TO SOLVE THESE PROBLEMS WHEN CALLED UPON . . . .

HOWEVER . . .

WHEN YOU ARE UP TO YOUR ASS IN ALLIGATORS, IT IS DIFFICULT TO REMIND YOURSELF THAT YOUR INITIAL OBJECTIVE WAS TO DRAIN THE SWAMP.

If education departments—large as well as small, rich as well as poor—typically act to avoid uncertainty, as organizational theory contends and my data suggest, then it should be less than surprising that Title V was used largely to react to a series of short-term problems. And if organizations typically behave according to standard operating procedures and traditions, then it also should not be surprising that short-term problems were met for the most part by marginal adaptation of ongoing activities.

A third working hypothesis is that standard procedures for recruiting personnel would not be affected by the availability of new resources.

Title V apparently had little direct impact on changing the caliber or qualifications of SEA employees. Hiring procedures were not altered as a

[38]William C. Enderlein, ed. *Comprehensive Planning in State Education Agencies,* Communication Technology, 1969, p. 19.

result of discretionary federal funding. This conclusion is consistent with that of the Campbell Report, which expressed concern about the use of Title V for the "perpetuation and reification" of 1965 hiring practices.[39]

It is important to point out, however, that the quality of SEA personnel in some states did improve. The reasons probably include the increased importance of certain SEAs within the structure of state government, the greater number of interesting positions available in SEAs given their new responsibilities in administering federal programs, and the enlarged pool of potential SEA employees because of nationwide economic recession and growing oversupply of professional educators. But it was these factors rather than the stimulus of Title V that seem to explain the personnel improvements.

A fourth working hypothesis is that organizational stakes would carry funded projects beyond the point where benefits outweigh costs. Projects would tend to become permanent.

Once Title V staff positions were filled, the jobs by and large continued from year to year with little evidence of careful evaluation. Even the New York SEA, which had a unit for evaluating its own programs, failed to terminate any ongoing Title V projects. "It's hard to identify a program that doesn't meet some kind of need somewhere," noted a staffer in the evaluation unit.[40] As another New York official put it, "Almost the last thing you drop are people."[41]

As a result, the original flexibility of Title V was short lived. The program turned into a source of general operational support, largely for projects designed to meet 1965 needs. This finding, combined with the fact that the initial projects would have been somewhat different if there had been a different cast of characters arguing their needs in 1965, leads to a curious result which pierces the aura of organizational rationality. In the words of Richard M. Cyert and James G. March, "The 'accidents' of organizational genealogy tend to be perpetuated."[42]

But not all of Title V resources were allocated for permanent staff positions. The three SEAs studied in depth in effect used a small portion of the money as a contingency fund to meet crises as they arose. This was accomplished in part without a formally earmarked fund. Job vacancies freed previously budgeted resources for new activities, and other budgeted items often were not spent completely during the year. As a result, Title V frequently was available to meet the cost of small new endeavors in the middle of the fiscal year.

[39]Campbell, Sroufe, and Layton, p. 75.
[40]Interview with New York SEA official, 1971.
[41]Interview with New York SEA official, 1971.
[42]Cyert and March, p. 34.

The sequence of events leading to these Title V expenditures should be emphasized. A need developed within the SEA. Then an appropriate funding source was sought. Since Title V was the most unencumbered source of funds available to SEAs, it could support activities which could not be funded appropriately through other more restricted federal categorical aid programs. Also, Title V could be used to pay expenses when state funds were not budgeted for that purpose. What this meant, of course, was that projects were simply labeled as a Title V effort because of the money's availability.

It should not be surprising that some SEAs used Title V in this fashion. As an experienced bureaucrat in Texas said: "Every level of government I've ever been involved with has had a slush fund. How it works depends on the ingenuity of the finance man."[43]

Fifth, SEA goals and activities would change slowly over time as a result of experience. Dramatic change usually would result only after heavy pressure from outside the organization.

The evidence is consistent with this working hypothesis. When Title V funds became available in Massachusetts, for instance, the SEA had just undergone a reorganization ordered by the legislature. But things seemed to return to business as usual when the reorganization was completed. There was no continuing legislative interest in SEA improvement, and only limited funds were provided to implement organizational changes. Moreover, little change took place in the number of bureaucratic hurdles required for hiring staff or in the entrenched tradition of localism which had previously resulted in an insignificant role for the SEA. Within this context the SEA changed somewhat from 1965, but continued in 1971 to be a second-class citizen in the state.

When Title V reached New York, by contrast, the SEA was a stable, well financed, sophisticated organization and not under significant pressure to institute major organizational changes. The SEA used Title V to make a series of marginal improvements, with the agency changing slowly over the years. The advent of Title V certainly did not precipitate any thorough overhaul or reevaluation of its needs or its direction. But recent extra-agency forces seem to be highly related to the department's declining influence with the legislature. A fiscal crisis in state government, a growing concern with the requests of educators and with the department's far-flung activities, and the demise of a once monolithic state school lobby have taken their toll on the SEA despite the continuing high competence of its staff and the influx of federal dollars.

[43]Interview with Texas SEA official, 1971.

In South Carolina—the state that changed the most—the SEA received its Title V apportionment just as the state was undergoing a political, economic, and social transformation in an attempt to meet well-recognized deficiencies. Pressure for economic expansion, the 1964 Civil Rights Act, the 1965 Voting Rights Act, massive federal aid, and reapportionment all had challenged traditional South Carolina ways. This economic and political ferment, coupled with demands for departmental change and leadership from a strong governor who viewed education as central to economic growth, provided SEA officials with the opportunity and necessity to develop a stronger SEA. Title V funds *facilitated* the development of an SEA that was ready to grow, with a new, management-minded superintendent and a new team of well-informed aides. Had Title V come five years earlier, the program probably would have had only marginal impact. At that time the agency had not yet reached a point where substantial change was demanded or was even possible. Coming when it did, the program translated the opportunity for progress into action.

The extent of Title V's success, then, depended mainly on local factors. These factors—economic changes, state fiscal problems, political shifts, a breakdown in traditions—were beyond manipulation by the federal government. Also, even when the conditions were right for strengthening an SEA's management and for upgrading its professional competence, there was no guarantee that this would result in a position of increased influence for the department with a state legislature. This suggests that rapid governmental reform is extremely difficult to accomplish. It depends on the right combination of local preconditions, political circumstances, and unpredictable events. Over time, pouring federal money into this mix will likely result only in marginal changes, unless the money is the only missing ingredient. Money is just not the key to reform that some would like to believe.

This discussion goes a bit further than the earlier "blame" explanations. But two qualifications need to be made. First, the fit between theory and practice was not always perfect. Some Title V projects, for instance, were not simply responses to short-term problems. The theory suggests typical institutional tendencies rather than precise predictions for all organizations. Second, I do not mean to imply that major change through federal discretionary funds cannot occur in the absence of external pressure. Under certain circumstances, it definitely can.

Existing organizational orientations and routines are not impervious to directed change. Careful targeting of major factors that support routines—such as personnel, rewards, information, and budgets—can affect major change over time. But the terms and conditions of most political leadership jobs—short tenure and responsiveness to hot issues—make effective, directed change uncommon.[44]

To a resourceful leader, who has both time and a clear sense of direction, unrestricted aid can provide long-term flexibility. But such situations are the exception rather than the rule.[45]

These qualifications notwithstanding, the theory does add an important, missing dimension to the discussion of Title V. The underlying reason why Title V did not result often in basic changes may have as much to do with the way complex organizations behave as with particular institutional or individual shortcomings. Stated differently, even with imaginative SEA leadership, modern and well-run SEAs, ample time for developing proposals, and no other new programs to implement, the chief focus in 1965 might still have been on "greasing squeaky wheels" rather than on selecting among fundamental innovations.

IMPLICATIONS

The widespread assumption that competently led bureaucracies operate like goal-directed, unitary decision-makers may well be a major barrier to dealing with problems of bureaucratic change. Both program evaluations and reform efforts must come to grips explicitly with the enduring attributes of organizations. In general these attributes include: differing organizational cultures, each with its own history, traditions, norms, and standard operating procedures; a pattern of bargaining among subunits, which have conflicting demands, expansionist tendencies, and a preoccupation with short-term crises; an inability to be comprehensive, leading to the search for solutions that are good enough rather than optimal; and a tendency to foster the continuation of ineffective programs and discourage candid evaluations. These organizational complexities are overlooked if we believe that properly functioning organizations proceed in a rational fashion and change flexibly to meet new priorities.

There are several possible ways to begin to deal with such generalized organizational phenomena. One way is through improved planning, which may enhance the capacity of SEAs to make and implement better decisions. A parallel strategy is to develop external sources of information that may lead to more candid analyses of governmental action. While space does not permit a full exploration of these approaches here, a few observations can be made.

[44]Allison, pp. 94–95.
[45]Katz and Kahn, pp. 446, 449.

In the case of planning, my investigation leads me to be deeply suspicious of much of the current literature on SEA planning which talks of the "science of long-range planning,"[46] "identification of overall, long-range goals"[47] for SEAs, and "comprehensive and continuous planning."[48] Such an approach falls prey to the assumption that bureaucracies can be made to operate in a rational and unitary fashion. Even putting aside the organizational constraints on such behavior, there are other major barriers to broadscale SEA planning. If it calls for the reallocation of public resources, planning encounters major political hurdles, especially with the current stiff competition for limited tax dollars. Moreover, finding solutions to educational problems is much more complicated today than it was 10 or 20 years ago. If the recent research on the effectiveness of schooling has told us anything, it is that conventional solutions—more money, smaller classes, and better trained teachers—do not seem to work the way people thought they did.

Intelligent SEA planning must deal explicitly with these awkward facts. Doing so is no simple matter of preparing planning documents. Instead, it will take time, resources, and a lot of hard thought about the complexities involved. This suggests to me that SEAs should concentrate their planning efforts at any given time on the thorough analysis of a *limited* number of problems, such as the equitable distribution of school aid to localities, a reworking of state programs for the disadvantaged, or other important issues of well-defined dimensions. In dealing with these issues, the analysis ideally should challenge assumptions, discuss values, and explore a number of alternative approaches. Modern technologies of planning should be used to the extent feasible, but the main concern should be with exploring good questions. As an example, what might it mean to achieve equitable distribution of school expenditures? Can we outline competing models of equity? What differences would each make, for whom? Is it worth the effort to further implement one of the models, and if so, how should we proceed?

Policy analysis calls for careful attention to the organizational problems of implementation as contrasted with simply logistical ones. Graham Allison has listed some of the questions an analyst needs to ask.

[46]Sam P. Harris, *State Departments of Education, State Boards of Education, and Chief State School Officers*, Washington, D.C., U.S. Government Printing Office, 1973, p. 27.

[47]Yeuell Y. Harris and Ivan N. Seibert, ed., *The State Education Agency: A Handbook of Standard Terminology and a Guide for Reading and Reporting Information about State Education Agencies*, Washington, D.C., U.S. Government Printing Office, 1971, p. 89.

[48]Edgar L. Morphet, David L. Jesser, and Arthur P. Ludka, ed., *Planning and Providing for Excellence in Education*, Denver: Improving State Leadership in Education, 1971, p. 44.

Is the desired action on the agenda of issues that will arise in the current climate? If not, can it be forced onto the agenda? . . . Which players will have to agree and which to acquiesce? What means are available to whom for persuading these players? Is the desired action consistent with existing programs and SOPs [standard operating procedures] of the organization that will deliver the behavior? If not, how can these organizational procedures be changed?[49]

Finally, in selecting problems for analysis, targets of opportunity need to be identified, with political considerations specifically built into final choices. Planning activity in a certain area might be opportune because of expiring legislation, a hot political issue, a breakdown in standard operating procedures, or new research findings. At any time, certain policies are more susceptible to change than others.

This view of SEA planning is purposely narrow. It will be viewed by some as a retreat from the notion of comprehensive planning, and it could become ineffectual if planning became too fragmented or too factional as a result of excessive or prolonged focus on a few issues at the expense of others. Nonetheless, moving in the direction of incremental, problem-oriented policy analysis now seems the most sensible way for SEAs to deal with the constraints created by the enduring attributes of organizations, the vicissitudes of local politics, and the great uncertainty surrounding educational problems. If this approach were adopted we realistically could expect modest changes in a few areas.

There are several ways to develop external sources of information. One approach is to expand the role of state audit agencies, or other similar bodies outside the SEA, to conduct performance audits: They would make "qualitative judgments about the effectiveness of [SEA] policies and actions."[50] As an alternative, SEAs could be required to undergo an annual performance audit by some recognized extra-governmental organization, such as a university or a consulting firm. Another possibility is to use federal research money to support evaluations of SEA operations. Candid, independent reports on SEA activities could be the first step toward the termination of outmoded programs and perhaps could lead to better decisions about allocation of agency resources.

At present, SEAs seem primarily accountable to one constituency—their professional peers in the schools. The development of other constituencies also might be useful, generated by creating countervailing sources of power outside the SEAs. One analogue for such an effort might be the Office of Economic Opportunity legal services program, where lawyers have brought suits or threatened legal action to encourage gov-

---

[49] Allison, p. 268.
[50] Frazar B. Wilde and Richard F. Vancil, "Performance Audits by Outside Directors," *Harvard Business Review*, 50, July-August, 1972, p. 113.

ernment agencies to pursue certain priorities. A second analogue might be the program advisory councils which currently exist to oversee implementation of certain federal programs conflicting with state priorities. A third approach could be through the creation of private, nongovernmental research–action agencies. "Nader's Raiders" provide one model for such activities. These agencies might conduct studies of the responsiveness of SEAs to particular minority groups, to consumers, and to the general public.

All of these ideas, of course, raise a number of complicated issues and face many obstacles in their implementation. It is not clear that most SEAs have the resources to do the type of policy analysis outlined above. Also, the development of external sources of information and power might not produce more effective SEA action but simply make SEA officials more defensive about everything they do. Nevertheless, the ideas briefly listed here seem worthy of careful exploration.

The present research also has direct bearing on the current debate about the inefficiencies and problems created by federal categorical aid programs. Like the framers of Title V, the current proponents of less restricted aid assume that competently led institutions, provided the freedom to plan without narrow federal requirements and red tape, will develop flexible strategies for institutional change.[51] This assumption is clearly illustrated in President Nixon's message to the Congress on Education Revenue Sharing:

> . . . Rigid qualifications for grants frequently stifle creative initiative . . . the present fragmented procedures virtually eliminate . . . a comprehensive, coordinated program. . . .
>
> . . . Education Revenue Sharing . . . would enhance flexibility in the application of funds for education, and permit the states to make substantial adjustments in their education plans as their educational needs require.[52]

But my investigation shows that discretionary aid falls short of expectations for many of the same reasons as categorical aid. Both foster narrow units within bureaucracies; both lead to activities that outlive their usefulness; both lead to organizational "add-ons" that do not affect basic SEA structures; neither necessarily leads to coordinated and comprehensive planning; neither seems especially effective in fostering creativity. Flexibility in the funding source, in short, does not necessarily lead to greater flexibility in recipient organizations.

---

[51]Of course, these current proposals, as with Title V in 1965, are multipurpose. Other purposes include simple fiscal relief, providing additional services, sharing in rising costs, and political decentralization.

[52]President's Message to Congress on Education Revenue Sharing, April 6, 1971.

The nature of the bureaucratic problem in implementing governmental programs has been obscured. Blame has been placed on the inefficiencies of the federal aid delivery system, when in fact major faults associated with categorical aid appear to be general features of public bureaucracies. As long as the investigation of the problem of governmental paralysis is reduced to a search for scapegoats, at the expense of attempting to understand organizational behavior, we can expect only limited improvements in the way educational bureaucracies work.

ACKNOWLEDGMENT

The author wishes to express his appreciation to David Cohen and John Steinbruner of Harvard University for their helpful suggestions on earlier drafts.

REFERENCES

Allison, G. T. 1971. *Essence of decision: Exploring the Cuban missile crisis*. Boston: Little, Brown.

Berke, J. S., & Kirst, M. W. (Ed.). 1972. *Federal aid to education: Who benefits? Who governs?* Lexington, Mass.: D. C. Heath.

Campbell, R. F., Sroufe, G. E., & Layton, D. H. (Ed.). 1967. *Strengthening state departments of education*. Chicago: University of Chicago, Midwest Administration Center.

Cyert, R. M., & March, J. G. 1963. *A behavioral theory of the firm*. Englewood Cliffs, N.J.: Prentice-Hall.

Derthick, M. 1970. *The influence of federal grants: Public assistance in Massachusetts*. Cambridge, Mass.: Harvard University Press.

Katz, D., & Kahn, R. L. 1966. *The social psychology of organizations*. New York: John Wiley and Sons.

March, J. G., & Simon, H. A. 1958. *Organizations*. New York: John Wiley and Sons.

Sarason, S. B. 1971. *The culture of the schools and the problem of change*. Boston: Allyn and Bacon.

Schick, A. 1971. *Budget innovations in the states*. Washington, D.C.: The Brookings Institution.

Schultze, C. L. 1968. *The politics and economics of public spending*. Washington, D.C.: The Brookings Institution.

Simon, H. A. 1957. *Administrative behavior* (2nd ed.). New York: The Free Press.

Steinbruner, J. *The Cybernetic Theory of Decision: New Dimensions of Political Analysis*. Princeton, N.J.: Princeton University Press, 1974.

Wildavsky, A. 1964. *The politics of the budgetary process*. Boston: Little, Brown.

5

FOLLOW THROUGH
PLANNED VARIATION*

Richard F. Elmore

PLANNED VARIATION, POLICY RESEARCH,
AND IMPLEMENTATION

In late 1967 a loosely constructed coalition of federal policymakers converged on the idea of designing a federal compensatory education program around systematic, or planned, variations in program content. Instead of simply dispersing federal money to local educational agencies and relying on each one to develop its own program, a limited number of "program models" would be developed by a group of educational research and development specialists, and each model would be implemented in a

*This paper, prepared especially for this volume, is a major revision of a paper that appeared earlier as, "Lessons from Follow Through," *Policy Analysis*, vol. 1, no. 3 (Summer 1975), 459–84. Some portions of the earlier paper are reprinted here with permission of The Regents of the University of California. A more detailed analysis of the Follow Through experiment can be found in Richard F. Elmore, *Follow Through: Decisionmaking in a Large-Scale Social Experiment* (unpublished doctoral dissertation, Harvard Graduate School of Education, 1976. The author wishes to thank the Lyndon Baines Johnson Library, Austin, Texas, and personnel of the Follow Through program for their assistance in securing the unpublished documents cited in this article.

number of settings. Planned variations in program content, it was hoped, would provide an opportunity to learn more about the specific characteristics of successful programs for educationally disadvantaged children.

The planned variation idea grew out of two distinct, but complementary, trends in federal policymaking during the middle and late 1960s—the failure of early attempts to evaluate federal education programs, and the growth of rational choice, or policy analysis, in the domestic agencies of the federal government. The enormous burst of new social programs that characterized the first years of Lyndon Johnson's Great Society was followed almost immediately by a sober appraisal of the gap between expectations and performance. In the field of education, the two most prominent Great Society programs—Head Start and Title I of the Elementary and Secondary Education Act—attracted the greatest attention. Early evaluations of both programs proved disappointing. Head Start evaluations produced a bewildering array of findings, suggesting that the program was neither consistently effective nor altogether ineffective.[1] Title I evaluations were much more depressing. After roughly two years of concerted effort, evaluators not only were unable to document the program's effectiveness, but also were unable to establish whether or not there was even a program in place at the local level. Title I funds, it seems, had simply disappeared into the quagmire of local school systems, leaving only an occasional trace of something that could reasonably be called a compensatory education program.[2]

But the inadequacy of program evaluations would not have become a public issue if it were not for the growth of rational choice, or policy analysis, in the federal domestic agencies. Largely as a result of attempts to transplant Planning, Programming, and Budgeting Systems (PPBS) from the Defense Department to the domestic agencies, there developed within the Office of Economic Opportunity (OEO) and the Department of Health, Education, and Welfare (HEW) a relatively small nucleus of people whose main concern was the systematic assessment of policy alternatives in light of their anticipated or actual effects. For these policy analysts, the failure of early attempts to evaluate federal education programs was attributable to a weakness in the design of the programs, not to a failure of evaluative technique. The evaluations failed to yield useful results because the programs themselves were poorly specified and implemented.[3] Hence, the

---

[1]See, e.g., Edith Grotberg, *Review of Research, 1965 to 1969, of Project Head Start,* Washington, D.C., U.S. Department of Health, Education, and Welfare, June 1969.

[2]See Milbrey McLaughlin, *Evaluation and Reform: The Elementary and Secondary Education Act of 1965, Title I,* Cambridge, Mass., Ballinger, 1975.

[3]See Alice Rivlin, *Systematic Thinking for Social Action,* Washington, D.C., Brookings Institution, 1971, 83–4.

way to assure useful evaluation results was to design a program around the requirements of good research design. Planned variations in program content, implemented systematically in a number of settings, would provide detailed information about what kind of compensatory education programs would work best for disadvantaged children. This became the distinguishing characteristic of the Follow Through program.

The design and conduct of the Follow Through planned variation experiment raise a number of issues that are basic to social policy analysis. The most obvious of these is the relationship between social science methodology and program administration. To what extent can the conventions of social science inquiry be used to structure the administration of a large-scale social intervention program? Planned variation experimentation was intended to be a major quantum jump in the sophistication of social program evaluation. But its success depended in large degree upon the ability of program administrators to adapt the design of the program to the requirements of social science methodology. Administrative decisions had methodological consequences, some of which were appreciated by program administrators and some of which were not. An examination of these decisions and their consequences provides useful information for the conduct of future program evaluations.

More importantly for the purposes of this book, though, Follow Through provides an excellent case of program implementation. There are actually two distinct implementation problems in the Follow Through program. The first, more specific problem is the implementation of program models, addressed briefly in the latter part of this chapter and extensively in the chapter by Weikart and Banet.[4] Each program model had to be developed and implemented in a number of diverse settings, and this process raised a number of difficult conceptual and practical problems. The second implementation problem is the more general one of how an innovation in federal programming is conceived and administered. The planned variation idea was a significant departure from earlier federal education programs. As such, it presented substantial organizational and political problems.

The methodological and implementation problems of Follow Through are essentially inseparable, since the successful execution of a planned variation experiment depends as much upon building and maintaining an evaluation design as it does on skillful program administration. In fact, concern over the implementation issue was largely a product of the increased methodological sophistication of planned variation. As attention

---

[4]David Weikart and Bernard Banet, "Planned Variation from the Perspective of the Model Sponsor," in this volume.

became focused on testing systematic variations in program content, it
became increasingly important to understand how those variations were to
be translated from ideas into practice.

This paper concentrates on five issues that proved to be important in
the design and conduct of Follow Through: (1) the tension between social
action and experimentation; (2) the selection of sites and assignment of
program models; (3) the selection and specification of program models; (4)
the implementation of program models; and (5) the use of evaluation
results. Each of these issues illustrates the mix of methodological and
implementation problems that confronted Follow Through administrators.

SOCIAL ACTION AND EXPERIMENTATION

Early in 1967, Lyndon Johnson asked Congress to authorize an
amendment to the Economic Opportunity Act that would provide for
extending Head Start-type programs into the early grades.[5] His proposal
had considerable political appeal. First, it was designed to capitalize on the
immense popularity of Head Start at a time when other parts of the
community action program of the U.S. Office of Economic Opportunity
(OEO) were coming under attack from state and local government officials
who resented federal sponsorship of local community action agencies.
Second, it was a direct response to the concern that the benefits accruing to
disadvantaged preschool children as a result of their participation in Head
Start were being dissipated by the children's subsequent placement in
substandard elementary schools. The new Follow Through program was to
have all the essential features of Head Start—extensive parental involvement; health, nutritional, and social services; and coordination with existing programs sponsored by local community action agencies. The critical
difference between Head Start and Follow Through lay in the fact that
Follow Through's target population was, ipso facto, in the established
public school system, while Head Start's was not. Perhaps for this reason
OEO agreed to delegate the administration of Follow Through to the U.S.
Office of Education (OE).[6]

[5] In his State of the Union Message, Johnson remarked: "We should strengthen the
Head Start program, begin it for children 3 years old, and maintain its educational momentum
by following through in the early years." *Congressional Record,* 90th Cong., 1st sess., 1967,
113, pt. 1: 37. In a later message, addressed exclusively to proposals for children and youth, he
asked Congress to "preserve the hope and opportunity of Head Start by a 'follow through'
program in the early grades," adding that "to fulfill the rights of America's children to equality
of educational opportunity the benefits of Head Start must be carried to the early grades."
Ibid., 113, pt. 2: 2882.

[6] The full text of the formal delegation of authority and of the memorandum of under-

Without waiting for congressional authorization of Follow Through, the project's administrators began a $2.8 million pilot program, involving 3000 children in 40 school districts during the 1967–68 school year, in expectation of an expanded $120 million program involving about 200,000 children in 1968–69. By late 1967, however, it was becoming clear that OEO's budget would not be increased enough to initiate a new program on the scale originally planned. When Congress finally passed the OEO appropriations bill in December 1967, the grim truth was that the agency would have to absorb a $10 million cut in existing levels of expenditure.

The budget cut was clearly the pivotal event in the development of Follow Through, for in the process of bargaining for the program's survival, OE administrators and the staff of the U.S. Department of Health, Education, and Welfare's assistant secretary for planning and evaluation had argued that Follow Through could be continued at a reduced budget level as an educational experiment to determine the most effective ways of educating disadvantaged children. In mid-December 1967, Robert Egbert, Follow Through's director, reported that funding for the program "appears to depend in large part on our ability to plan and carry through a program involving substantial variations among projects, which variations can be carefully evaluated in terms of the full range of Follow Through objectives." He continued: "We are eager to do this and are accepting the challenge of trying to bring it off despite fearful time pressures."[7]

While the budget cut may have provided the occasion for experimenting within Follow Through, it most certainly did *not* change Follow Through from a social action program into an educational experiment. The OE administrators charged with immediate responsibility for the program were strongly predisposed toward experimentation and indeed were enthusiastic about the idea. But their enthusiasm was based on a strictly instrumental view of the purpose of experimentation, as evidenced by Egbert's comments regarding the outcome of the budget cut. "The decision was therefore made and agreed to by OEO, HEW, USOE, and BOB [Bureau of the Budget] that Follow Through—*for the time being*—should be an experimental program *designed to produce information which would be useful 'when' the program was expanded to nationwide service proportions.*"[8] They saw experimentation as a means of developing program

---

standing between the director of OEO and the U.S. commissioner of education are in *Examination of the War on Poverty,* Hearings before the Subcommittee on Employment, Manpower, and Poverty of the Senate Committee on Labor and Public Welfare, 90th Cong., 1st sess., 1967, pp. 2257–60.

[7]Letter from Robert L. Egbert, director of Follow Through, to Gordon Klopf, dean of faculties, Bank Street College of Education, 14 December 1967.

[8]Robert L. Egbert, "Follow Through" (unpublished manuscript, 1971), p. 7. Emphasis added.

techniques and sources of information that would be useful to administrators embarking on a major educational intervention effort. The experimental phase of the program was a "holding action"—a means of keeping the program alive in the face of what was regarded as a temporary budget cutback. The object of the experiment was much less to discover systematic relationships between certain school factors and pupil outcomes than it was to develop a new intervention strategy for federal compensatory education programs. By agreeing to continue Follow Through as a planned variation experiment, the program administrators did not substitute the goals of dispassionate, scientific inquiry for those of social action. The basic federal commitment to compensatory education was a given and was not subject to experimental proof or disproof. Only specific programmatic techniques were to be the object of experimentation.

Nowhere are the consequences of this point of view more evident than in the willingness of Follow Through administrators to accept the constraints on experimentation entailed in the statutory requirements of the Economic Opportunity Act (EOA). The administrators made no attempt to secure special legislative authority, or exemption from certain provisions of the EOA, in order to conduct an experiment. As a consequence, Follow Through was subject to the same statutory requirements that applied to the other community action programs authorized under the EOA—an allotment formula for program funds based on the relative incidence of poverty among states, a requirement that local community action agencies be involved in project planning, and a requirement that every project provide for substantial parental involvement. In addition, the administrative guidelines for the program, developed jointly by OE and OEO, called for a "maximum feasible social, economic, and racial mixture of children," "ample parent participation in classroom and other project activities," and a "comprehensive program" of instructional, dental, nutritional, psychological, social, and staff-development services.[9] Finally, because Follow Through was a joint undertaking involving OEO, OE, state departments of education, local education agencies, ánd local community action agencies, the initial process of organizing the program, as will be seen in the next section, was enormously complex.

Because no exemption was sought from the provisions of the EOA, every local Follow Through project was required to have all the basic components of a comprehensive social action and social service program; there would be no attempt to vary systematically the kind or quantity of the social action and social service activities required by the act.[10] The

---

[9]*Follow Through Program Manual,* Washington, D.C., U.S. Office of Education, 1972, pp. 4, 14, 16–21.

[10]The Follow Through guidelines are quite emphatic on this point. They are devoted

"planned variations" that formed the basis of experimentation were strictly limited to the *educational* component of each project. A number of sponsoring institutions—college- and university-based research organizations, private educational foundations, federally funded research centers—were designated to develop and implement these educational programs. But the planned variations in the content of the educational programs were to take place within the bounds of a wide range of social action and social service activities that could not, strictly speaking, be considered part of the planned variation experiment, since no attempt would be made to vary them in any systematic way.

Since Follow Through's administrators regarded planned variation experimentation as simply a prelude to an expanded service program, there was a practical logic to their willing acceptance of the substantive policy constraints entailed in social action programs. They were interested in determining the performance of a number of educational program models under conditions as similar as possible to those that would prevail in an expanded program. Eliminating the policy constraints imposed by the EOA would have created an artificial environment for testing instructional models and would have meant the loss of a great deal of practical administrative experience that would be useful in an expanded program.

Whatever the practical advantages, however, such policy constraints create fundamental problems of evaluation design and inference, posing a dilemma that might be stated as follows: If social services and parental involvement have a positive educational effect on children, then the effects of these unsystematically varied program components will be confounded with the effects of planned variations in educational programs. If, on the other hand, such services have no demonstrable educational effect and hence do not confound the effects of educational programs, then it makes very little sense to include them as part of an educational program in the first place. Actually, we have no way at present of estimating the effect of unsystematically varied services in Follow Through because existing data on these services are suspect.[11] Evaluations of educational outcomes in Follow Through simply have ignored this problem, making no attempt to establish a causal link between social services and educational outcomes or to estimate the extent to which unsystematic variations in services are likely to affect measures of the performance of educational programs.

The instrumental view of experimentation held by Follow Through administrators had other consequences for the program's structure, espe-

---

almost exclusively to a description of the community action and social service components that each project must have, with only perfunctory mention of curriculum variations.

[11]The only data collected thus far on social services have come from project applications, specifying what a given community plans to do over the course of a school year. No data have been generated from direct observation of local programs.

cially notable in its scale and complexity. As the program developed, during the first 3 years of its existence, it mushroomed into a very large and complicated administrative apparatus. The number of program sponsors grew from 12 to 22; the number of participating school districts grew from 91 to 158; the number of children in the program grew from 15,000 to 70,000; and the number of staff members employed by the evaluation contractor to collect data on program effectiveness grew from 500 to 3000. As the organization grew, more and more administrative discretion was concentrated in the hands of program sponsors and local school districts, and less and less control was exercised by central administrators. Each sponsor developed a large organization, in some instances larger than the entire federal program staff, to deal with problems of model implementation. Each local school system developed a program organization consisting of a local director, a team of teachers and specialists, and a parent advisory group. The more the scale and complexity of the program increased, the less plausible it became for Follow Through administrators to control the details of program variations, and the more difficult it became to determine whether the array of districts and sponsors represented "systematic" variations in program content.

Finally, the tension between social action and experimentation was demonstrated to Follow Through administrators in an early confrontation over the program's purposes. Only a month after the beginning of the planned variation experiment, a meeting was held in Atlanta, Georgia, to familiarize a broad range of participants in the program with the program models and the structure of the evaluation. The meeting was no sooner underway than it became apparent that some local project personnel and some consultants to local projects objected strongly to the constraints imposed by planned variation experimentation on local decision making. The content of local programs, they argued, should be determined by parents and community representatives, not by federal administrators and program sponsors. Hence, the basic principle on which the planned variation idea was based—systematic variations in program content across a number of local settings—proved to have very limited appeal for local program participants. In the eyes of its local constituency, Follow Through was primarily a social action program, *not* a planned variation experiment.

These three problems—the confounding of planned variations in educational program content with unsystematic variations in other services, the scale and complexity of the Follow Through organization, and disagreement over the program's purpose—all tended to undermine planned variation experimentation. They all had their basis in a more general phenomenon of public policymaking and administration—the specification problem. It is generally not necessary for policymakers to agree specifically on what they intend to do in order to initiate a new program, but as programs develop and implementation progresses, it becomes increasingly difficult to avoid the consequences of poor specification. Follow Through administrators initially were able to finesse the conflict between social action and experimentation by adopting an instrumental view; the planned variation experiment would be a prelude to an expanded program. But their failure to confront the conflict early in the program's history led to an accumulation of decisions that later made it extremely difficult to conduct a planned variation experiment. Follow Through administrators were simply unwilling to concentrate on the central problem of the planned variation experiment—testing the relative effects of alternative educational models—if it meant compromising the possibility of turning Follow Through into a broad-scale social action program. Ironically, the program never did expand beyond the scale it assumed after its third year of operation. It was too large to be a coherent planned variation experiment and too small to be a broad-scale social action program.

SELECTION OF SITES AND ASSIGNMENT OF MODELS

The process of selecting participating school districts and pairing them with program sponsors illustrates another set of methodological and implementation problems. From the point of view of evaluation design, selection and assignment procedures should reflect as nearly as possible the requirements of experimental method. That is, the sample of sites should be constructed so as to maximize its representativeness and minimize the possibility that evaluation results will reflect an atypical compatibility between sites and sponsors. Random selection of participating districts from a population of potentially eligible districts and random assignment of sites to program models would serve this purpose. Within sites, eligible children ideally would be assigned randomly to treatment and control classrooms to minimize the possibility that evaluation results might be attributable to the background characteristics of children rather than to the program models. From the point of view of program implementation, however, the important consideration is not methodological purity but cooperation and concurrence. Decision-making authority in educational matters tends to be concentrated in the hands of local school personnel. Federal administrators are able to exercise only minimal control at the local level. The process of implementing a large-scale federal program, whether it is experimental or not, is characterized by a limited exercise of central control.

In view of the fundamental role that random selection and assignment play in the conventions of experimental design, it is of some interest to examine the calculatedly nonrandom selection and assignment procedures used in Follow Through. In mid-December 1967, OE asked the chief state school officers and OEO technical assistance officers in each state to nominate school districts for possible participation in the Follow Through program. These nominations produced a list of 225 districts, from which 51 were chosen as grantees at a mid-January conference by representatives from the OE and OEO regional offices. The criteria used in selecting the districts indicate that the program administrators were less concerned with the effect of the selection process on the external validity of the results than they were with choosing districts with a high probability of success in the first year of the program. The criteria stated, for example, that candidates were to be capable of mounting a comprehensive social service program in a relatively short period of time, that they had to be willing to participate in an experiment not yet fully designed, and that they had to have a well-established, cooperative relationship with the local community action agency. The same selection process was repeated in two successive years—60 districts were added in 1969–70, and 12 more in 1970–71. No new districts have been chosen for Follow Through since 1970–71, although there has been an annual increase in the number of children in the program because of the addition of grade levels within sites.

The first districts chosen were paired with program sponsors at a single, hectic, four-day meeting in Kansas City, Missouri, in late February 1968. The first two days of the meeting were devoted to discussions with the original forty pilot districts, which were encouraged, but not required, to affiliate with a sponsor. The remaining two days were given over to discussions with the newly selected districts, which were required, as a condition for participating in the program, to select a sponsor.

This process of selection and assignment is important, not because it represents a particularly unique way of allocating federal funds or because there is anything in it that recommends itself for future educational experiments, but because it illustrates the extent to which selection and assignment procedures are based on quite deliberate and rational assessments of the conditions necessary for the success of a complex administrative undertaking. At the same time, it also shows why random selection and assignment in large-scale educational experiments is likely to be enormously difficult to accomplish.

Faced with an educational system in which most of the important administrative decisions are made at the local level and in which state educational agencies, although relatively weak, are far more influential than the federal agencies, federal program administrators must rely on persuasion, consultation, and monetary incentives to elicit the cooperation of state and local school officials. These conditions are hardly conducive to the kind of centralized control that is needed for randomized processes of selection and assignment. Yet the selection and assignment procedure of Follow Through is most likely the norm against which state and local school officials will judge more tightly controlled attempts at selection and assignment in the future.

Furthermore, there is a rationality in the Follow Through selection and assignment approach that is easily overlooked by focusing simply on the mechanical application of the conventions of experimental design. At one point or another, virtually every political unit that might be in a position to influence the success or failure of the program—local school boards, local school administrators, parents, community action agencies, statewide professional associations, state education agencies—was included in the selection procedure. In a situation in which there is little or no hierarchical control, success or failure in an administrative endeavor as complex as Follow Through is determined by the extent to which those who are in a position to damage the program can be involved in allocation decisions and thus have a stake in the program's success.

In this particular experiment, the demands on local school systems were especially heavy, for the commitment to participate meant agreeing to allow an outside organization to intervene in and restructure a part of the local school program, an arrangement for which there was little precedent at the time that Follow Through was begun. Hence, as a minimum condition for assuring that some good-faith attempt would be made to implement a program model, Follow Through administrators thought it necessary to offer local districts a free choice in the selection of the model. Self-selection of program models by districts, then, represents not only the reality of decentralized power in educational decision-making but also a powerful incentive for districts to undertake the complex task of implementing a program model.

The idea of incentives for good-faith participation in large-scale experiments applies with special force to the problem of securing adequate comparison groups. In the case of Follow Through, the evaluator chose comparison groups from the non–Follow Through population within the same community or from a population in another community which the evaluator judged to be similar to the Follow Through community. Treatment and comparison statuses were not randomly assigned. Regardless of the nature of the selection process, there is no strong incentive for cooperation on the part of comparison groups. When comparison groups are designated within participating school districts, the chance of "contamination" among treatment and comparison groups is increased by the fact that local school administrators have no inclination or incentive to exclude certain schools from the presumed benefits of a program model. And when comparison groups are in school districts other than those in which program models are being implemented, local school administrators are being asked, in effect, to suffer the inconvenience of periodic interviews and testing without any of the presumed benefits of participating in the program.

The consequences of the purposely nonrandom selection and assignment procedure for the Follow Through evaluation are, of course, quite serious. They have been reviewed at length elsewhere[12] and will be noted here only briefly. First, self-selection results in unknown and unmeasurable selection-by-treatment biases of program effects. Second, Follow Through models are confounded with a number of critical background variables: region, school entry level, prior preschool experience, and ethnicity, to name a few. Some models are concentrated in the North, others in the South; some in areas where strong preschool programs are readily available, some not; some in predominantly black population areas, some in Caucasian areas, some in Spanish-speaking areas. Third, there are large, systematic differences in important background variables between treatment and comparison groups. In most cases, these differences probably bias the results in the direction of showing no treatment effects.[13] Finally, for some models there are not enough replications to make reliable model-to-model comparisons.

On the one hand, then, the selection and assignment procedures used in Follow Through are based on a quite rational assessment of the distribution of power in education and of incentives for participation under conditions of very weak centralized control. On the other hand, the procedures result in problems of confounding, lack of adequate comparison groups, and insufficient replication of treatments, which make strong conclusions regarding program effects impossible.

Follow Through illustrates something quite important about the conduct of social experiments in education and the implementation of social programs in general. There is no substitute for a detailed understanding of the structure of power relationships and incentives that surrounds every social intervention.[14] Very plausible program ideas—for example, planned

[12]See, for example, David K. Cohen, "Politics and Research: Evaluation of Social Action Programs in Education," *Review of Educational Research*, vol. 40 (1970), 213–38; and Joseph Wholey et al., *Federal Evaluation Policy: Analyzing the Effects of Public Programs*, Washington, D.C., The Urban Institute, 1970, pp. 32–33, 92–93.

[13]See Egbert, "Follow Through," p. 52; and Stanford Research Institute, "Evaluation of the National Follow Through Program, 1969–1971," Menlo Park, Calif., August 1972, pp. 11–18.

[14]See John Pincus, "Incentives for Innovation in the Public Schools," in this volume.

variation experimentation—that are predicated on a high degree of central control for their implementation simply may not be practical, given the existing distribution of power and the incentives available for altering that distribution. A careful assessment of this issue in the planning stages of a program could do a great deal to influence both the content of the program and the expectations with which it is undertaken.

SELECTION AND SPECIFICATION OF PROGRAM MODELS

When federal policymakers decided to undertake a planned variation experiment, they assumed that sufficient knowledge existed in the educational research and development community to meet the need for a wide variety of program models. Soon after the planned variation idea was conceived, the Follow Through staff set about looking among researchers and practitioners for potential program sponsors. In January 1968, while participating school districts were being selected, 26 potential program sponsors were invited to two meetings in Washington to discuss among themselves and with the Follow Through staff the idea of planned variation experimentation.[15] Among those invited were representatives of every conceivable school of thought and opinion on the subject of compensatory education. Some presented models based on adaptations of various theories of learning;[16] some advocated what could only be called general philosophies of schooling;[17] for some the idea of social action and community involvement in educational decision-making superseded any concern for school programs;[18] a good many others were so eclectic as to defy categorization.

The diversity of program models reflected a more general confusion and lack of agreement among educational researchers and practitioners over the preferred outcomes of schooling and what features of schools and communities needed to be changed to bring these outcomes about. Under such circumstances, it is not surprising that there was some ambiguity as to

[15]This account is based on transcripts of these meetings filed at the Lyndon Baines Johnson Library in Austin, Texas: Department of Health, Education, and Welfare, Office of Education, *Transcript of Proceedings: Follow Through Planning Meeting,* January 5, 6, 26, and 27, 1968.

[16]Seigfried Engleman, University of Illinois; Donald Baer and Donald Bushell, University of Kansas; David Weikart, High/Scope Educational Research Foundation.

[17]Elizabeth Gilkeson, Bank Street College of Education; Ronald Henderson, University of Arizona; Alan Leitman, Educational Development Center.

[18]Kenneth Haskins, Morgan Elementary School, Washington, D.C.; Tom Levin, Albert Einstein College of Medicine; Anthony Ward, Harlem Block School, New York City.

what was meant by planned variation experimentation. In fact, at least two distinctly different ideas of planned variation experimentation were expressed in the early stages of Follow Through. One approach, outlined separately by Cohen and Bronfenbrenner, in two memoranda written for the 1967 White House Task Force on Child Development,[19] would have begun with a set of predefined dimensions of variation and would have specified fairly clearly what variations were being tested. Cohen and Bronfenbrenner suggested that it might be possible to vary systematically components of school structure such as pupil–instructional staff ratio, teacher ability, socioeconomic mix of classrooms, extent and type of parental involvement in school program, and extent and type of nonparent, paraprofessional involvement.

There would have been several advantages to this approach. First, a planned variation experiment based on these dimensions of variation would have been, in effect, a more controlled test of some of the major findings of the Coleman study.[20] In other words, it would have expanded existing research on the relationship between school-structure variables and pupil outcomes. Second, variations in school structure, as opposed to variations in the substance of school program, would have been, according to Cohen, (1) "less dependent for their successful implementation upon the ability of a given school staff"; (2) more "susceptible of implementation with relative consistency in a variety of situations"; and (3) more "susceptible to evaluation, given the existing difficulties in measuring educational change."[21] It is impossible to say, of course, whether this approach would have worked any better than the one eventually adopted, but undeniably it had the further initial advantages of simplicity in design and clarity in the definition of independent variables.

The idea of planned variation experimentation adopted by Follow Through was, of course, very different. Instead of prespecifying dimensions of variation and attempting to limit the experiment to those programs most susceptible to definition and replication, the Follow Through administrators tried to select what appeared to them to be promising, innovative program models, leaving the question of how these models differed to a later time. This "all comers" approach to selection was structured by no particular preconception on the part of the administrators of what the major dimensions of variation should be. Of the 26 potential sponsors who attended the planning meetings, 18 were invited to submit proposals for

---

[19]David K. Cohen, "Variation in the Structural Features of School Programs," 16 October 1967; and Urie Bronfenbrenner, untitled memorandum, October 19, 1967.

[20]James S. Coleman et al., *Equality of Educational Opportunity*, Washington, D.C., U.S. Department of Health, Education, and Welfare, Office of Education, July 1966.

[21]Cohen, "Variation in the Structural Features of School Programs."

participation in the program, 16 responded to the request, and 14 of the 16 were finally selected. During the following year, 6 more sponsors were added to the original 14 in an effort to give representation to 3 additional groups—state education agencies, minority colleges, and profit making companies. The main criterion used in selecting the first group of sponsors was that they appear to have an interesting idea for a program; for the later group, the criterion was a potential sponsor's being in some sense "representative" of an important or interesting educational constituency. As a result, it is far from clear what the dimensions of variation were.

Even if it were impossible to specify dimensions of variation in advance, it might have been possible to arrive at a fairly systematic evaluation design by defining each model in detailed operational terms and looking for naturally occurring variations among models, which could then be associated with expected outcomes. Quite early in the process of selecting sponsors, however, Follow Through discovered that none of the existing program models was sufficiently well developed to allow for detailed operational descriptions at the outset:

> It was obvious that despite the growing interest in this field and despite extensive publicity given various new programs, no one was fully prepared to move into the primary grades with a completely developed, radically different program.[22]

If there was to be any attempt to describe program models in detail and to specify what, if any, variations were represented in the sponsors selected for the program, it would have to be incorporated into the program's overall evaluation plan. One of the earliest evaluation planning memoranda for Follow Through stated the problem in this way:

> Although many of those in institutions currently sponsoring Follow Through projects have been working for long periods in the field of early childhood education, we have been impressed, in our discussions during this year, with the extent to which they seem to operate on the basis of intuitive judgment rather than explicit principle. There is clear need for support which will enable those with long experience but still unsystematic knowledge to delineate more clearly the elements of their programs which they regard as essential to optimum development of the child. . . . The goal . . . is the development of operational procedures for the definition and measurement of program characteristics to which our measures must in the final analysis be related.[23]

Research and development funds that were allocated to sponsors

[22]Egbert, "Follow Through," p. 10.
[23]Memorandum from John F. Hughes, U.S. Office of Education, Division of Compensatory Education, to Karl Hereford, director, Program Planning and Evaluation, Bureau of Elementary and Secondary Education: "Follow Through Research, Development, and Evaluation Plans for Fiscal Year 1969–70," May 20, 1968.

were supposed to be used in part to provide the specification of models that was considered essential to a well-designed evaluation, but as late as February 1973 the program's evaluators were explaining that:

> It is important to recognize that even if the number of significant effects were strikingly greater, we would still have difficulty interpreting how or why such results occurred because, at present, our current knowledge of the treatments is confined almost exclusively to the sponsors' descriptions of them. . . . To interpret how and why results occur, we now need clear operational statements of what a sponsor does when he is installing and maintaining a project.[24]

The results of several successive Follow Through evaluations have been reported, without a clear specification of program models, simply by associating outcomes with particular program labels. Since these results tell us only that certain effects are associated with certain descriptive labels, policymakers and program administrators who want to make use of the results are left with no choice but to assume that each program model constitutes a "black box" whose contents are largely unspecified but whose effects are known to some degree. They cannot offer programs that replicate specific causal relationships of treatment and result, but rather must market black boxes. While this arrangement might appeal to program sponsors, who have a proprietary interest in their products, it is not a sophisticated application of social science to a problem of social policy. Presumably, since planned variation experiments are not simply exercises in product development, they should be designed to provide specific information that will be useful in structuring school programs, quite apart from indicating the superiority of one product over another. This all suggests that if the technique of planned variation experimentation is to become a routine feature of social program evaluation, some means ought to be developed for prespecifying dimensions of variation and for translating them into operational model descriptions.

The Follow Through program's experience with model selection and specification also suggests a more general lesson for social program implementation. Frequently policy decisions are based on overly optimistic assumptions about the state of existing knowledge. In the case of Follow Through, the initial decision to undertake a planned variation experiment was based on a very sketchy and inadequate understanding of the actual capacity of educational researchers to develop systematic program variations. By the time Follow Through administrators discovered how little actually was known, they were committed to proceed with the planned variation experiment. Where the application of prior research is an integral

---

[24]Stanford Research Institute, "Evaluation of the National Follow Through Program, 1969–71," Menlo Park, Calif., February 1973, pp. 4–5.

part of a program implementation strategy, it would seem wise to anticipate the possibility that the research simply will not support program activity.

MODEL IMPLEMENTATION

The issue of model implementation in the Follow Through planned variation experiment had both methodological and administrative implications. Being certain that a program model actually has been put into operation is an important minimum condition for determining the effects of alternative models in planned variation experiments. If the evidence from experimentation is to be convincing, each treatment must be implemented in its essential respects, and for each there must be several essentially identical replications. These are considerations of design; they describe the assumptions an evaluator must make about a treatment in order to conclude that the results of his evaluation are, in fact, valid comparisons of program models. In addition, the results of planned variation experiments are meant to be useful in a programmatic sense; hence, it is important to learn something about the *process* of model implementation. If a given model raises particular difficulties, for example, those difficulties can point to the kind of administrative problems that might arise in disseminating the model beyond the bounds of the experiment. Evidence of this kind also can tell us something about the capacity of local school systems to adopt and execute the kind of innovations that planned variation models represent.

Implementing a program model in a number of diverse local settings is likely to be an enormously complex administrative task. Even assuming that the model is fairly well defined (a tenuous assumption in light of the discussion above), it is unlikely that most administrators will have the capacity to deliver such a model with consistency to a number of school systems. And the way in which a program's implementation affects its results is uncertain. It has been suggested that the effects of even a well-implemented program innovation are apt to be quite modest:

> Most innovations don't work, even when they are introduced with the best will in the world, are carefully thought out, and vigorously and expertly executed. . . . Why are educational innovations frequently ineffective? . . . When someone looks at a going school system and suggests that it be changed to make it better . . . he has two strikes against him. First, . . . the system is running now, and the proposed innovations can possibly reduce its effectiveness. Second, the people who formerly ran and are now running the school will have put a strong effort into doing what they can to make the system pay off well. So at best the change is only going to take up part of the slack between how well the system works now and the best it could do.[25]

[25] John Gilbert and Frederick Mosteller, "The Urgent Need for Experimentation," in Frederick Mosteller and Daniel P. Moynihan, eds., *On Equality of Educational Opportunity,* New York, Random House, 1972, p. 379.

Reasoning of this kind leads in a number of directions. It suggests that our expectations about the magnitude of effects resulting from even a well-implemented program innovation should be quite modest. We already have reason enough for modesty, based on the findings of previous research on the effects of schooling. Gilbert and Mosteller suggest an additional reason stemming from the problems of institutional change. All changes in ongoing educational systems are fundamentally incremental; they represent *not* the difference between treatment and nontreatment but rather the marginal effect of some complex change in an existing treatment. Thus, any study of the effects of program innovation ought to take into account the incremental nature of change in educational institutions. In practical terms, this means that program models probably ought to be judged in terms of what was there before the innovation, what sort of changes are entailed in the innovation, the extent to which these changes actually are implemented in any given case, and the relationship between changes and measures of outcome.

One further complicating factor in any attempt at large-scale intervention in the established organizational routines of a number of school systems is the variable institutional resistance to, and selectivity of, parts of the innovative program. This invites the question of the possibility, or even desirability, of creating several virtually identical replications of the same program model. On the one hand, it would be far easier to interpret the results of evaluation if there were some assurance that the same program was operating in each setting where it was implemented. But, as Williams observes in his concluding chapter in this volume, what is *practically* desirable is some reasonable approximation to the program model, taking into account differences in the political and bureaucratic characteristics of each setting.

Simply raising the problem of model implementation leads us to question not only our ability to influence school outcomes through planned intervention but also our ability to apply the principle of replicability in large-scale social experiments that require institutional change. There is, in short, far more at stake in studies of implementation than simply establishing the presence or absence of an experimental treatment. Planned variation experiments are, perhaps more importantly, tests of a particular strategy of educational change and a specific technique of program evaluation. If evaluations of planned variation experiments were to indicate, for example, that it was impossible to implement program models consistently in a number of settings or that the level of implementation bore little or no relationship to differences in educational outcomes, then we would have grounds for rethinking both the conception of educational change underlying planned variation experiments and our use of the techniques of large-scale experimentation as an evaluation tool.

Follow Through's administrators were not unaware of the difficulties of implementing a model when they began the experiment. They proposed to do a series of community case studies that would detail the process of model implementation in a number of settings. The results of these case studies would then be used "to identify those variables that markedly affected program implementation" and "to work toward an integrative model which would describe the institutional changes associated with Follow Through and which might then be employed in data collection efforts at a larger number of sites."[26] In its execution, however, this plan of study became something quite different from an analysis of model implementation. It was transformed over time into a study to explain the relationship between parent participation and institutional change in school districts.[27] Little remains in the existing Follow Through evaluation that specifically addresses the problem of how well, and by what process, program models are implemented.

In neither Follow Through nor Head Start planned variation was an attempt made to structure a systematic study of implementation around a sequential set of problems: What was there before the innovation? To what extent were models implemented? What was the relationship between level of implementation and outcomes? A number of observational techniques—including those developed expressly for planned variation experiments—might have been used to detect changes in classroom behavior if a concerted attempt had been made to observe classrooms *before* as well as after the introduction of a program innovation. Our capacity to detect less easily defined institutional changes is, of course, quite primitive. But the task can be lightened if, during the planning and development of an experiment, the major actors in the implementation process are identified precisely and descriptive studies are constructed around the central problem of defining their role in the process. Two recent single-school case studies of educational innovation and one classic application of role theory to the analysis of school organization indicate that we are not entirely without methodological resources in this area.[28] The basic precon-

[26]Stanford Research Institute, "Longitudinal Evaluation of Selected Features of the National Follow Through Program," Menlo Park, Calif., January 1971, Appendix F: Case Studies, 1969–70, p. 3.

[27]Stanford Research Institute, "Evaluation of the National Follow Through Program, 1969–71," Menlo Park, Calif., August 1972, Appendix E: Follow Through Community Studies.

[28]Neal C. Gross, Joseph Giacquinta, and Marilyn Bernstein, *Implementing Organizational Innovations: A Sociological Analysis of Planned Educational Change*, New York, Basic Books, 1971; Louis Smith and Pat Keith, *Anatomy of Educational Innovation: An Organizational Analysis of an Elementary School*, New York, John Wiley & Sons, 1971; and Neal Gross, Ward Mason, and Alexander McEachern, *Explorations in Role Analysis: Studies of the School Superintendency Role*, New York, John Wiley & Sons, 1964.

dition for any study of implementation is, of course, a detailed knowledge of the essential components of what is to be implemented. From that, it should be possible to determine the level of implementation and the relationship between level of implementation and measures of outcome.

THE USE OF EVALUATION RESULTS

The difficulties of design and analysis that have become apparent in the course of the Follow Through evaluation would seem to dictate caution in drawing policy-relevant conclusions from the evaluation results. Yet proposals have been made within the U.S. Office of Education (OE) that involve short-term use of Follow Through results to restructure compensatory education programs. In February 1972 the Office of Education's Division of Compensatory Education announced a plan to extend the sponsored-model approach of Follow Through, over a 5-year period, to the 16,000 school districts and more than 250,000 children then covered by Title I of the Elementary and Secondary Education Act.

In the fall of 1972, however, this plan apparently was superseded by another, whose object was to use incentive grants to encourage local districts to adopt successful, innovative compensatory programs. Follow Through was seen as only one of many possible sources of "validated" program models.[29] It is not clear at the moment what, if any, effect the recent reports of Follow Through results have had on OE's dissemination plans. But it *is* clear that there is potentially a rather large and precarious gap between the desire of program administrators to control and shape compensatory programs and the capacity to produce validated program models. Indeed, if the results of planned variation in Follow Through conform to the pattern of other research on the effects of schooling, it seems highly unlikely that anything like "validated" program models will be available for dissemination in the near future.

Moreover, it is unrealistic to expect that educational experimentation will ever produce unequivocal evidence of program effects. Under the best of circumstances, there will always be some fuzziness and uncertainty in the analysis and interpretation of results of large-scale educational experiments. Even if the design and administration of such experiments can be improved, the constraints imposed by our lack of centralized control and by the weakness of the knowledge base in education make it highly unlikely that results will be unambiguous. This suggests that, rather than concen-

[29]Thomas C. Thomas and Meredith L. Robinson, "Analysis of Issues in the Implementation of a Program of Matching Incentive Grants, Part B of Title I ESEA," prepared for the U.S. Office of Education, Office of Program Planning and Evaluation, by the Educational Policy Research Center, Stanford Research Institute, Menlo Park, Calif., 14 September 1972.

trating on strategies for disseminating results, time might be spent better in determining what use, if any, can be made of ambiguous results.

Observing the ambiguity of program evaluations and the decidedly unscientific nature of the process of public decision-making, a number of commentators have suggested the need for some institutionalized structure for discussing the meaning of evaluation results. Cain and Hollister note a proposal by Kenneth Arrow that the use of evaluation results be structured around the model of advocacy implicit in the court system, with open debate on the meaning of evaluation results for particular substantive policy questions and the development of "rules of evidence" to guide the use of these results.[30] Gilbert and Mosteller have also argued for an "adversary procedure so that an administrator could fairly hear the sides of a difficult question argued by prepared experts, with help of his own experts to guide some part of the questioning."[31] The argument can be carried even further than this. It would be possible to provide for more than one analysis of evaluation results without markedly increasing the cost of the evaluation, since data collection is far more costly than data analysis. In secondary analyses of data from the Coleman study[32] and the Westinghouse-Ohio evaluation of Head Start,[33] the payoff was high in terms of both exploiting the ambiguities of the data and answering important basic research questions on the effects of schooling.

In an important sense, all the methodological and administrative problems of planned variation experimentation come to roost on the issue of how evaluation results are to be used. If there is substantial ambiguity and disagreement on the purposes of the program, if selection and assignment procedures make it difficult to draw firm conclusions about program effectiveness, if program models are poorly specified, and if there is only a limited knowledge of the process by which models are implemented, then it is unlikely that planned variation experiments—or social programs in general—will provide useful information for policymakers.

CONCLUSIONS

There are two ways of interpreting the Follow Through experience. The first is to judge its success as a planned variation experiment. In this

[30]Cain and Hollister, "Methodology of Evaluating Social Action Programs," pp. 135–36.

[31]Gilbert and Mosteller, "The Urgent Need for Experimentation," p. 377.

[32]The Coleman reanalysis is reported in Mosteller and Moynihan, eds., *On Equality of Educational Opportunity,* and in Christopher Jencks et al., *Inequality: A Reassessment of the Effect of Family and Schooling in America,* New York, Basic Books, 1972.

[33]Marshall S. Smith and Joan S. Bissell, "Report Analysis: The Impact of Head Start," *Harvard Educational Review* 40, February 1970: 51–104.

sense, it is fair to say, Follow Through has fallen far short of expectations. It has not offered any definitive solutions to the evaluation problems which it originally addressed. In fact, it has raised a number of new evaluation issues that were only dimly appreciated at its outset. But it cannot be said that the Follow Through experience has been completely without value or that it conclusively demonstrates the uselessness of the planned variation strategy. In principle at least, the planned variation strategy is still an appealing approach to program design and administration because it draws attention to so many basic issues. It forces program administrators to think in terms of specific program alternatives rather than global abstractions. It provides a means of systematically sorting more- and less-effective program components. And it draws attention to program specification and implementation, because it is impossible to speak of systematic variations in program content without addressing the issue of how they are to be defined and put in place. In practice, though, Follow Through demonstrates the vulnerability of the planned variation strategy to a variety of constraints that commonly operate on social programs—which leads us to the second way of interpreting the Follow Through experience.

The problems confronted in Follow Through are in fact no different from those encountered in any large-scale social intervention program. They are, however, made more apparent by the fact that the program was conceived of as a planned variation experiment. The tension between social action and experimentation in Follow Through, for example, is a manifestation of a more general problem in social program administration. Ambiguity of purpose has an important political function for policymakers and administrators because it allows them to hold people with divergent interests together in a stable coalition. A certain amount of ambiguity of purpose is inevitable in any large-scale social program, but as implementation progresses it becomes increasingly difficult to avoid its negative consequences. The unwillingness of Follow Through administrators to focus specifically on the task of conducting a planned variation experiment, and their insistence on viewing the experiment as a prelude to an expanded program meant that the program's content, scale, and complexity were allowed to develop in a way that was contradictory to the logic of planned variation experimentation. The point is that, even though a certain amount of ambiguity is inevitable, administrators can exert some control over specific aspects of the program's structure. In Follow Through, the failure of administrators to exercise any control at all over program content, scale, and organizational complexity essentially undermined the possibility of conducting a planned variation experiment.

The selection of participating school districts and their assignment to models in Follow Through illustrates the importance of basing an implementation strategy on a detailed understanding of the distribution of power and the incentives available to influence that distribution. The planned variation strategy was predicated on a much higher degree of central control than actually existed, and it is not clear how the skillful use of incentives might have affected the distribution of power. This problem is not unique to the planned variation strategy. It is difficult to think of a single social intervention program that does not take place in an environment of decentralized decision-making, but it is a relatively rare occurrence when program administrators actually plan an implementation strategy around a careful assessment of their ability to influence the distribution of power.

The selection, specification, and implementation of program models in Follow Through illustrates the importance of closely examining assumptions on which policy decisions are based before those decisions are translated into programs. The decision to undertake a federally sponsored planned variation experiment in Follow Through was based on a very limited understanding of the capacity of educational researchers to develop and implement program models. By the time Follow Through administrators discovered the limits of existing knowledge, they were irrevocably committed to launching the experiment. Even after model specification and implementation problems were acknowledged, only limited progress was made in solving them. An early analysis of the state of existing knowledge might have led to a more deliberate and systematic approach to specification and implementation.

6

PLANNED VARIATION FROM THE PERSPECTIVE OF A MODEL SPONSOR*

David P. Weikart and Bernard A. Banet

The idea of planned variation may have been logical at the national level, but at the sponsor level it was mystifying. The January 1968 meeting in Washington of prospective sponsors to present our various orientations to curriculum, the idea that evaluation could be done by a third agency, the meeting in a hotel room to add a Head Start planned variation experiment, and the assumption that each sponsor had a complete package to present—all created a feeling of bewilderment and even of madness. It was a credit to everyone that something happened: a project was born, and people worked extraordinarily hard to fit the pieces into a constantly changing jigsaw puzzle.

The amazing thing about both of the planned variation experiments—Head Start and Follow Through—was that they occurred and that thousands of people became deeply involved in making them work. Statistical outcomes stand pale beside this outpouring of commitment.

*Copyright © 1975 by The Regents of the University of California. Reprinted from *Policy Analysis*, Vol. 1, No. 3, by permission of the Regents.

To promote an understanding of some of the complications and forces that affected the implementation of both of the planned variation experiments, we will discuss here several important problems faced in developing our model and implementing it in the field, and their eventual impact on us as a sponsor. While all sponsoring groups did not have the same experience, it may be helpful to examine one such group in looking at the future of planned variation studies and the prospects for educational reform.

DEVELOPMENT OF THE MODEL

Our early work in preschool education had a decisive influence on the development of our Follow Through model.[1] In 1968 we had completed a 5-year study of preschool education and had just launched our own mini-planned variation preschool study, as well as a study of infant and mother support programming. The idea of moving into the elementary schools was almost frightening. We reluctantly accepted three Follow Through sites the first year (1968–1969).

We were deeply immersed in Piagetian theory[2] at the time and had been fighting an amiable battle with preschool educators who felt that our model was too structured for children to thrive in. Our preschool data, however, were leading us to some heady conclusions about what would work with children; we were getting consistent and repeated increases in measured intelligence scores and significant increases in long-term academic achievement as well. However, as we moved to the field, we found our methods woefully lacking in the capacity to meet the needs of teachers faced with daily classroom programming.

Our basic approach—the "cognitive curriculum"—places both the teacher and the child in active, initiating roles; it attempts to blend purposeful teaching with open-ended, child-initiated activities. The curriculum framework, based in part on Piaget's developmental theory, focuses on the underlying cognitive processes that are basic to acquiring and organizing knowledge. Implementation of the curriculum centers on training of the teaching staff in the goals, methods, and attitudes required for a program with a "cognitive" orientation.

[1]For a description of the model, see D. Weikart et al., *The Cognitively Oriented Curriculum: A Framework for Preschool Teachers*, Washington, D.C., National Association for the Education of Young Children, 1971.
[2]J. Piaget, *The Psychology of Intelligence*, New York, Harcourt, Brace, 1950; B. Inhelder and J. Piaget, *The Growth of Logical Thinking from Childhood to Adolescence*, New York, Basic Books, 1958.

At first, we thought that we could run workshops for teachers, explaining our basic theory of education and the essentials of the cognitive curriculum, and that they would then be able to "graft" the cognitive curriculum onto what they normally did in the classroom. We soon discovered, however, that this grafting would create an impossible conflict between teaching styles, content orientation, and roles of classroom participants. The advice we received from local sites was that we ran impressive workshops but gave little help to the teacher in organizing her day. Administrators told us that teachers were generally unable, on their own, to map out whole new approaches to teaching, and that we should give them very explicit directions and offer specific materials and activities.

While administrators raised questions about the usefulness of theory, a "surrender phenomenon" seemed to prevail among teachers who had made the commitment to the curriculum theory. Instead of developing a strong, independent teacher who knew theory and how to apply it in her classroom, we seemed to have had the opposite effect; we took away the confidence the teacher had and replaced it with dependence and frustration.

Our response to this problem, and our second phase of evolution, was to find commercial materials that reflected the theory we wanted to implement, that could be introduced into the classroom quickly, and that would meet local school district needs. This brought us to the position of suggesting a total curriculum that would reflect our cognitive orientation throughout the day.

Adding commercially available material to our Piaget-based, cognitively oriented approach made sense to the teaching staffs and was the beginning of a genuinely independent program. But a coherent, attractive educational alternative was not yet realized. We recognized the need to increase the practical application of our theory base, and actually to offer an alternative method, but we were not yet willing to take that position to its logical conclusion and throw out all traditional classroom methods. What we did was move to reorganize the classroom and the class day. This sounds simple, but in fact we had cut through to a basic truth. The obvious elements of support for teachers are administrators, parents, and other teachers; less obvious are the physical environment and daily routine. Altering room arrangements by removing individual desks and establishing interest centers for child-initiated activities, and suggesting a daily routine with emphasis on children planning their own activities, carrying out those plans, and reviewing their work in relation to their plans, revolutionized the implementation of our model.

In rapid succession there were several dramatic changes: Teaching was now focused on divergent questioning; classroom dominance by the teacher was reduced (now a teacher's voice could be heard only by the several students with whom she was involved); and there was parallel teaching by paraprofessionals and parent volunteers rather than serial teaching (observing while waiting your turn). These changes in classroom structure and routine began to produce change in programs and classrooms which had previously been immune.[3]

By the end of this phase of program evolution, it had become apparent that the model had moved from (1) the assumption that a teacher's understanding of theory automatically would lead her to practice it in the classroom, through (2) the altering of classroom operations and the addition of commercial materials compatible with theory to replace traditional materials, to (3) the current phase, where we are beginning to see the potential of our curriculum as an educational alternative. It may seem strange that after 5 years we are just now at the threshold of what is possible with our model, but that is our position and probably that of most of the sponsors who have elected to follow a developmental approach.

The planned variation studies represent the first major attempt to examine the clash of philosophies among educational reformers. The basic problem is that the further one moves from accepting technological "containers" for traditional school content, the more the program has to be accepted as a personal act of faith, because it is not an obvious extension of what we always have tried to teach.

FIELD IMPLEMENTATION AS TEACHER
TRAINING

Under pressure to mount programs in the field, with practically no lead time, almost all the traditional procedures for training teachers were discarded in planned variation. Unlike conventional teacher education, most of the training that occurred in the planned variation sites was in-service. Teachers learned a model by teaching in it; they actually con-

---

[3]In one school system each classroom in an old building was a beautiful mix of alcoves, window ledges, and plenty of floor space. However, the school kept 50 desks bolted to the floor in all classrooms. With the change in the classroom arrangement and daily routine, the desks became intolerable. How can you run a class around the edges of a classroom? After viewing the room with the principal and hearing all the reasons why it takes 12 years for the system's union glazers to replace the broken windows in the school (90% of the windows were broken) and 7 years for the carpenters to remove the desks and fill in the holes in the floor even if policy could be changed, Weikart offered to remove the desks himself that evening. "Oh no," the principal said, and the next week all the desks disappeared. No wonder teachers always refer to their administrators as "they."

fronted, in the classroom, the task of applying strategies and objectives identified by the sponsor.

The planned variation experiments created a training environment guaranteed to produce frustration and struggle, but also one that was more likely than a survey or methods course in a school of education to produce real growth in teaching skills. The planned variation environments were among the first in which preschool and early elementary school teachers were exposed to systematic feedback over time, from knowledgeable adults, concerning their classroom performance in relation to more or less explicit criteria provided by a model.

A welcome aspect of this training was that the commitment to a model had been legitimized if not yet internalized. In the foreign soil of traditional teacher-training programs and staff in-service workshops, our experience, as representatives of a model, has been that eclecticism reigns supreme. Anyone with a model is suspected of neglecting "the whole child" or of threatening the academic freedom of a teacher to develop her own class in her own way. The planned variation experiments gave several coherent approaches to preschool and early elementary education at least a fighting chance to be tested.

EARLY EXPECTATIONS

The revolutionary assumptions about teacher training imposed by the constraints of planned variation gradually had their full impact on the sponsors. How can in-service training be carried out with teachers in distant sites without the apparatus of credit hours, examinations, and so on? To our embarrassment we must admit that our assumptions about training 5 years ago were that (1) one could describe a "model" in largely verbal terms, with perhaps a few charts and diagrams; and that (2) this simple verbal description, presented before a gathering of teachers in a preservice workshop, should persuade them to modify radically their teaching behavior in the coming year. Of course, this modification would need constant support from the project director and curriculum assistant, but it could, we thought, be accomplished in a magic 5-day week as our field consultants descended on the school system or Head Start site.

We learned the hard way that these expectations were absurd. Financial and verbal commitment to a model by a school district did not mean that anyone, least of all teachers, needed only to be told about the model in order to implement it. There were problems both of motivating teachers to change their teaching styles and of supporting orderly change in the classrooms rather than expecting the revolution to come overnight. Our early workshops featured discussions of Piagetian theory and videotaped or demonstrated examples of classroom applications. We felt that this approach had enough power to ring all sorts of bells in the teachers' heads, stimulating them to create open, active classroom environments where before there had been teacher domination and reliance upon highly abstract materials. The preservice workshops we ran in both Follow Through and Head Start were well received. Everyone expressed enthusiasm about the new ways of doing things; but when we visited classrooms a few months later, change was difficult to detect.

PROBLEMS IN IN-SERVICE TRAINING

There was a vast gulf between the smiles and nods of workshop sessions and actual classroom implementation of a model. This led us to wonder about the relation between the traditional teacher-training activities and the actual job performance of teachers. Apparently a teacher's repertoire and the constraints she perceives on her role, as emphasized by the local school authorities and some parents, are not amenable to lightning-fast change. This is true especially if one is expecting the teacher to be able to apply the most abstract theoretical principles after a few hours of workshop experience that is itself remote from the classroom. Not surprisingly, our training began to be focused increasingly on concrete teaching strategies that put into practice our theoretical conceptions, and on concrete examples provided by classroom settings, either at the center or on film or videotape.

We learned that there are some high-priority issues in in-service training that must be dealt with from the beginning. Two of these are the physical arrangement of the room and the structure of the daily routine. Modifying these structures did not guarantee that anything more than superficial change would occur; for example, it is possible to teach reading in the same old way even if the teacher is working with only five children at a time instead of the whole class. But it is not possible to move toward an individualized learning setting without first modifying the physical environment and the time schedule of a classroom.

We learned that changes that modify the kinds of feedback teachers get from children must be initiated. Children can be powerful shapers of adults in a classroom. If processes such as the planning that children themselves do in our model can begin to operate, the teacher begins to see that the children are capable of making choices and decisions, and is willing to support and extend these skills. But the teacher must first give the new process a chance.

In implementing a model, teachers can become quite paranoid. They are under constant observation, and they notice that a number of people have explicit but differing expectations about how they should be functioning as teachers. We found that one way to reduce this inevitable paranoia is to talk about activities and classroom practices in terms of providing better learning experiences for children; with this focus, teachers are less likely to perceive evaluative discussion as subtle attacks on their professional competence.

Often the teacher must face the critical opposition of people outside the model. Principals may want things done the old way. One teacher was told by her principal to "do things the way those Ypsilanti people want them done" only when the High/Scope consultants were in the school. Head Start teachers face the scorn of kindergarten and first grade teachers who feel that they are not "preparing" children for further schooling if the children cannot read and write by age five and are not used to sitting quietly for long periods of time. Fourth grade teachers have a knack for threatening the first or second or third grade teacher who is trying innovative methods. That "the children won't know how to deal with the traditional fourth grade" becomes a source of great anxiety.[4]

COUNTERFORCES

Effective training can mobilize a number of counterforces to these pressures. One, as we have mentioned, is the children themselves. A classroom that is aglow with the excitement of active learning, and a child who is proud of accomplishing something he has planned give the lie to criticisms that the children do not learn self-discipline or do not learn to work independently. Another counterforce is the mutual support within the teaching teams created in many of the planned variation settings. The addition of an aide or another teacher to a classroom will provide emotional and intellectual help to a teacher learning a new method.

Not only were teachers and/or paraprofessionals in our classrooms organized into teaching teams, they also were given much closer supervision in program implementation than ever before. For perhaps the first time in many of these schools there was someone other than the teacher who was vitally concerned with the content and processes of classroom learn-

[4]One non-model teacher complained that Follow Through had not taught the children self-discipline and that they were very hard to handle; but his definition of self-discipline was that children would do exactly as they were told. In another site, several successful Follow Through children were failing during their fourth grade year until they learned to sit in their seats and follow directions.

ing. The curriculum assistant, as we called him, was not, like most principals, concerned only with the smooth functioning of the physical plant and with reducing conflicts and responding to requests. Rather, he spent a significant amount of time in each classroom each week, raising curriculum questions and helping teachers plan and evaluate.

The full potential of the curriculum assistant's role is just beginning to be realized. In Head Start the inexperienced paraprofessional teachers were especially responsive to the leadership of the curriculum assistants. Previously in Head Start there had been education directors who were assigned to many more classrooms than were the curriculum assistants, or the project director had assumed the training and supervision responsibilities along with all of his other administrative duties. In most public schools the principal only nominally supervises the teaching staff; no one really is concerned with the classroom teaching of individual teachers unless the class disrupts other classes or the building routine. Teaching under these circumstances can be a very lonely occupation indeed. The field implementation model used by a number of sponsors, in which classroom teachers are teamed up and supervised by a program specialist or curriculum assistant, deserves further study for clues as to roles and functions that simply are not performed in U.S. schools.

The curriculum assistant, supported by visits from the field consultants and given additional training in workshops, was the core of the training process that evolved in the planned variation programs. He made it possible for training to be an ongoing process, related to classroom experience rather than just to theory. Especially valuable as training for the curriculum assistants was their experience as classroom teachers using our model. We learned, however, that the teacher who enjoys the classroom and is effective there does not necessarily, without further training, become an effective supervisor of other teachers. Changing the behavior of classroom teachers without alienating them must be done most subtly. It is easy to be a hostile critic or to be a "nice guy" who says that everything is being done perfectly. The honest but helpful teacher trainer cannot be mass produced, but we can point to some individuals who have shown considerable growth in that role and some who are naturally good at it.

In an open-framework program we try to have teachers apply certain strategies to the design of educational environments and activities, and we try to have them understand, evaluate, and apply developmental goals appropriate to individual children. It took us longer than one might expect to become clear about what these goals and strategies are. In the Follow Through age range we were hampered by not having a functioning prototype. It is difficult to train teachers and supervisors to implement a model that consists only of some basic hunches about good education. As we developed a prototype at our High/Scope Staff Training and Curriculum Development Center, we could show rather than just tell, and teachers and curriculum assistants from our 10 Follow Through sites could experience what we were trying to get across.

As our model became clearer to us, it was easier for us to explain it to others. Although the process of developing the model as we tried to train others to use it put a strain on everyone—most notably our field consultants—it did help us to see that what we were developing was an implementation package and not simply a "curriculum" to be used in a classroom. It also prevented the model from becoming a static derivation from theory, a set of a priori assumptions. We are stronger by virtue of the trial by fire in the field.

Ultimately each teacher must experiment in the classroom, within the framework of the model, to discover the most effective approaches for his or her particular group of children. We think we can give teachers some useful guidance, but our training is effective only when it leads to new approaches in the classroom that are initiated to meet needs that the teachers themselves perceive. This is a long-term process involving several adults as well as the children. We think it would be a good way to conceptualize *any* teacher training program.

IMPLEMENTATION: THE REALITIES

The selection of a model sponsor by a community was the first major test of the political realities of planned variation. Generally speaking, the choice of one model over another was based on trivial reasons. One state official promoting our model in a remote area confided that he knew it was "all right" because he had graduated from the nearby university and knew our area. At times, however, the decision was made on the basis of a hard-fought election. In Seattle, we and a competing model made a debate-style presentation to the parent board responsible for selection of the sponsor. The contrast between a hard-line academic program and our more open, process-oriented approach led to bitter and angry arguments among parents. An election was held, and although the electors chose our model, four years later elements of that battle are still being fought. Other sponsors could describe equally difficult situations.

When a model was selected as the Follow Through guidelines suggest, a careful study was made of the sponsor's approach. A planning committee from the community usually visited the sponsor, looked at whatever educational programs were under way, and discussed the sponsor's educational philosophy. School officials, teachers, and parents generally were represented. However, there was often little that these persons really could grasp about the model. Moreover, the concept of a "marriage" between an independent school system and an outside sponsor for a period of years was foreign to a generation raised on the one-day-wonder, consulting–training approach. Even more than the concept of parent participation in local project decision-making, the role of the sponsor was enigmatic to the planning committee.

Why did many of the schools agree to participate in these projects? The reasons seemed to range from a genuine desire to improve education in the community for all children, especially poor children, to a clear intent to obtain the funds and then ignore regulations, guidelines, sponsors, and parents. "I thought Follow Through was to buy equipment for the schools, not employ people," was the comment of one school board member in a small western community. Communities with limited employment opportunities desperately needed job openings; some were in active competition with nearby communities, and they could chalk up an easy victory in the intercommunity balance by accepting Follow Through.

Once established, Follow Through became a focus of hostility in many communities, for a wide range of reasons. Basically, the minority groups are right: There *is* a vast reservoir of anger and hostility toward low-income people, particularly those who are members of minority groups. Follow Through and Head Start, as programs for such groups, attracted major opposition simply because "they get too much already." One community was upset because of the dental treatment program for the youngsters: "They should take care of their own problems." Another was angered because of the free lunch provided to guideline children: "If you feed them now, they'll expect it later." Attempts were made to divert Follow Through dollars to other community needs; requirements that Follow Through funds actually be used as the federal program intended were resented and resisted.

As these programs became established, the general hostility toward the participants (more common in small southern and western communities than in the problem-plagued great cities) often became particularly intense as the Follow Through parents, building on the guidelines, began to be more active politically. One school board member commented that "the parents can ask, but they had better not try to tell us anything." A superintendent said that Follow Through was a squeaky wheel on the wagon. "Now, there is no point," he said, "to a squeaky wheel. We'll just take it off the wagon." Ultimately, politically active parents became recognized forces in their communities. Indeed, in the spring of 1973, one Follow Through site, when the board refused to meet its request for continuation of the project, initiated a recall election to replace the board members with their own community representatives.

CONSTRAINTS ON MODEL IMPLEMENTATION

A major force affecting the ability of sponsors to implement their programs as originally conceived is the growing pressure—from state legislators, school boards, and even commercial publishing houses—for educational "accountability." Basically, the idea is sound: Establish realistic goals for education, and then hold teachers and ultimately children accountable for reaching those goals. California has molded this concept into law; Colorado and Michigan, among others, have moved rapidly toward statewide systems that are based primarily on a patchwork of opinions from educators as to what constitutes minimally acceptable objectives for the various "domains" of education at each grade level. Accountability sounds like an excellent idea, especially when it is designed so that local school administrators set the standards of performance.

While the trend toward accountability has been running strong, an opposing trend, toward open education, has also been gathering support. The consequence has been a serious threat to the integrity of the "open" planned variation models. Basically, the appeal of the accountability model is its use of technocratic solutions to educational problems. If we want children to read, the logic goes, direct teaching of reading is certainly the most effective way to accomplish that end. What could be simpler than to have the state pick up this theme and hold sponsors in the state responsible for reaching these goals? The instructional objectives against which programs and teachers are usually held accountable best match those of the programmed models that follow "teacher-proof" curricula. This leaves the majority of Follow Through sponsors in a quandary. The overwhelming focus on the direct teaching of academic skills has to be carefully side-stepped by all models with other means and other ends for education. Surprisingly, many parents and education officials are unaware of these differences among models. Our open-framework model was accused of failure in one community after it was announced that programmed instruction models funded under the OEO performance contract study had failed to show positive results. In general, a particular model is seen only within the context of local community concerns. When the parents of children in various models "get together," the focus is usually on political survival; to the dismay of sponsors, there is seldom time for or interest in discussing, say, the relative merits of a Piagetian and a Skinnerian solution to an educational problem.

Local school districts have placed difficult demands on Head Start centers, often as a result of their concern with academic degrees, tenure, and administration. Critical problems arose in connection with making home visits, with finding enough time in the official school day for staff planning, and with attempts by local districts to impose non-model classroom materials. An important factor was whether the program was run by a Community Action agency or by the local school system. Community Action programs tended to be less bound by public school traditionalism, but they did not escape pressures from the school, especially if they were dependent on the school for classroom space, cafeteria services, or transportation. Conflict that arose between Community Action and the local schools weakened and eventually eliminated a strong program in one of our planned variation sites; in this case, Community Action had goals relating to community organization that took precedence over the Head Start program.

THE BRIGHTER SIDE

One bright spot in the Head Start Planned Variation study has been the role of the general consultant. Many of us were deeply concerned when we found that supposedly neutral consultants were going into the communities to observe the work of the model sponsor. We were even more concerned when we found that their travel budget for on-site time frequently exceeded ours! However, we found that these general consultants were remarkable in their ability to intervene neutrally or supportively even when their viewpoint differed from that represented by the model. In our opinion, this was a major contribution by a dedicated group of professionals.

The role of the general consultant has been more ambiguous in Follow Through. Many of these consultants have been unable to leave their theoretical bias behind and support the project as it is operating. One consultant felt that our reading program was not effective, so he set up a review session with the teachers to introduce alternatives. Another left flyers concerning a commercial reading program. Still another found that our focus was not sufficiently behavioral, so he introduced training sessions for the staff on the preparation of behavioral objectives.

We do not mean to leave the impression that these problems always occurred or that they were never solved. Many general consultants have saved our programs from certain death by timely and professional intervention. Many have added greatly to our understanding of the teacher learning process. It is true, however, that we have at times felt corralled by forces and individuals—politically inspired or simply opportunist—and that, in Follow Through, general consultants have contributed to this feeling.

Pressure from the state for accountability, the conflict with university and regional personnel, and confusion at the local level with the standard school programs were nothing compared to the force that the participants in the project exerted on the model. If our model is typical, the pressure by the local participants is sufficiently unique in its effect to warrant major attention as a way of shaping effective education. Usually implementation of an educational experiment or program is accomplished at one site by a group of outsiders on their own initiative and for their own purposes. It is well known that reform in education is seldom accomplished by outsiders; that reform in education is almost *never* accomplished by local people alone is perhaps recognized but rarely conceded. It is essential that a process of interaction be established for effective change.

A "one-site/one-shot" philosophy has done much to shape educational research and reform. Fortunately, Head Start and Follow Through are different. First, there is the long-term funding for the participants; in spite of Follow Through's current economic and political ill health, half a decade of consistent developmental work under demanding circumstances has produced change. Second, there is the opportunity for a sponsor to work at many sites instead of only at one. Third, and most important, the arrangements with communities are almost in the form of "marriages" that cannot be annulled without danger of a collapse of funding; this forced togetherness over five years has given us ample time to see issues come and go, to gain perspective on the central problems, and to develop programs and services.

OUR MINI–PLANNED VARIATION STUDY, 1968–70

Since 1962, Weikart and staff have been developing the High/Scope Cognitively Oriented Curriculum as a preschool model, based on the theories of Piaget as well as on ideas drawn from teachers' experience. In 1967 we decided to run a tightly controlled study of model differences, selecting a programmed model (the Language-Training Curriculum) designed by Bereiter and Englemann, then at the University of Illinois; a child-centered model (the Unit-Based Curriculum) drawn from the traditional concerns and methods of preschool educators; and our own open-framework model (the Cognitive Curriculum). The experiment was designed with an initial wave and two replications. As in the national planned variation studies, the children were selected from the low-income families in the community, but in contrast to the national studies, we were able to assign children randomly to each of the three treatment groups. For funding reasons, we were limited to children who scored below 85 on the Stanford–Binet Intelligence Test.

The results of the study are shown in Tables 1 and 2. While the

TABLE 1

Stanford–Binet Intelligence Test Results for the Ypsilanti Preschool Curriculum Demonstration Project

	Fall, Entering Year		Spring, Entering Year			N	Spring, Current Year		
	Mean	Standard Deviation	Mean	Standard Deviation	Col. 3 — Col. 1		Mean	Standard Deviation	Col. 7 — Col. 1
Wave 5[a] (1968)									
Cognitive (N = 11)[b]	75.3	6.1	98.6	12.8	+23.3	11	84.5	13.2	+ 9.2
Language (N = 8)[c]	73.9	5.3	98.2	9.4	+24.3	7	79.0	11.8	+ 5.6[e]
Unit-Based (N = 8)[d]	76.4	4.5	94.1	2.4	+17.7	8	86.5	9.4	+10.1
Wave 6 (1969)									
Cognitive (N = 5)	83.2	4.8	110.8	12.3	+27.6	5	97.6	19.5	+14.4
Language (N = 8)	84.4	3.2	114.6	6.1	+30.2	7	100.1	12.4	+15.4[c]
Unit-Based (N = 8)	73.6	6.9	101.1	7.1	+27.5	6	93.3	13.9	+18.1[c]
Wave 7 (1970)									
Cognitive (N = 7)	79.9	7.3	102.3	13.8	+22.4	6	88.3	5.6	+10.0[c]
Language (N = 9)	78.3	6.0	102.3	13.9	+24.0	9	97.2	14.5	+18.9
Unit-Based (N = 8)	84.3	3.6	101.9	7.4	+17.6	8	95.3	6.6	+11.0

[a]Wave 5 is the transition wave from the 1962–67 Ypsilanti–Perry Preschool Project.
[b]Attended 2 years of preschool as 3- and 4-year-olds.
[c]Tested only as 3-year-olds, attended language program as 4-year-olds.
[d]Tested only as 4-year-olds, Fall 1967; attended unit-based program as 4-year-olds.
[e]Difference scores obtained only on children tested in both time periods.

138

TABLE 2

California Achievement Test Results for the
Curriculum Demonstration Project

	Grade 1		Grade 2		Grade 3	
	N	Raw Score	N	Raw Score	N	Raw Score
Wave 5 (1968)						
Cognitive	10	81	11	151	11	167
Language	7	83	8	153	7	172
Unit-Based	8	65	8	151	8	192
Wave 6 (1969)						
Cognitive	5	144	5	195		N/A
Language	6	119	7	178		
Unit-Based	6	147	4	173		
Wave 7 (1970)						
Cognitive	6	103				
Language	9	104		N/A		N/A
Unit-Based	8	116				

NOTE: At no grade level do these group differences reach statistical significance.

number of observations is small and a full longitudinal analysis is not available, there are two principal findings from the project that are worth noting.

1. On the whole, there were no initial or subsequent differences among the models on either intellectual or achievement tests. Children in all three programs did very well on both.

2. The supposed advantages of direct teaching of academic skills in the language-training curriculum simply do not occur, and, furthermore, the widely reported inability of traditional child-centered curricula to produce effective results is not supported by these data.[5]

Our interpretation is that specific curricula may have less impact on the general success or failure of various models than does the matrix of demands and expectations that surround the operation of a complex project. In light of this, certain principles may be derived from this mini–planned variation experiment.

First, a high-quality staff is important to the success of any project: quality is defined in terms of willingness to operate within the context of the

[5]These results stand in contrast to our predictions as well as to results obtained in second-year Head Start Planned Variation wherein the High/Scope model showed improvement on cognitive measures while programmed models were effective in teaching recognition of letters and numbers but not general cognitive skills.

project, to accept supervision, to be part of a working team, and to evaluate activities constantly. Traditional indices of quality, such as academic degrees, teaching certificates, tenure, and administrative experience, are less relevant.

Second, the work must be public, that is, open to observation and challenge by all participants in the project at all times. The staff must participate in a process of planning and evaluation where the focus is not on whether something is right or wrong, but on detail, completeness, adherence to the curriculum theory, and knowledge of the children.

Third, the typical goal of project administration—a high degree of organization and efficiency—is what kills the outcome, since, paradoxically, the better organized a project becomes, the less pressure there is on the staff to appraise critically their work and their program. What produces effective education is a project in transition toward high-quality service to children, firmly anchored in curriculum theory and supervised by experienced staff capable of building progress out of problems.

It was difficult for us at the end of this mini–planned variation study, as it was during its follow-up, to shift our focus from finding the "right" curriculum to examining the operation of a project, and to realize that the very outcome of an educational project is based on how the staff members conduct themselves. The failure of many programs has little to do with the children's "deficits" or even with the concept of the program but has much to do with the ways in which adults work together to accomplish their objectives and meet the needs of children. Schools don't work because adults don't work to solve the problems that must be solved to permit children to function.

THE VALUE OF COMPARING MODELS

The logic of the planned variation approach is compelling. It is, of course, an application of the basic logic of scientific verification; departures are made from true experimental procedures in the interest of preserving the relevance of the findings. The purpose of the experimental design is to relate the models (as predictor variables) to outcomes—usually child outcomes. However, the absence of clear model effects in our mini–planned variation study, and the paucity of useful findings in the entire literature on teaching methods force us to ask whether the planned variation methodology can be expected to yield useful data. Are researchers and policymakers doomed to findings of "no differences" among educational methods?

Our opinion is that the paradigm of scientific hypothesis-testing, the experiment, should not be abandoned, because differences among treatment groups are not readily apparent. Even if the tightly controlled experiment degenerates into a "quasi-experiment," like Follow Through or Head Start Planned Variation, it is not a new methodology we need. What is needed may be a clearer conceptualization of models, outcomes, and intervening processes, as well as better educational "treatments" for the researcher to evaluate—treatments that recognize the need for energizing frameworks as well as "validated" materials.

Using the so-called "models" as the treatments in the planned variation experiment was an informed strategy on the part of the designers of the planned variation studies. The models should introduce systematic variation, which should be fairly readily describable. If experimental effects are produced, the models should be explicit enough to provide a rich source of hypotheses about what specific aspects of the treatments worked. However, for this informed strategy to pay off:

1. The models actually must be implemented in the field situations or at least must produce evidence of having systematic effects on classrooms.

2. Outcome measures must reflect validly the central concerns of the policymaker or of the model sponsors and must include a search for *unintended* desirable and undesirable effects.

In practice, these criteria have not been fully met. Models, conceptualized as replicable treatments, seem to dissolve into unreality when poked. The gap between a model-as-conceived and a model-as-implemented may be traced to a number of points of slippage:

1. The model may be inadequately conceptualized and specified. This is especially likely to happen if the model developer is asked to implement a model in the field before he has a local prototype in operation.

2. The model may change over time so that the treatment will have a somewhat elusive character. There may even be a systematic convergence of the models over time due to uniform pressures from the field.

3. The model may be inadequately "delivered" via the training and monitoring systems.

4. The model may be understood but actively resisted by the classroom personnel and others responsible for its implementation.

Dilution of the treatment variable has occurred in *all* of these ways throughout the history of planned variation experiments. It is noteworthy, however, that data concerning the empirical question of whether distinct models actually are implemented in a planned variation experiment are being gathered with increasing frequency and sophistication. In the future, we should not have to guess at the relationship between a sponsor's prototype and the field models.

There may be important differences among model types (for example, programmed versus open-framework versus child-centered) in the extent to which a model can be specified behaviorally and rapidly implemented. A programmed model, aimed at removing inter-teacher variation, may be ready for summative evaluation long before an open-framework or child-centered model is. The latter do not produce automatic homogenization of teacher behavior by means of materials for children, equipment, or a "script" for the teacher. Open-framework and child-centered models may be more effective in the long run in some ways, but ease of implementation is not their strong point. A planned variation experiment that stresses initial results may miss this important fact. Follow Through fortunately is permitting adequate time for developing prototypes, delivery systems, and implementation. Head Start Planned Variation was heartlessly short. The success of the High/Scope model in Head Start Planned Variation may reflect the comparatively mature state of our preschool program prior to field implementation.

While treatment variables are less than adequately defined, outcome measures are even more of a problem. We seem to be embroiled in several dilemmas in this area.

We use available measures, such as IQ tests and standard achievement tests, rather than developing alternative instruments. It would be foolish to abandon planned variation methodology or intervention effects because we cannot produce IQ differences or differences in performances of Piagetian tasks. These kinds of measures are composed of items specifically selected for their relation to age rather than years of formal instruction. When we *can* produce differences in "unteachable" measures, it is usually a sign that there is a powerful method at work, but we should not despair because of a failure to differentiate models on the basis of those skills that are least susceptible to differences in educational treatment.

Reliance on standard achievement tests also works against the wider range of information we could get from a planned variation experiment. Many models would not normally aim at producing higher achievement test scores in the earliest years, so why judge them on these criteria alone? We do need better measurements, but these *should* develop naturally out of the objectives specified by the "nontraditional" models. The High/Scope Foundation, for example, is working on measures of productive communication skills to supplant conventional reading achievement tests.

To date, it does not seem as if planned variation results have helped us to identify superior and inferior ways of accomplishing important long-run educational objectives. The specific outcomes seem simply to result from the emphasis or de-emphasis within a model on behaviors related to the criterion measures. Empirically as well as logically, the less "teach-

able'' the criterion tasks and the more universal the criterion-related behaviors, the less likely it is that the planned variation technique will yield
differences.

We need to look not only at skill outcomes but also at affective ones
—intended and unintended. Are children doing well on reading achievement tests but learning to hate reading and fear school? And we need to
look at whether we are creating acceptable (''humane'') *environments* as
well as immediate outcomes.

It is possible that studies like the planned variation experiments
are most useful as prods to curriculum development, the refinement of
evaluation techniques, and the generation of new hypotheses about changing individuals and institutions. Rather than producing conclusive validation of methods, they may serve as stimuli to important further work. The
heuristic value of the inconclusive experiment is obvious in other sciences.
There may be a wider understanding of this phenomenon now than at the
beginning of the planned variation efforts. Further planned variation experiments should take this into account. To translate this statement, we are
saying that the formative feedback obtained from planned variation should
be much more explicitly built into the process and seen as of prime importance, as opposed to the emphasis on summative evaluation. As an example, mountains of narrative accounts as well as quantitative data already
have been collected. Model sponsors for the most part have not benefited
from these reports. A less rigid conception of the planned variation research might have led to feedback of data to the sponsors who were in the
process of developing delivery systems.

IMPLICATIONS FOR PLANNED VARIATION
RESEARCH

After 5 years of experience in planned variation experiments both on
the national scale and in one mini-project, what are some of the central
conclusions or implications we can draw?

1. There are phases in the research–dissemination cycle that cannot
be tampered with. (See Figure 1.) They begin with a tightly controlled
research project, move through the development of training materials to
demonstration and field testing, and finally to the dissemination phase.
Because of the pressure for policy information, most planned variation
sponsors bypassed the early phases and began the field test phase without
any prior development. Many of the dilemmas in interpreting data from the
planned variation experiments are the result of this situation. In future

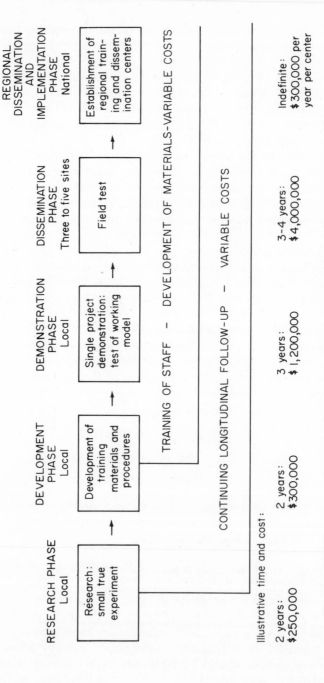

Figure 1. High/Scope research dissemination procedure: stages in the development of an intervention project.

144

studies it is essential that adequate time and resources be devoted to preparation. The more complex the proposed ideas and the more they diverge from current practice, the greater is the need for this.

2. To develop true alternatives to current educational practices, developers must be cast into a dynamic system. This means allowing for and responding to pressure from the participants—teachers, parents, administrators, and the children themselves. Educational programs must be a synthesis of theory and practice and must continually be reshaped by developers and participants alike if they are to remain effective. Once the developer is committed to a dynamic system, he must have enough time to produce the changes he desires.

3. It is apparent to those of us who have participated in planned variation experiments that there is a need for new attention to major changes in education. Programs with what are really minor differences in methods of teaching phonics to first graders have never produced significant differences in the past. Why should they in Follow Through? The need is for whole new educational systems with broadly differentiated goals and outcome effects. The grafting of various program parts—of teachers with the traditional training, school structures with standardized space and equipment, a fairly uniform school day (5 hours) and year (900 hours)—is not the best way to produce radically new approaches. New systems must evolve that represent dramatically different ways of approaching and supporting child development. Why teach reading as such at all? Where does the responsibility lie for a child's learning, and how soon and in what way does *he* become able to assume this responsibility? Those of us who have participated in the planned variation experiments represent a level of situation-induced training and experience that is unique in education. From our point of view, we have just begun an extended process of development, rather than having completed a demonstration of what exists. New planned variation experiments must accept this difference.

4. When planned variation experiments began, we thought that much of our problem would be in training teachers. This was a correct prognosis except that we were unprepared for the extraordinary difficulty of altering teaching behavior. We believe that teacher behavior is shaped to an important extent by the expectations of parents, peers, administrations, and, indeed, by the children themselves. There is no such thing as a "trained teacher"; we had to construct a training system that was continuous. Such a system must begin with the teacher at his or her point of need and then gradually shift as the teacher gains sophistication in the methodology.

5. Along with the evolution of global research methods, there is a pressing need to develop new assessment strategies. The way we evaluate competence in school has little relation to the long-term objectives most

parents and educators really hold for children. Reading is not marking the appropriate box on the multiple choice test; most Americans don't read regularly. Mathematics is not the multiplication table; whole segments of our society fear numbers and numerical operations. New evaluation tools are needed that tap the broader social goals of education. The direction seems to be toward radically different measurement objectives (for example, using writing as a test of reading) and toward recognizing that curriculum evaluation cannot be accomplished without some measurement of degree of implementation. This calls for the development of observational and situational testing procedures that would capture a program in process, the conditions under which children are functioning. We also need to look at longitudinal effects. We have found, for example, that children who had a successful preschool experience ten years ago in our Ypsilanti–Perry Preschool Project are placed less frequently in special education classes than children from the "no treatment" control group. Longitudinal follow-up is critical for assessing the optimal ages for learning specific skills and the unexpected effects in areas not directly related to treatment.

Planned variation experiments are a solid method for developing alternative educational procedures. The statistical data produced by this first round may be unclear, but that is the fault of our conception of the methodology. What planned variation did produce was a base for more effective future experiments and for effective educational alternatives.

APPENDIX: RESEARCH DISSEMINATION SYSTEM

We propose a five-phase research dissemination procedure to guide the development and implementation of effective educational programs. The model is presented in Figure 1.

Phase 1. This stage must be a tightly controlled research study, guided by as close adherence to true experimental design as possible. This calls for the random assignment of simple, clearly stated objectives, carefully documented procedures, formative evaluation with special emphasis on nonquantitative information, and basic summative or outcome evaluation if instruments exist for assessing the program goals effectively. While the program should provide high-quality service to the participants, the purpose is frankly experimental, and the specific outcomes of the work are truly unknown.

Phase 2. This stage is for developing training materials and methods that will serve as the basis for program implementation in Phase 3. Based on the needs identified in the experimental study, a wide range of training materials and methods will be developed. These methods may include film, videotape, manuals, handbooks, reading lists, and suggested practical systems for gaining actual experience rapidly. The materials will be used in both preservice and in-service training, and they will be directed toward assisting trainees in achieving competence-based criteria. They are critical to Phase 3, but the development of training materials will continue throughout the remaining phases, since this work must constantly be adjusted to meet the needs of different staff and situations. Instrument development, based on the data collected in the experimental phase, continues. The essential function of this phase, then, is to prepare the materials that will provide the basis for developing the program implementation staff in Phase 3.

Phase 3. In Phase 3 the developed educational program is demonstrated in a natural setting that approximates conditions of regular field operation. While still "at home" and not in distal sites, the characteristics of the personnel operating the project are as close as possible to those of the people who are expected to operate such a project in the field. For example, paraprofessionals are used if that is intended in the final operational model. The basic purpose of the phase is to complete the development of five essential components for effective field operations so that they will be ready for Phase 4. These are: the curriculum to be delivered, the system to deliver that curriculum, the training procedures that must be used if the program is to be implemented successfully, the staff model to be used, and the quality control methods to accompany the field implementation to insure the success of the program. A wide range of "adaptations" and "improvements" are made within the framework of the original research project, to build on the experience of the original project and to meet practical political and other demands. However, the central focus of the project is retained, and these additions can be seen as "practical" and "responsive," rather than as changes in the basic design. This phase is perhaps the most critical because retention of the intent of the original "at home" project under the pressures of the more open situation in the field is most difficult. Research is directed to special objectives: validation of training systems, further instrument development, and replication of original findings. Formative evaluation is maximized to serve as a basis for quality control recommendations and to link specific project procedures with desired outcomes.

Phase 4. This stage represents a limited field test under natural circumstances. The number of sites cannot be so large that effective control is lost. The training methods and materials are ready for field use, and the five components listed in Phase 3 are ready for implementation. The research revolves around large policy issues, such as the potential impact on populations to be served, and so on. The quality control procedures are primarily designed to produce monitoring information and to indicate comparability with the original study and demonstration project. Through this stage the original sponsor is usually active.

Phase 5. The education program is now ready for dissemination to many sites. The curriculum, training program, delivery system, staff model, and quality control procedures are clearly known and available. Continued research on the effect upon differing populations and under differing circumstances may be continued, but the basic program is well documented and can achieve the intended results. At this stage, sponsorship is broadened, as is program operation.

There may be many ways to develop effective educational curricula. The course outlined above is a 12-year sequence, which certainly does not provide information quickly for policy decisions. Nevertheless, it has as its goal the effective delivery of an educational program with the ability to obtain consistently the desired results.

7

IS REAL-WORLD EXPERIMENTATION POSSIBLE? THE CASE OF EDUCATIONAL PERFORMANCE CONTRACTING*

Edward M. Gramlich and Patricia P. Koshel

Policy analysts these days are quick to call for government to experiment with social policies. Rather than simply launching national programs, analysts argue, the government should try them out on an experi-

*Copyright © 1975 by The Regents of The University of California. Reprinted from *Policy Analysis*, Vol. 1, No. 3, by permission of The Regents. This chapter is excerpted from the authors' *Educational Performance Contracting: An Evaluation of an Experiment*, Washington, D.C., The Brookings Institution, 1975. The authors note that if some topic appears to be treated too cursorily here, there is at least a chance that it is discussed at greater length in the Brookings publication.

At the time of the performance contracting experiment, Dr. Gramlich was director of, and Ms. Koshel was in, the Policy Research Division of the Office of Economic Opportunity. Neither was directly involved in the experiment, but both became familiar with its operations. This article and the manuscript from which it is excerpted were prepared after both had left OEO. The views expressed are those of the authors and do not reflect the opinions of the officers or trustees of the Brookings Institution, the National Institute of Education, or the Edna McConnell Clark Foundation, which supported some of the work.

mental basis to see if they work. Rather than simply accepting the provisions of new and existing programs, the government should test these provisions and alternative ones on an experimental basis to see if the provisions produce the intended effects and if there are other ways of achieving the same ends.

The age of experimentation with government social policies has lasted for five years now, and it is time to examine the early experiments to see what they have taught us about behavioral responses to these alternative policies and about policy implementation. Not surprisingly, they have taught us much in both respects. With regard to behavioral responses, most experiments, in areas as diverse as income maintenance and educational enrichment, have generated results which Walter Williams has described as "macro-negative"—that is, the policies under investigation have not caused large changes in human behavior.[1] As for implementation, the experiments have shown both that it is difficult to implement policies satisfactorily and that it is difficult to measure the effect of policies because of uncertainty as to whether they are being implemented as intended. In one area after another, a major difficulty in designing effective social policies has been the seemingly straightforward task of assuring that policies operate as they are supposed to.

In this article we use one of the early social experiments—the Office of Economic Opportunity (OEO) project in educational performance contracting—to illustrate these implementation difficulties. First we examine the climate for the experiment and then the experiment's design and results. Then we recount some of the difficulties encountered in actually carrying out the project. These difficulties, ranging from problems in launching the experiment to problems in operating the programs to problems in analyzing test scores, confounded the results of the experiment seriously in many ways. At least in this case, the process of social experimentation turned out to be a good deal less precise than was suggested by early rhetoric on the topic.

THE CLIMATE FOR THE EXPERIMENT

The term "performance contracting" describes an arrangement whereby agents are paid on the basis of results instead of cost inputs. In the area of education, a performance contracting arrangement is one under which teachers may be rewarded handsomely if their students learn well

---

[1]Walter Williams, *Social Policy Research and Analysis*, New York, American Elsevier, 1971, pp. 7–8.

but not if they do not learn well. There are obviously many types of such arrangements—the teaching agents can be teachers themselves or private companies, student gains can be measured in various ways, payment schedules can feature various types of monetary incentives. But whatever the scheme, the general idea is that basing payment on educational output instead of cost input will elicit better teaching and provide a means of introducing market incentives into education.

Modern interest in performance contracting was first evoked by a project in Texarkana, Arkansas. The Dorsett Company, a private firm operating under a performance incentive contract, received a great deal of publicity in the winter of 1970 for generating what at first appeared to be very large gains in student learning. Although these gains later proved impossible to verify, the Dorsett experience did excite many local boards. In the first year of Dorsett's operation, over 100 school districts planned to follow the Texarkana lead in making some contracting arrangement with a private company.

There was also a receptive audience at the federal level. The Texarkana story came out just as President Nixon released an important congressional message on education, which featured the statement that local systems should be held "accountable" for their performance.[2] Similar speeches were being made by many other officials in both the Office of Education and OEO.[3] The fact that companies teaching under performance contracting would not be paid unless results showed they merited it meant that the concept of incentive contracting was ideally suited to the emerging "accountability" theme. The fact that the companies were private, demonstrating the fruits of free enterprise, made the idea even more attractive to Republican policymakers.

Performance contracting was also appealing to those who felt that teachers lacked sufficient monetary incentives to improve their teaching, focus on disadvantaged students, try new methods, or whatever. Teachers were simply paid according to seniority scales, which were alleged to place more of a premium on doing things in traditional ways and not causing trouble than on anything else. An institutional change under which firms and ultimately their teachers would be paid only according to how well they taught might break this conservatism and make it to the real advantage of

[2]Message to the Congress by President Richard M. Nixon, "Education for the 1970s: Renewal and Reform," March 1970.

[3]See: Donald Rumsfeld (director of OEO), "Experiments in Education" (Speech given at the Urban Roundtable, San Francisco, 23 September 1970); and Leon Lessinger, "Engineering Accountability for Results in Education," in *Learning C.O.D.: Can the Schools Buy Success?*, eds. J. A. Mecklenburger, J. A. Wilson, and R. W. Hostrop, Hamden, Conn., The Shoestring Press, 1972.

these firms to improve their methods. In fact, in the longer run a system of monetary incentives such as this could lead to even more fundamental changes in existing educational systems. Those firms which proved to be successful at teaching underprivileged children (and for that matter all other children) would thrive and expand; those which did not would drop out of the industry. Local school boards would be given a chance to purchase educational materials on the basis of outputs instead of inputs, to select from competing sources of supply, to buy materials from firms with real experience in teaching and a tradition of success, and to write incentive contracts which could encourage a focus on disadvantaged students.

The most vociferous opposition to the concept came from the major national teachers' unions. After all, incentive contracts do not guarantee anybody's pay; they only make it possible to earn more if students do well, which the teachers deemed a rather unlikely prospect. Teachers undoubtedly felt threatened by the specter of private firms competing for their jobs and by some of the early speeches of government officials about contracting, which may have been more challenging and contentious than necessary.[4]

The upshot of this strong but less than unanimous interest was a decision to make educational performance contracting the focus of a social experiment. OEO, at that time in the process of being transformed from an agency that actually operated national programs to one that carried out mainly research, evaluation, and program development activities, seemed like an ideal place in which to house such an experiment. OEO was interested and experienced in the area of social experimentation, having recently begun a widely publicized income maintenance experiment. Moreover, it was interested in performance contracting, it was less beholden to the teachers' unions and educational establishment generally than the Office of Education might have been, and it had enough money to begin the project right away. Rigorous evaluation of social programs had become the word of the day at OEO, and a controlled experiment with performance contracting looked like the perfect way to start.

DESIGN AND RESULTS

An experiment to test the idea of performance contracting could have been designed in two quite different ways. At one extreme, the possible long-run advantages of introducing market incentives into education could

---

[4]"The Performance Contract: Innovation or Hucksterism," an American Federation of Teachers pamphlet, undated, is one sample of the teacher opposition to performance contracting.

have been examined through an experiment in which private firms or teachers entered into incentive contracts with school boards, had time to alter their methods in response to successes or failures, and, in the case of firms, even had time to expand or contract their business and enter or leave the industry. This type of experiment would feature incentive contracts, would involve no control by OEO of the teaching methods used in the experimental classrooms, and would presumably last for several years. At the other extreme, the more immediate advantages of teaching students by the new and innovative methods used by the private firms could have been examined in an experiment which contained no incentive contracting and lasted for a much shorter time; here the methods of instruction used in both experimental and control classrooms would be determined beforehand, held to throughout the experiment, and carefully documented.

As it was, the experiment was a generally unsatisfactory mixture of these two ingredients. It was like a test of incentives in featuring contracts whereby both private firms and, in a few cases, local teachers were paid according to how well their students did. Although there was an attempt to enroll a range of firms using somewhat different approaches, these firms were free during the course of the experiment to alter their procedures if they felt that certain changes would be more successful. Nor did OEO make any attempt to restrict or monitor the instructional methods used by the control schools, which were free to teach in ways every bit as new and innovative as those used in the experimental classrooms.

But the experiment fell short of a test of an educational incentive system in one crucial respect. Because it would have been costly to do as a multiyear experiment (the annual cost was about $6 million), and because it would have been politically embarrassing to give private firms several years to accomplish what many were saying they could do in one year, and because school boards wanted quick results, OEO limited the experiment to one year. This meant that while the firms did have time within the experiment to correct obvious problems with their methods of instruction, there clearly was not enough time to test many of the supposed longer-term advantages of performance contracting.

Thus, the experiment was really a test of the learning technology and management abilities of the outside private firms as of 1970, and of the value of profit incentives in the short run. This ambivalent position was not very satisfactory either to those interested in organizational change or to those interested in teaching method. But in a more down-to-earth sense, it was still of value to the many local school boards that in 1970 were faced with the decision of whether or not to sign up with an outside contractor: By waiting only a year, they would have much better information on which to base such a choice.

The Design

The experiment was designed to be both general and rigorous. To attain generality, OEO decided to enroll a number of private firms (six) in a number of sites (three per contractor) and to have the contractors teach in a number of grades in both elementary and junior high school (first, second, third, seventh, eighth, and ninth grades). Late in the planning period, the experiment was expanded to include two more sites. Here the incentive contracts would be signed with local teacher organizations in order to determine the separate contributions of private firms and incentive contracts to any educational successes.

The rigorous aspect of the experiment was in its attempt to make careful comparisons between experimental and control students. Large numbers of control students were included. They were in the same grades and sites as the experimental students, selected from the same population of underprivileged students, and tested with the same tests on the same dates as the experimental students.

The experiment was conducted entirely within the regular public school system. In schools designated as experimental, 100 of the most academically deficient students in each grade were taken out of their regular classrooms and instructed in reading and math by the companies in special classrooms for an hour a day, roughly the length of time that other students were being taught the same subjects. Whenever these students dropped out of the school or the program during the year, their positions were filled by other students, so that total educational gains attributable to the firms could be measured. All experimental students were pretested in the fall and posttested in the spring for reading and math achievement. In the schools designated as control, everything ran as it normally would have, except that 100 of the most deficient students were also pretested in the fall and posttested in the spring with the same tests taken by the experimental students. The educational success of the companies was measured by comparing the test gains of experimental and control students.

The firms operated under contracts which rewarded them according to how much their students had gained during the year. As it turned out, these contracts were not very favorable to the firms—probably because the firms were so confident of their success that they were willing to take on substantial risks. The typical contract stipulated that a firm would get no payment at all for any student who failed to gain 1.0 grade equivalent units;[5]

---

[5]Grade equivalent unit is a commonly used educational concept referring to the gains which would be realized by an average student for that grade on that achievement test during one school year.

a lump sum payment of approximately 43% of the contractor's eventual per-student instructional cost in the experiment, for students who just reached this level; and a further payment for gains above this level. There was a ceiling on the government's liability which averaged $200 times the number of students in the classroom, or 15% more than the average firm's total cost. In addition, 25% of the contractor's maximum pay was to be based on the results of 5 interim-performance objective tests (IPOs), to be given throughout the year to measure mastery of curricular skills specific to the contractor's program. Even if a student earned the full IPO payment for a company, he would have to gain 1.6 grade equivalent units, about two and a third times what would have been expected on the basis of past performance for a student of this rank, just for the contractor to break even on him. And all students in the class would have to gain an average of 1.9 grade equivalent units for the firm to earn its maximum payment, which exceeded its total cost by only 15%.[6] Thus, under these arrangements there was much for the contractors to lose and little for them to gain—a fact which later caused both the contractors and OEO serious problems in negotiating the final settlements of the contracts.

The Results

To make a long story short, the performance contracting experiment did not provide any evidence that private companies could outperform the normal public schools. A large number of comparisons were made: between experimental and control groups overall; broken down by subject, grade, company, and site in various combinations; between relatively good and relatively bad students; and using subtest components and even attendance data. All comparisons indicate that there were at best very slight differences between experimental and control students.

Summary results are given in Table 1. The first row of the table gives the difference between experimental and control gains, by grade and subject, in grade equivalent units and after a statistical adjustment to account for the fact that experimental students were chosen from a slightly lower-ranking population. These numbers indicate that in 6 of the 12 grade-subject cases, there was no difference at all between experimental and control gains; in 1 case there was a gain of .2 grades (about 2 months worth of learning for the normal student), in 4 cases a gain of .1 grade, and in 1 case a loss of .1 grade. The average over all 12 cases was a relative experimental gain of .04 grades, or about 2 weeks of normal learning.

[6]For a more extensive treatment of these matters, see Gramlich and Koshel, *Educational Performance Contracting*, chap. 2.

TABLE 1

Mean Achievement Gain of Experimental Students Less Mean Gain of Control Students, by Grade and Subject, in Grade Equivalent Units, Adjusted for Initial Differences

(R = reading; M = math)

Item	Grade											
	1		2		3		7		8		9	
	R	M	R	M	R	M	R	M	R	M	R	M
1. Mean gain difference	0.0	0.0	0.1	0.0	0.1	0.0	0.2	0.0	0.0	−0.1	0.1	0.1
2. Adjusted mean gain difference at bottom of distribution	0.1	0.1	0.0	0.0	0.1	0.0	0.3	0.2	0.1	0.2	0.1	0.3
3. Adjusted mean gain difference at top of distribution	−0.1	−0.2	0.1	0.0	0.1	0.0	0.1	−0.2	0.0	−0.5	0.1	−0.1

SOURCE: Edward M. Gramlich and Patricia P. Koshel, *Educational Performance Contracting: An Evaluation of an Experiment* (Washington, D.C.: The Brookings Institution, 1975), chap. 4.

Viewed in a different way, whereas the control students in this sample could be expected to gain about .67 grade equivalent units in 1 year—and in fact did gain almost exactly this amount in the experiment—the experimental students gained .71 (.67 + .04) grade equivalent units. They gained either 6% more than the control students (.71–.67), or eliminated 12% of the normal deficit (.04–.33), depending upon one's perspective. While the gains were positive and sometimes statistically significant, they did fall well short of what most people were anticipating the experiment would show—thus leading to the widespread perception that the firms had "failed."[7]

Rows 2 and 3 of Table 1 display the results in a slightly different light. Here the same gains are tabulated for students at the bottom and at the top of the distribution of pretest scores, to see if the performance contracting firms were any more successful at teaching good or bad students. Again there were no very striking findings—in 4 of the 12 cases, the relative gains were the same for low-ranking as for high-ranking students, in one case the relative gains were greater at the top of the distribution, and in 7 cases they were greater at the bottom. There is a suggestion—but only a suggestion—that performance contracting may be better for students who are more deficient academically.

Finally, we have tabulated the site-by-site results to see if any companies achieved unusual success (see Table 2). These comparisons are somewhat more tenuous than the others because of some serious testing problems at individual sites, but the results in Table 2 still do not indicate that great disparities are being hidden within the overall results. The best firm, Quality Education Development Corporation (QED), was responsible for relative gains of .31 grade equivalent units. The worst, Singer-Graflex and Westinghouse, were responsible for losses of .14 and .13 grades. The others produced close to a tie with the control students. QED may have been doing something right, but it was the only one of the six firms that did so.

IMPLEMENTATION DIFFICULTIES

If what we have already described were all there was to it, the experiment would appear to be giving a rather clear verdict: Performance contracting is no better than the status quo—neither private companies nor

---

[7]These results are described in detail in Gramlich and Koshel, *Educational Performance Contracting*, chap. 4. The adjustment for differential populations used there is developed and defended in a technical article by Irwin Garfinkel and Edward Gramlich, "A Statistical Analysis of the OEO Experiment in Educational Performance Contracting," *Journal of Human Resources*, Summer 1973.

TABLE 2

Individual Site Results, Adjusted Mean Gain Differences,
in Grade Equivalent Units, by Site and Contractor

(R = reading; M = math)

Site and Contractor	Adjusted Mean Gain Difference
Learning Foundations	
Bronx, N. Y.	−0.18
Jacksonville, Florida	0.21
Hammond, Indiana	0.01
Average	.01
Westinghouse	
Philadelphia, Pennsylvania	−0.28
Fresno, California	0
Las Vegas, Nevada	−0.11
Average	− .13
Quality Education	
Development Corporation	
Dallas, Texas	0.28
Anchorage, Alaska	0.35
Rockland, Maine	0.30
Average	.31
Alpha Learning Systems	
Grand Rapids, Michigan	0.05
Hartford, Connecticut	−0.05
Taft, Texas	0.18
Average	.06
Singer-Graflex	
Seattle, Washington	−0.41
Portland, Maine	−0.13
McComb, Mississippi	0.12
Average	− .14
Plan Education Centers	
Wichita, Kansas	−0.02
Athens, Georgia	0.19
Selmer, Tennessee	0.26
Average	.14
Teacher Incentives	
Stockton, California	0.12
Mesa, Arizona	0.04
Average	.08
Overall Average	0.05

SOURCE: Edward M. Gramlich and Patricia P. Koshel, *Educational Performance Contracting: An Evaluation of an Experiment* (Washington, D.C.: The Brookings Institution, 1975), chap. 4.

teachers operating under incentive contracts could teach students better than they were taught in the control public schools. But of course this may not be all there is to it. One of the sad lessons of the performance contracting experience is that these experiments are incredibly difficult to organize and encourage. There were at least three important types of difficulties. These involved the haste with which the experiment was done, the actual operation of the companies' programs, and the analysis of results. These difficulties proved serious enough to raise the major question of whether the experiment was implemented sufficiently well to allow for a valid test of the concept of performance contracting.

Haste in Conducting the Experiment

The first reason why the experiment may not have been an entirely accurate test is that the companies may not have been given sufficient time to implement their programs properly. Beyond raising the more basic issue of whether one year was long enough for the companies to organize their instructional programs properly, one can question whether they even had time before the start of the year to set up their programs.

With regard to the beginning difficulties, in its haste to do an experiment while performance contracting was a hot issue, OEO undoubtedly rushed things. The agency made its first visit to Texarkana in March 1970, approved the experiment in April, and simultaneously sent requests for proposals to a list of private companies. At about this time it also awarded a contract for management support in running the experiment to Education Turnkey Systems, Inc., the firm that had handled the Texarkana arrangements. The extensive company selection process was completed in just 2 months, as was the process for selecting school districts. Most of the performance contracts between the companies, school districts, and OEO were signed by July, when the agency also began to select the testing and evaluation contractor. Battelle Memorial Institute was awarded this contract in August and was in the field doing the pretest just 2 weeks later. Thus, with the August starting date, the experiment began barely 6 months after the OEO staff had first heard of Texarkana.

Although the original model for performance contracting, the Dorsett program in Texarkana, had started in even less time, and although the 6 private firms had advertised their teaching experience when bidding for the OEO contracts, by August most of them were still not sufficiently prepared to begin teaching in 3 separate sites and about 20 different schools. They found it very difficult even to hire enough local teachers to staff their programs, let alone to obtain the advice and support of local teachers and other school officials. There were also cases of the necessary equipment and instructional materials not arriving at the sites in time, necessitating hasty revisions in the teaching programs.

The school districts encountered similar problems. The schools were asked to do a considerable amount of work in preparation for the start of the experiment—they had to prepare lists of students who might be participating in the project, provide a project director and two aides to run the experiment, and secure the cooperation of teachers and principals in the schools where the experiment would take place. They managed to complete the first two tasks by the fall, but they were unable to do much in the way of preparing the teachers and principals, most of whom did not even find out about the project until they returned from their summer vacations.

The initial problems were especially bad in the teacher-incentive sites. OEO had decided to include two sites in which incentive contracts would be signed directly with the local teachers' unions, but this decision was not made until very late in the planning period—during the summer before the experiment was to begin—which meant that the number of districts responding was very small. In fact, only two districts submitted formal proposals—Mesa, Arizona, and Stockton, California—and both, necessarily, were included in the experiment. Because of the late start, the project was delayed considerably in these sites. By fall, both sites were still securing formal approvals from teachers' organizations, state and local boards of education, governors, and community groups, and both were still negotiating their incentive contracts into November. Mesa did not even receive the advance on its incentive payments until almost Christmas.

A final set of problems involved the pretesting of students at the start of the experiment. Battelle Institute, which was not awarded this contract until just before it was to begin testing 27,000 children, had had no experience in organizing such large-scale testing programs and had little time to schedule the exams, arrange for rooms, and train the test administrators. As a consequence, testing conditions for the pretest were poor in many sites, in both experimental and control classrooms. The Battelle test report notes many instances of lack of discipline, overcrowded conditions, and excessively hot classrooms, and isolated instances of minor student riots. There was even a fire drill in the middle of a test period. In a few cases the problems were so severe that the students had to be retested a few weeks later.[8]

Operating the Companies' Programs

The second difficulty concerned the operation of the six companies' programs. The general goal of each of these programs was to increase the

[8]See: Battelle Memorial Institute, *Office of Economic Opportunity Experiment in Educational Performance Contracting*, Columbus, Ohio, 1972, pp. 47 ff.

student's motivation. All attempted to avoid the allegedly stifling traditional classroom atmosphere where the teacher worked with the entire group, students were at attention, and desks were lined up neatly in straight rows. The performance contracting programs instead featured individually prescribed lesson plans, students working on their own projects at their own pace, much more casual classroom atmospheres, and also much noisier classrooms. Rather than having one fully licensed teacher in every classroom, many of the companies tried to replace and supplement these teachers as much as possible with aides, paraprofessionals, and a range of teaching machines, audio-visual tutors, and cassette recorders. The firms also insisted on refurbishing the classroom facilities with small tables and chairs or learning carrels which could be grouped in many ways depending upon the day's activities, sometimes with carpets to cut down the noise.

Within these broad outlines, there were of course important differences among the six companies' programs. The six firms differed in the degree to which they replaced regular teachers with paraprofessionals and hardware. They also differed in their philosophy of providing incentives by rewarding students for completing lessons: some firms, such as Learning Foundations and Alpha Learning Systems, made extensive use of tangible incentives like toys, small games, and candy bars to maintain the students' interest in the instructional program; others, such as QED, attempted to provide intangible incentives—for example, free time to play educational games, listen to music, read, or take part in other activities; while still others, such as Plan Education Centers, thought that the sheer satisfaction of learning would make for its own incentives and did not use student rewards at all. The companies also differed in the extent to which they relied on their own or on commercially available instructional programs and in the degree to which their programs relied on the imagination and expertise of the teachers.

While the firms were initially chosen partly because they planned to do things in different ways, the basic idea of performance contracting was that they were free to modify their programs, and as the year went on they certainly did. Sometimes these modifications were due to conscious deliberation, but more often they seemed to be forced by management breakdowns of one sort or another. The firms which relied heavily on their own instructional programs generally were not able to supply these materials on schedule and had to permit their teachers to use some other commercial materials. The firms that relied on teaching machines and other hardware could not keep their equipment in good repair and generally had to resort to less capital-intensive ways of teaching. In Las Vegas, for example, Westinghouse had to abandon its reel-to-reel tape recorders when it found that students learned how to erase the tapes and were recording obscenities. The programs that relied on incentives to teachers could not make these incentive payments when it became apparent that they were causing too much hostility among the teachers. The programs that relied heavily on tangible student incentives could not continue this when the rewards failed to arrive in time—Learning Foundations kept certain students in Jacksonville waiting until October of the following year for their rewards.

The extent to which firms were able to rise above these problems was determined in large part by the local project director. This person, usually someone who had been an administrator or teacher in the district, was responsible for making the project run smoothly, keeping records, assisting the firms, and stepping in when things did not seem to be going well. Some of the more successful project directors in fact took on so much responsibility for the success of the companies that OEO feared that the experiment might be contaminated. The project director in Athens, Georgia, for example, was so concerned about how the project was going in the beginning of Plan Education's project there that he threatened to terminate the experiment unless the firm made certain revisions. He recommended additional teaching materials, enlisted consultants from the University of Georgia to assist the contractor, and saw to it that Plan Education hired more teaching staff. As Table 2 shows, this was one of the most successful sites in the experiment. Other project directors played this role to a lesser degree.

A related problem was teacher hostility. This hostility was partially a reflection of inadequate attempts to enlist the cooperation of local teachers at the start of the experiment, but for the most part it was probably inevitable: The regular teachers did not particularly enjoy competition; they were envious of the experimental teachers, whether brought in from the outside or hired locally, who received higher salaries from the companies; and they were upset by the scheduling disruptions caused by the presence of experimental classrooms in their schools. Even such seemingly reconcilable matters as the fact that experimental teachers often did not have cafeteria duty often snowballed into great problems.

Problems at Specific Sites

A few sites suffered extraordinary difficulties, much beyond anything that might have been anticipated beforehand, and sometimes so serious as to make the test results next to meaningless. By all odds, the worst of these cases was the Bronx. In the late 1960s the New York City school system had moved toward a decentralized, community-controlled system, which antagonized its strong local teachers' union, the United Federation of Teachers. This union, a chapter of the American Federation of Teachers, was strongly opposed to performance contracting; its president, Albert Shanker, announced on a radio broadcast that he believed the Bronx program to be illegal, and he threatened action to prevent its continuation. The teachers in the experimental schools took this cue and were continually at loggerheads with the contractor, Learning Foundations. There were reports that they threw some of the Learning Foundation equipment out of second-story windows and told students to throw away their parent questionnaires. Discipline in the junior high schools involved in the experiment became so bad at one point early in the fall that all testing and instruction was halted and a full-time policeman had to be stationed in one school. Instruction could be resumed only when the president of Learning Foundations, Fran Tarkenton, at that time also a quarterback with the New York Giants football team, was able to rally community support for the project. Even so, records from the project are very incomplete. In one school the posttests were given in a ballroom a few blocks from the school and many students never made it from the school to the testing room. In another, some students were not posttested because the principal had assigned Battelle a testing date which was after the school year was over. Fortunately, this sort of experience was extraordinary: if it were not, there would be no point in even attempting social experiments.

The situation in Hartford and Philadelphia was almost as disorganized. In Hartford, a strike closed both the experimental and control schools for 13 days, and the contractor claimed that another 14 days had been lost because of classroom disruptions. Furthermore, there were reports that about 75 of the 300 elementary experimental students did not start the program until late in October, more than a month after the other students had begun. In Philadelphia, there was also a short school strike, much of the teaching equipment was vandalized and the contractor's junior high school staff walked off the job to protest the firing of one person. There was also considerable conflict between the contractor's staff and school personnel.

Disruptions occurred at a few other sites as well. In Taft, Texas, a number of Mexican-American parents pulled their children out of a ninth grade class because the class consisted of only Mexican-Americans. Taft also had a hurricane which blew the roof off one of the schools at the start of the experiment. And the beginnings of the experiment in Wichita were confused by the fact that the district was then redrawing school zone lines to correspond with a court integration ruling.

Difficulties in Analyzing the Results

Analysis of test scores is made possible in an experiment such as this by the law of large numbers: Test-score gains for any individual student are not very reliable because of testing problems at pretest or posttest time, because the student may not have been feeling well when the test was given, because there may have been a fluke question which he could not answer even though he knew the material, or for many other reasons. While this is true for any one student, however, when groups of students are averaged the individual peculiarities are canceled out and the test scores become much more reliable.

It is likely that this fact implies that reasonable confidence can be placed in the overall results given in Table 1. The numbers in row 1 are based on averages for 2500 students in each grade, and it would be most extraordinary if these results did not depict quite accurately what happens when companies and control public schools teach underprivileged students in this way for a year. Yet an equally important goal of the experiment was to examine experiences on a site-by-site basis, and for this the results of the experiment are much less reliable. Not only is the sample size reduced by a factor of 20 (to 125 students, on the average), but also there is a much stronger possibility that testing disturbances have affected a whole site and made the entire comparison of gains meaningless at that site.

The Battelle report cited above indicates that there were many instances of subpar testing conditions. With some exceptions, however, it is vague concerning whether disturbances existed in the control or experimental testing room, or during the pretest or posttest. Even if the report were more specific, in principle it would be impossible to know whether a disturbance was normal or was so great as to make the classroom results useless. Therefore, we were forced to adopt statistical procedures for examining the site-by-site results to see if these problems were serious. Problems in testing the control students can be ascertained by comparing a site's experimental gains with the gains of control students across the whole experiment, not only at that site. When this is done, between a third and a half of the small number of cases where the experiment did appear to be unusually successful or unsuccessful disappear—leading to the suspicion that many apparent program successes were really failures in testing control students properly. This technique cannot be used to uncover problems in testing experimental students, because it becomes conceptually impossible to distinguish uniqueness in testing conditions from uniqueness in instructional program. But it is possible to compare test gains with gains on other tests given for purposes of computing company performance payments. Differences in types of tests used made these comparisons very unreliable, but, in any case, there was again a very loose correlation between gains.[9] The upshot is that because of these testing problems, the specific site results from the experiment must be treated with very great caution.

[9]See: Gramlich and Koshel, *Educational Performance Contracting,* chap. 4.

LESSONS FROM THE EXPERIENCE

Whatever the cause, the idea of incentive contracting in education suffered a very fast turnabout from the time in 1970 when it seemed to be sweeping the country. Only 1 of the 20 OEO sites signed a performance contract in the year following the experiment, and none have performance contracts now. The same has been true in the locally initiated projects analyzed by Rand, which now have been converted generally to cost-plus arrangements if the contractor is still there at all.[10] Even the Banneker School in Gary, site of the most publicized and extensive illustration of performance contracting, closed down its program in the fall of 1972, a year ahead of schedule, because of the same contractual and educational problems encountered in the OEO experience. The only persisting interest involves writing incentive contracts with teachers, which many school districts are still attempting.

There is no precise way to determine whether the demise of performance contracting is due to problems with the concept or to unwarranted negative publicity from the experiment. While for certain sites the experimental results are no doubt useless, in most sites the experiment did proceed at least fairly smoothly and should have provided at least some useful information. But it is difficult to know how much, how literally the results of the experiment should be interpreted, and, indeed, whether it is a good idea even to attempt to conduct experiments which are so publicized yet so difficult to organize and manage.

This pessimistic appraisal of the merits of experimentation emerges despite the fact that the performance contracting project was a relatively straightforward experiment. Unlike tests of specific instructional programs, the firms, and not OEO, were responsible for what actually went on in the classroom. Needless to say, this took a great load off the shoulders of OEO. But even then the experience demonstrated the incredibly complex range of details which must be attended to in a social experiment. There must be careful planning, careful preparation of firms, school districts, teachers, and testers, and large enough sample sizes so that if things become disrupted at certain sites, for certain students, on certain tests, there will be still other measures to analyze. The process is risky enough to make it advisable for the experimenter to *assume* that various things will not work out and to build certain fallback procedures right into the experiment.

[10]See: Polly Carpenter and George R. Hall, *The Evolution of Educational Performance Contracting in Five School Districts, 1971–72,* Santa Monica, Calif.: The Rand Corporation, 1972.

It should also be clear from this experience that experimenters should not proceed too quickly. There are powerful pressures to try to accelerate the process of gaining knowledge, to come up with information while the need for it is most urgent. While these pressures should not be resisted totally, it is important to recognize that attempting to do experiments too quickly may frustrate the whole enterprise. This mistake was made in two important ways in the performance contracting experiment: The experiment was launched too quickly, resulting in inadequate time to plan the enterprise, and it was limited to a 1-year period, making it impossible to test the long-run advantages of a performance incentive system. Although we have argued elsewhere that performance contracting would not have looked any more appealing even with more time for planning and running the experiment,[11] it is clear that the haste with which the experiment was launched and completed did not give the concept a very fair test. There is a large risk, in other words, that an inadequate experiment may be worse than no experiment at all if the trial is not long enough to give the policy under investigation a chance to work as it should.

Finally, one of the important lessons of the experience is that the experimental strategy is no panacea. The fact that it is so difficult to conduct experiments, even ones which seem straightforward, implies that social scientists should be very modest about their ability to do good experiments. The present state of the art of experimentation indicates that it simply may not be clear whether the results of the experiment—whether macro-negative or micro-positive—are valid or are merely a function of some unintended defects in the experiment. Until the state of the art improves, there is a very great risk that potentially promising programs will be rejected because of inadequacies in the experiment. Experimenters must keep this risk in mind and choose their ground very carefully.

[11]See: Gramlich and Koshel, *Educational Performance Contracting,* chaps. 5 and 6.

8

IMPLEMENTATION AS MUTUAL
ADAPTATION: CHANGE IN CLASSROOM
ORGANIZATION*

Milbrey McLaughlin

Most observers believe that the educational innovations undertaken as part of the curriculum reform movement of the 1950s and early 1960s, as well as the innovations that comprised the initiatives of the "Education Decade," generally have failed to meet their objectives. One explanation for these disappointments focuses on the *type* of innovations undertaken and points out that until recently few educators have elected to initiate innovations that require change in the traditional roles, behavior, and structures that exist within the school organization or the classroom. Instead, most innovative efforts have focused primarily on *technological*·

*Reprinted with permission from *Teachers College Record*, Vol. 77, No. 3, February 1976. This chapter is a revision of a paper presented at the March 1975 American Educational Research Association Meetings in Washington, D.C. It is based on the data collected for the Rand Corporation study of federal programs supporting educational change. However, the interpretation and speculations offered in this paper are my sole responsibility and do not necessarily represent the views of the Rand Corporation, or the study's sponsor, the United States Office of Education, or my colleague Paul Berman, who has been so helpful in formulating this paper.

change not *organizational* change. Many argue that without changes in the structure of the institutional setting, or the culture of the school, new practices are simply "more of the same" and are unlikely to lead to much significant change in what happens to students.

Since about 1970, however, a number of educators have begun to express interest in practices that redefine the assumptions about children and learning that underlie traditional methods—new classroom practices that attempt to change the ways that students, teachers, parents, and administrators relate to each other. Encouraged and stimulated by the work of such writers as Joseph Featherstone, Charles Silberman, and William Glasser, some local schoolmen have undertaken innovations in classroom organization such as open education, multiage grouping, integrated day, differentiating staffing, and team teaching. These practices are not based on a "model" of classroom organization change to be strictly followed, but on a common set of convictions about the nature of learning and the purpose of teaching. These philosophical similarities, which can be traced to the work of the Swiss psychologist Piaget, are based on a belief that humanistic, individualized, and childcentered education requires more than incremental or marginal change in classroom organization, educational technology, or teacher behavior.

Because classroom organization projects require teachers to work out their own styles and classroom techniques within a broad philosophical framework, innovations of this type cannot be fully specified or packaged in advance. Thus, the very nature of these projects requires that implementation be a *mutually adaptive process*. Specific project goals and methods must be made concrete by the users themselves as they acquire the skills appropriate to the innovation.

Classroom organization projects were among the local innovations examined as part of Rand's Change Agent Study.[1] Of the 293 projects surveyed, 85 could be classified as classroom organization projects; 5 of our 30 field sites were undertaking innovation of this nature. The findings of the Change Agent Study suggest that the experience of these projects should be examined in some detail. At the most general level, the change study concluded that implementation, rather than educational treatment, level of resources, or type of federal funding strategy, dominates the

---

[1]The conceptual model, methodology and results of the first year of the Rand Change Agent Study are reported in four volumes: Volume I, *A Model of Education Change* (R-1589/1-HEW); Volume II, *Factors Affecting Change Agent Projects* (R-1589/2-HEW); Volume III, *The Process of Change* (R-1589/3-HEW); Volume IV, *The Findings in Review* (R-1589/4-HEW). Four technical appendices to Volume III describe in detail the federal program management approach, state education agency participation, and case studies for each of the programs in the study.

innovative process and its outcomes. The study found that the mere adoption of a "better" practice did not lead automatically or invariably to "better" student outcomes. Initially similar technologies undergo unique alterations during the process of implementation, and thus their outcomes cannot be predicted on the basis of treatment alone. Further, the process of implementation that characterized successful classroom organization projects was found to describe effective implementation generally. Specifically, the Change Agent study concluded that *successful implementation is characterized by a process of mutual adaptation.*

Contrary to the assumptions underlying many change strategies and federal change policies, we found that implementation did not involve merely the direct and straightforward application of an educational technology or plan. Implementation was a dynamic organizational process that was shaped over time by interactions between project goals and methods and the institutional setting. As such, it was neither automatic nor certain. Three different interactions characterized this highly variable process.

One, *mutual adaptation,* described successfully implemented projects. It involved modification of both the project design and changes in the local institutional setting and personnel during the course of implementation. A second implementation process, *co-optation,* signified adaptation of the project design, but no change on the part of the local staff or the institutional setting. When implementation of this nature occurred, project strategies simply were modified to conform in a pro forma fashion to the traditional practices the innovation was expected to replace, either because of resistance to change or inadequate help to implementers. The third implementation process, *nonimplementation,* described the experience of projects that either broke down during the course of implementation or simply were ignored by project participants.

In short, where implementation was successful, and where significant change in participant attitudes, skills, and behavior occurred, implementation was characterized by a process of mutual adaptation in which project goals and methods were modified to suit the needs and interests of the local staff and in which that staff changed to meet the requirements of the project. This finding was true even for highly technological and initially well-specified projects; unless adaptations were made in the original plans or technologies, implementation tended to be superficial or symbolic, and significant change in participants did not occur.

Classroom organization projects provide particularly clear illustration of the conditions and strategies that support mutual adaptation and thus successful implementation. They are especially relevant to understanding the operational implications of this Change Agent study finding for policy and practice not only because mutual adaptation is intrinsic to change in classroom organization, but also because the question of institutional receptivity does not cloud the view of effective implementation strategies afforded by these projects.

The receptivity of the institutional setting to a proposed innovation varied greatly among the projects we examined—from active support, to indifference, to hostility. The amount of interest, commitment, and support evidenced by principal actors had a major influence on the prospects for successful project implementation. In particular, the attitudes and interest of central administrators in effect provide a signal to project participants as to how seriously they should take project goals and how hard they should work to achieve them. Unless project staff perceived that Change Agent projects represented a school and district educational priority, teachers were often unwilling to put in the extra time and emotional investment necessary for successful implementation. Similarly, the attitudes of teachers were critical. Unless teachers were motivated by professional concerns (as opposed to more tangible incentives such as extra pay or credit on the district salary scale, for example), they did not expend the extra time and energy requisite to the usually painful process of implementing an innovation.

Classroom organization projects were almost always characterized by high levels of commitment and support for their initiation, both at the district and at the building level. This is not surprising when we consider the risk and difficulty associated with these projects; it is unlikely that a district would elect to undertake a project of this nature unless they believed strongly in the educational approach and were committed to attempting the changes necessary to implement it.

In fact, classroom organization projects possess none of the features traditionally thought to encourage local decisionmakers to adopt a given innovation:

1. Ease of explanation and communication to others.
2. Possibility of a trial on a partial or limited basis.
3. Ease of use.
4. Congruence with existing values.
5. Obvious superiority over practices that existed previously.[2]

Innovations that focus on classroom organization are at odds with all five of these criteria. First, since there is no specific model to be followed, it is difficult to tell people how these approaches operate. Advocates can only

[2]M. Rogers and F. Shoemaker, *Communication of Innovation,* New York, The Free Press, 1962.

offer general advice and communicate the philosophy or attitudes that underlie innovation in classroom organization and activities.

Second, although open classroom or team teaching strategies can be implemented slowly, and can be installed in just one or two classrooms in a school, it is generally not possible to be "just a little bit" open or just a sometime part of a team teaching situation. The method is based on fundamental changes, which are hard to accomplish piecemeal.

Third, change in classroom organization is inherently very complex. Innovations of this nature require the learning of new attitudes, roles, and behavior on the part of teachers and administrators—changes far more difficult to bring about than the learning of a new skill or gaining familiarity with a new educational technology. Classroom organization changes also typically require new arrangements of classroom space, the provision of new instructional materials, and usually new school scheduling and reporting practices.

Fourth, strategies of open education or team teaching are a radical departure from the traditional or standard practices of a school, district, or teacher. Change in classroom organization means changing deeply held attitudes and customary behavior. These projects, by attempting to change organizational structure and goals, attempt to affect the fundamental nature of the organization and are therefore basically incongruent with existing values.

Fifth, although proponents argue that humanistic, child-centered education represents a big advance, the objective evidence is ambiguous. Most evaluations of informal classrooms conclude that participating children do better on affective measures, but there is little evidence of significant cognitive differences that confidently could be attributed to open classrooms themselves. Thus, an administrator contemplating a change in classroom organization is confronted with a complicated innovation that shows no clear advantage over existing practices—at least in the ways that often matter most to school boards, voters, and anxious parents.

Thus, given the complex, unspecified, and inherently difficult nature of these projects, they rarely were initiated without the active support and commitment of district officials and participants. Consequently, the insufficient institutional support that negatively influenced implementation in other projects and so made it difficult to obtain a clear picture of the strategic factors affecting project implementation (i.e., did disappointing implementation result from a lack of enthusiasm or from inadequate training?) generally was not a problem for classroom organization projects. Variance in implementation outcome of classroom organization projects, consequently, can be attributed in large measure to the project's particular implementation strategy.

For classroom organization projects, as for other change agent projects, *institutional receptivity was a necessary but not a sufficient condition for successful implementation*. Unless project implementation strategies were chosen that allowed institutional support to be engaged and mutual adaptation to occur, project implementation foundered. A project's particular implementation strategy is the result of many local choices about how best to implement project goals and methods. What seems to be the most effective thing to do? What is possible given project constraints? What process fits best with local needs and conditions? Decisions about the type and amount of training, the planning necessary, and project participants are examples of such choices. They effectively define how a proposed innovation is put into practice. Implementation strategies are distinguishable from project treatment. That is, the educational method chosen for a project (i.e., team teaching, diagnostic–prescriptive reading) is different from the strategies selected for implementing the method. No two reading projects, for example, employ quite the same process or strategy for achieving their almost identical goals.

Each project employs its own combination of strategies that effectively define its *implementation strategy*. Thus, in addition to identifying especially effective component strategies, it is meaningful to examine how and why the various individual strategies interact with each other to form a "successful" implementation strategy and to promote mutual adaptation. The experience of classroom organization projects suggests at least three specific strategies that are particularly critical and that work together to form an adaptive implementation strategy: local materials development; ongoing and concrete staff training; iterative, on-line planning combined with regular and frequent staff meetings.

Local Material Development

In almost all of the classroom organization projects, the staff spent a substantial amount of time developing materials to use in the project classrooms. These materials either were developed from scratch or put together from bits of commercially developed materials. Although these activities were sometimes undertaken because the staff felt they couldn't locate appropriate commercial materials, the real contribution lay not so much in better pedagogical products but in providing the staff with a sense of involvement and an opportunity to learn by doing. Working together to develop materials for the project gave the staff a sense of pride in its own accomplishments, a sense of "ownership" in the project. It also broke down the traditional isolation of the classroom teacher and provided a sense of professionalism and cooperation not usually available in the school setting. But even more important, development of materials provided an opportunity for users to think through the concepts which underlay the project in practical, operational terms—an opportunity to engage in experience-based learning. Although such "reinvention of the wheel" may not appear efficient in the short run, it appears to be a critical part of the individual learning and development necessary to significant change.

Staff Training

All the classroom organization projects we visited included both formal and informal, preservice and inservice staff training. For example, one project's formal training took place in a 2-week summer session before the project began; its informal development activities have been extensive, providing for almost constant interaction between project staff. Most all of these projects provided preservice training that included observations in operating classrooms. One open classroom project staff even participated in a trip to observe British infant schools. All projects also have conducted regular workshops throughout the first 3 years of project implementation.

Training heavily concentrated only at the beginning of the project was not effective. Although such training designs have the virtues of efficiency and lower cost, they ignore the critical fact that project implementors cannot know what it is they need to know until project operations are well underway. This is generally true for all innovative efforts, but particularly salient in the case of amorphous classroom organization projects. There is just so much that a would-be implementor can be taught or can understand until problems have arisen in the course of project implementation and solutions must be devised. Similarly, it is difficult to anticipate in advance exactly what implementor needs might be at different points in project implementation. Training programs that attempt to be comprehensive and cover all contingencies at the outset are bound to miss their mark and also to be less than meaningful to project participants.

Project staffs agree that staff development and training activities were a critical part of successful implementation. They also agree that some kinds of training activities are more useful than others. With few exceptions, visits by outside consultants and other outside "experts" were not considered particularly helpful. Teachers in all the change agent projects we examined complain that most visiting consultants could not relate to the particular problems teachers were experiencing in their classrooms, or that consultant advice was too abstract to be helpful. Where outside experts were considered useful, their participation was concrete and involved working closely with project teachers in their classrooms or in workshops. However, it was unusual for consultants to have either the time or the inclination to provide assistance outside the lecture format. Such expert delivery of "truth and knowledge," however, was seldom meaningful to participants, and foreclosed important learning opportunities.

The sessions participants thought were most useful were regular meetings of the project staff with local resource personnel in which ideas were shared, problems discussed, and support given. Materials development often provided the focus for these concrete, how-to-do-it training sessions. Visits to other schools implementing similar projects were also considered helpful; the teachers felt that seeing a similar program in operation for just a few hours was worth much more than several days of consultant talks on philosophy.

Some commentators on the outcomes of planned change contend that where innovations fail, particularly innovations in classroom organization, they fail because their planners overlooked the "resocialization" of teachers. Even willing teachers have to go through such a *learning (and unlearning) process* in order to develop new attitudes, behavior, and skills for a radically new role. Concrete, inquiry-based training activities scheduled regularly over the course of project implementation provide a means for this developmental process to occur.

Adaptive Planning and Staff Meetings

Because of their lack of prior specification, almost all classroom organization projects engaged in adaptive or on-line planning. Planning of this nature is a continuous process that establishes channels of communication and solicits input from a representative group of project participants. It provides a forum for reassessing project goals and activities, monitoring project activities, and modifying practices in light of institutional and project demands. Planning of this nature has a firm base in project and institutional reality; thus issues can be identified and solutions determined before problems become crises. Just as intensive, "one-shot" training activities can neither anticipate the information needs of implementors over time nor be comprehensible to trainees in the absence of direct experience with particular problems, neither can highly structured planning activities that attempt extensive prior specification of operational procedures and objectives effectively address all contingencies in advance or foresee intervening local conditions. Often problems arise and events occur during the course of implementation that are unexpected and unpredictable. As a result, project plans drawn up at one time may or may not be relevant to project operations at a later date. Planning activities that are ongoing, adaptive, and congruent with the nature of the project and the changing institutional setting are able to respond to these factors better.

Frequent and regular staff meetings were often used as a way to carry out project planning on a continuous basis. Projects that made a point of scheduling staff meetings on a frequent and regular basis had fewer serious implementation problems and greater staff cohesiveness. Staff meetings not only provided a vehicle for articulating and working out problems, but they also gave staff a chance to communicate project information, share ideas, and provide each other with encouragement and support.

Finding time for these meetings or planning activities was a problem that some districts were able to solve and others were not. One classroom organization project, for example, arranged time off one afternoon a week for meetings. Project participants almost universally singled out these meetings as one of the most important factors contributing to project success. Such time to share ideas and problems was, in the view of all classroom organization respondents, especially important in the rough and exhausting first year of the project. Where meetings were infrequent or irregular, morale was noticeably lower and reports of friction within the project were higher.

Past research on implementation is almost unanimous in citing "unanticipated events" and "lack of feedback networks" as serious problems during project implementation.[3] Routinized and frequent staff meetings combined with ongoing, iterative planning can serve to institutionalize an effective project feedback structure, as well as to provide mechanisms that can deal with the unanticipated events that are certain to occur.

CASE ILLUSTRATIONS

The critical role that such elements of an adaptive implementation strategy play in project implementation and outcomes is best illustrated by describing the experiences of two open classroom projects that were similar in almost every respect—resources, support and interest, target group background characteristics—but differed significantly in implementation strategy and in implementation outcome. The Eastown (project and site names are fictitious) open education project had extensive and ongoing

[3]See, for example, W. W. Charters et al., *Contrasts in the Process of Planning Change of the School's Instructional Organization, Program 20*, Eugene, Ore., Center for the Advanced Study of Educational Administration, 1973; O. Carlson et al., *Change Processes in the Public Schools*, Eugene, Ore., Center for the Advanced Study of Educational Administration, 1971; M. Fullan and A. Pomfret, Review of Research on Curriculum Implementation, Toronto, The Ontario Institute for Studies in Education, April 1975; M. Shipman, *Inside a Curriculum Project*, London, Methuen & Co., 1974; N. C. Gross et al., *Implementing Organizational Innovations*, New York, Basic Books, Inc., 1971; L. M. Smith and P. M. Keith, *Anatomy of Educational Innovations: An Organizational Analysis of an Elementary School*, New York, John Wiley & Sons, Inc., 1971.

staff training, spent a lot of staff time and energy on materials development, arranged for staff to meet regularly, and engaged in regular formative evaluation. This project was also well implemented, running smoothly, and meeting its objectives. In fact, this project received validation as a national exemplary project in its second year—a year before it theoretically was eligible.

The very similar Seaside project, in contrast, did not employ such an implementation strategy. Because of late funding notification, there was little time for advance planning or preservice training; project teachers were asked to implement a concept that they supported, but that few actually had seen in operation. The planning that was done subsequently was mainly administrative in nature. The in-service training was spotty and was offered almost totally by "outside experts." The Seaside project did no development of materials but instead tried to convert traditional materials to the goals of open education. This project has not only been less successful than hoped, but, in our judgment, its central percepts and objectives yet to be fully implemented. Teacher classroom behavior exhibits only a very superficial understanding of the rhetoric of open education; our observations led to the conclusion that teachers had yet to understand the practical implications of the tenets of open education and have made only symbolic use of the more standard methods. For example, in many of the classrooms we visited, although the teacher had set up interest centers, these centers had not been changed in 6 or 7 months. Thus they failed to serve their purpose of providing a continually changing menu of material for students. Teachers in the Seaside project had dutifully rearranged their classroom furniture and acquired rugs—as befits the open classroom—but even in this changed physical space, they continued to conduct their class in traditional manner. A student teacher commented that many of the teachers in this school conducted their class in the small groups or individualized manner appropriate to this educational philosophy only on visitors' day. In our judgment, many of the teachers in the school honestly wanted to implement open education, and many sincerely believed that they had accomplished that goal. But, in our view, implementation in this project was only pro forma, largely because of the absence of implementation strategies that would allow learning, growth and development, or mutual adaptation to take place.

SUMMARY AND GENERAL IMPLICATIONS

In summary, overcoming the challenges and problems inherent to innovations in classroom organization contributes positively and significantly to their effective implementation. The amorphous yet highly complex nature of classroom organization projects tends to *require* or *dictate* an adaptive implementation strategy that permits goals and methods to be reassessed, refined, and made explicit during the course of implementation, and that fosters "learning-by-doing."

The adaptive implementation strategies defined by effectively implemented local projects were comprised of three common and critical components—local materials development; concrete, ongoing training; on-line or adaptive planning and regular, frequent staff meetings. These elements worked together in concert to promote effective implementation. Where any one component was missing or weak, other elements of the overall implementation strategy were less effective than they might be. A most important characteristic these component strategies hold in common is their support of individual learning and development—development most appropriate to the user and to the institutional setting. The experience of classroom organization projects underlines the fact that the process of mutual adaptation is fundamentally a learning process.

It is useful to consider the implications of the classroom organization projects and the general Change Agent study findings in the context of the ongoing debate about the "implementation problem."

The Change Agent study is not the first research to point to the primary importance of implementation in determining special project outcomes.[4] A number of researchers and theoreticians have come to recognize what many practitioners have been saying all along: Educational technology is not "self-winding." Adoption of a promising educational technology is only the beginning of a variable, uncertain, and inherently local process. It is the unpredictability and inconsistency of this process that have generated what has come to be called the "implementation problem."

There is general agreement that a major component of the "implementation problem" has to do with inadequate operational specificity.[5] There is debate concerning *who* should make project operations more specific, *how* it can be done, and *when* specificity should be introduced.

One approach prescribes more specificity prior to local initiation. Adherents of this solution ask that project planners and developers spell out concrete and detailed steps or procedures that they believe will lead to successful project implementation. It is hoped that increased prior operational specificity will minimize the necessity for individual users to make

[4]See especially the analysis of this debate in Fullan and Pomfret, op. cit.; see also E. C. Hargrove, *The Missing Link: The Study of the Implementation of Social Policy*, Washington, The Urban Institute, 1975, Paper 797–1; W. Williams, "Implementation Analysis and Assessment," this volume.

[5]See Fullan and Pomfret, op. cit.

decisions or choices about appropriate project strategies or resources as the project is implemented. This essentially technological approach to the "implementation problem"—exemplified at the extreme by "teacher-proof" packages—aims at standardizing project implementation across project sites. It is expected that user adherence to such standardized and well-specified implementation procedures will reduce local variability as project plans are translated into practice and so lead to predictable and consistent project outcomes, regardless of the institutional setting in which the project is implemented.

A second approach takes an organizational rather than a technological perspective and focuses primarily on the development of the user, rather than on the prior development of the educational treatment or product. This approach assumes that local variability is not only inevitable, but a good thing, if a proposed innovation is to result in significant and sustained change in the local setting. This approach also assumes that the individual learning requisite to successful implementation can only occur through user involvement and direct experience in working through project percepts. Instead of providing packages which foreclose the necessity for individuals to make decisions and choices during the course of project implementation, proponents of this perspective maintain that implementation strategies should be devised that give users the skills, information, and learning opportunities necessary to make these choices effectively. This approach assumes that specificity of project methods and goals should evolve over time in response to local conditions and individual needs. This second solution to the "implementation problem," in short, assumes that mutual adaptation is the key to effective implementation.

The findings of the Change Agent study strongly support this second perspective and its general approach to the "implementation problem." We found that *all* successfully implemented projects in our study went through a process of mutual adaptation to some extent. Even fairly straightforward, essentially technological projects were either adapted in some way to the institutional setting or they were only superficially implemented and were not expected to remain in place after the withdrawal of federal funds. Where attempts were made to take shortcuts in this process—out of concern for efficiency, for example—such efforts to speed up project implementation usually led to project breakdown or to only pro forma installation of project methods.

Viewed in the context of the debate over the "implementation problem," these findings have a number of implications for change agent policies and practice. At the most general level, they suggest that adaptation, rather than standardization, is a more realistic and fruitful objective for policymakers and practitioners hoping to bring about significant change in local educational practice. Such an objective would imply change agent policies that focused on implementation not simply on adoption—policies that were concerned primarily with the development of users and support of adaptive implementation strategies. Specifically, the classroom organization projects suggest answers to the strategic issues of who, how, and when innovative efforts should be made operationally explicit, and of how user development can be promoted.

Furthermore, the classroom organization projects, as well as other innovative efforts examined as part of the Change Agent study, imply that the would-be innovator also must be willing to learn and be motivated by professional concerns and interests if development is to take place. Thus, change agent policies would be well advised not only to address the user needs that are part of the implementation process per se, but also to consider the developmental needs of local educational personnel that are a prerequisite for the initial interest and support necessary in change agent efforts. It is not surprising that teachers or administrators who have not been outside their district for a number of years are less eager to change, and less confident in their abilities to do so, than planners would hope. Internships and training grants for administrators, or travel money and release time for teachers to participate in innovative practices in other districts are examples of strategies that may enable educational personnel to expand their horizons and may generate enthusiasm for change.

The findings of the Change Agent study and the experience of the classroom organization projects also have implications for the dissemination and expansion of "successful" change agent projects. They suggest, for example, that an effective dissemination strategy should have more to do with people who could provide concrete, "hands-on" assistance than with the transcription and transferal of specific successful project operations. It is ironic that staff of the federal exemplary projects who last year pointed to the central importance of local materials development are this year packaging and disseminating their project strategies and materials without a backward glance. Indeed, the Change Agent findings concerning the importance of mutual adaptation and "learning by doing" raise a number of critical questions for educational planners and disseminators. For example, to what extent can this developmental process be telescoped as project methods are attempted in a new setting? What kinds of learning or advice can be transferred? If adaptation is characteristic of effective implementation and significant change, what constitutes the "core" or essential ingredients of a successful project?

District administrators hoping to expand successful project operations face similar issues. Our findings suggest that, even within the same district, expansion of "successful" programs will require that new adopters repeat in large measure the developmental process of the original site. While there are, of course, general lessons that original participants can transfer to would-be innovators, there is much that the new user will have to learn for himself.

In summary, the experience of classroom organization projects together with the general Change Agent study findings suggest that adaptation should be seen as an appropriate goal for practice and policy—not an undesirable aberration. These findings suggest a shift in change agent policies from a primary focus on the *delivery system* to an emphasis on the *deliverer*. An important lesson that can be derived from the change agent study is that unless the developmental needs of the users are addressed, and unless project methods are modified to suit the needs of the user and the institutional setting, the promise of new technologies is likely to be unfulfilled. Although the implementation strategies that classroom organization projects suggest will be effective represent "reinvention of the wheel" to a great extent—an unpalatable prospect for program developers, fiscal planners, and impatient educational policymakers—the experience of these projects counsels us that a most important aspect of significant change is not so much the "wheel" or the educational technology but the process of "reinvention" or individual development. This is not to argue that new educational technologies are not important to improved practice. Rather, it is to indicate that they can be neither effective nor sustained unless they are thoroughly understood and integrated by the user. The evidence we have seen strongly suggests that the developmental process of mutual adaptation is the best way to ensure that change efforts are not superficial, trivial, or transitory.

III

COMMUNITY-ORIENTED PROGRAMS

9

MAKING A NEW FEDERAL PROGRAM: MODEL CITIES, 1964–68*

Edward C. Banfield

During the evening of the first full day of Lyndon B. Johnson's presidency—at 7:40 P.M. on November 23, 1963, to be precise—Walter Heller, chairman of the Council of Economic Advisers, came to tell him that three days before his assassination President Kennedy had approved a suggestion that the Council and the Bureau of the Budget develop a program to alleviate poverty. They were thinking, Heller said, in terms of pilot projects to be tried in a few cities. The president was enthusiastic, but he wanted something "big and bold." A program for just a few cities could never be propelled through Congress and, in any case, it would be regarded as another example of "tokenism" by black leaders whose growing anger was a matter of concern to him. A few weeks later, in his first State of the Union Address, he declared "unconditional war on poverty in America." The Office of Economic Opportunity (OEO) was created almost at once.

This initial attack was to be followed by offensives along a broad front. The Vietnam war was expected to fizzle out shortly and the federal treasury to overflow with a "peace dividend" as the economy expanded.

*Edward C. Banfield, "Making a New Federal Program: Model Cities, 1964–68," in Allan P. Sindler (ed.), *Policy and Politics in America: Six Case Studies,* pp. 125–158. Copyright © 1973 by Little, Brown and Company (Inc.). Reprinted by permission.

No doubt, too, the president was confident that after the November election he would have comfortable majorities in both houses of Congress (as it turned out, he had the largest ones since 1937). Under these circumstances, he needed big ideas to put before the new Congress—a legislative program that would be distinctively his.

The following pages tell about one of the biggest and boldest of the programs that resulted—how the Model Cities effort was planned; how, through the intervention of the president himself it was pushed through a reluctant Congress; how its administrators grappled with dilemmas and constraints that were partly inherent in the conception of the program and partly in the harsh realities of the governmental system; and how, by the time the Johnson administration left office, the program had become very different from what its originators had intended it to be.

THE PROGRAM'S ORIGINS

Needed: The Best Thought

In May 1964, the president told a University of Michigan audience that it was in the cities, the countryside, and the classrooms that the Great Society was to be built. While the government had many programs directed at these "central issues," he did not pretend to have the "full answers." To get them he would establish "working groups" to make studies and hold White House conferences. "We are going," he said, "to assemble the best thought and the broadest knowledge from all over the world to find those answers for America." That there *were* "answers" to large social problems and that thought and knowledge could "find" them he seemed to take for granted.

The president knew that John F. Kennedy had used task forces in his 1960 campaign. Because these groups had been too heavily weighted with scholars, the president thought, "very few suggestions emerged that were practical enough to exploit." He intended his to have a broad balance of "thinkers" and "doers." The presidential assistant who played the leading part in making up the Metropolitan and Urban Affairs Task Force was Richard N. Goodwin, a young lawyer who had been in the Kennedy entourage and was now a Johnson speechwriter. Although there were "doers" in the group that he assembled, its most active members turned out to be mostly "thinkers."

One of these was the chairman, Robert C. Wood, an amiable man just entering middle age who was a professor of political science at M.I.T. Before beginning his scholarly career he had served for three years in the

Bureau of the Budget. His later work dealt largely with practical matters (his most recent book—*1400 Governments*—was an account of the intricacies of governmental organization in the New York region), and he had been active in the Kennedy advisory group during the 1960 election campaign. He could, therefore, be considered both a "thinker" and a "doer." The other members of the task force were Paul Ylvisaker, director of the public affairs program of the Ford Foundation; Raymond Vernon, a Harvard economist who had directed the study of the New York metropolitan region; Jerome Cavanagh, mayor of Detroit; Saul B. Klaman, director of research for the National Association of Mutual Savings Banks; Ralph McGill, editor of the *Atlanta Constitution*; Dr. Karl A. Menninger, chief of staff of the Menninger Clinic; and four members of the faculty of the University of California at Berkeley: Nathan Glazer, a sociologist; Norman Kennedy, associate director of the Institute of Traffic and Transportation Engineering; Martin Meyerson, dean of the School of Environmental Design, and Catherine Bauer Wurster, professor of city planning. William B. Ross, a career civil servant from the Bureau of the Budget, was executive secretary. Goodwin was White House liaison.

The task force had less than 3 months in which to work. By the middle of November 1964, Goodwin, along with the assistants assigned to the other task forces, would have to begin "feeding" the president paragraphs for use in the various messages he would send to Congress in January 1965. Despite the lack of time, the group produced a report running to seventy double-spaced pages with an additional 10 pages summarizing its recommendations. Often such reports consist largely of hot air; this one did not.

The report was politely but severely critical of the existing government programs for the cities. "Too frequently they operated within narrowly defined agency boundaries that fragment logically related services." This was true even of the newly created OEO ("admirable" but "designed to help primarily the temporarily disadvantaged"); the task of this and the juvenile delinquency programs "must be broadened to include health, education, recreation—the entire gamut of social development."

It went on to make many far-reaching proposals for change: The federal government should give block grants[1] to enable the cities to provide a wide range of services to all of their citizens as well as to care effectively for the poor; it should also make special grants for the support of community facilities (health stations, small parks, and so on); both the block and special grants should be contingent upon a *local* (this word was underlined) Social Renewal Plan (these words were capitalized); the government

---

[1]A "block" grant is one that may be used for any purpose by the recipient or, at least, for a very wide range of purposes. By contrast, a "categorical" grant may be used only for a specified—often very narrowly specified—purpose.

should also expand its technical assistance in many fields of public administration; and it should support planning by the cities, and endeavor in other
ways as well to strengthen the office of mayor (or manager).

In polite—and therefore not very vigorous or vivid—language, the
report said that most urban renewal projects had served the interests of
downtown department stores and real estate operators and that public
housing projects had not made a dent in the slums. If middle-income people
were to be lured back into the deteriorating areas of the larger, older cities,
a new strategy would have to be used. Timid efforts would be worse than
none. "What is needed is an intervention so large and so profound as to
alter the image of a neighborhood."

There were many other recommendations, including building large
new cities from the ground up, reorganization of housing finance, aid to rail
rapid transit, and creation of an Urban Affairs Council headed by the vice
president. The emphasis, however, was on making federal efforts more
comprehensive, improving their coordination, and giving local governments and the citizens most directly affected a greater share of control over
the federal government's undertakings. The task force expected, it said
(and these words were underlined),

> that the block service grants, the special local facility grants, the social renewal plan and
> the revised urban renewal plan would enable the mayor or other public bodies where
> appropriate, especially in larger cities, to bring together heretofore separate activities
> into a comprehensive strategy for local action.

Another report, this one prepared in the Bureau of the Budget and
taking the form of a 100-page book, went to the president in May 1965. It
reviewed various efforts to coordinate the many categorical programs
through the voluntary efforts of the agencies themselves. (These included
the Neighborhood Development Programs and One-Stop Welfare Centers.) These efforts had been almost fruitless and extremely time consum-
ing. The president, the Bureau of the Budget suggested, might deal with the
coordination problem in one or the other of two ways: either by giving the
cities block grants or by instituting a program under which they would be
helped to make comprehensive plans that, when approved by the White
House, would be implemented with federal funds.

The Two-Page Appendix

Whether because the president thought that they smacked more of
"thinkers" than of "doers" or for other reasons, neither the task force nor
the Bureau of the Budget report seems to have influenced his 1965 legislative program. Ironically, a proposal that was *not* among the task force's

many recommendations turned out to have great importance. In the course of its discussions, at least three members of the task force (Wurster, Meyerson, and McGill) had more or less independently suggested that the federal government "adopt" two or three large cities and in addition build a brand-new one in order to show what could be accomplished by well-conceived, large-scale, concerted effort.

A concrete proposal along these lines had come to the task force in the form of a two-page memorandum titled "Demonstration Cities" written by Antonia Chayes, a former student of Wood's, in collaboration with her boss, Leonard Duhl, a psychiatrist who was head of the Office of Planning of the National Institute of Mental Health. Mrs. Chayes and Dr. Duhl proposed that all relevant federal agencies join in sending a team of experts to three large cities to make comprehensive plans for dealing with their particular problems in a fundamental way. When the plans had been made, agencies would concentrate their resources in a coordinated effort to carry them into effect. This might involve a good deal of slum clearance and rebuilding as well as the repair of much dilapidated and blighted housing. The emphasis, however, would be shifted from the "bricks and mortar" approach of the urban renewal program to a "social and psychological" one involving the improvement of school and health facilities, provision of neighborhood recreation centers, better police–community relations, participation by neighborhood residents in decisions affecting them, and whatever else offered some hope of raising morale and creating self-confidence among those who lived in the poorest districts.

This proposal may have been influenced by what was then happening in New Haven. Beginning in 1959, that city had sharply redirected its efforts from slum clearance to a wide range of efforts to improve the opportunities of the chronically poor, especially the young among them. What was happening in New Haven probably influenced the conception of "youth development projects" that were begun in New York City in 1961 with the encouragement and support of Robert Kennedy, then the attorney general. The central ideas behind these developments—the prevention (as opposed to the "cure") of poverty, especially among the young, through concentration of efforts by a wide range of public and private agencies in order to change the character of an entire district in accordance with a carefully made plan—were also the basic principles of the proposal that Heller carried to President Kennedy and then, a few days later, to President Johnson. (A Bureau of the Budget memorandum of November 21, 1963, had recommended "human investment expenditures through education, training, and health" directed at "particular problem groups" or "where the yield will be high," with a focus on "human development" rather than physical facilities.)

The task force did not recommend the "adoption" of any cities; it attached the Chayes-Duhl memorandum to its report as an appendix, however. When Mayor Cavanagh showed the report to fellow Detroiter Walter Reuther, the president of the United Automobile Workers, it was the appendix that caught Reuther's eye. He and the mayor arranged to have a brochure prepared—"Detroit, A Demonstration City"—which they put before Robert C. Weaver, the head of the Federal Housing and Home Finance Agency, and later before the president. Presumably this is what Mr. Johnson refers to in his memoirs, *The Vantage Point,* where he says that in May 1965, Reuther gave him a memorandum warning of the "erosion of life in urban centers."

Another Task Force

When Reuther's memorandum reached him, the president was beginning to think about his legislative program for 1966. He had directed his special assistant, Joseph A. Califano, a 33-year-old lawyer who had recently moved to the White House from the office of the Secretary of Defense, to "perform the spadework on a full-scale domestic program." "Rebuilding the slums," the president thought, represented "the first challenge." To help meet it, a new task force was created late in the summer. It was to work closely with Califano, and have its recommendations ready by the end of November 1965.

Wood was to be chairman of the new task force, but "doers" were to dominate it. As the president wrote in his memoirs, "Business, labor, the construction industry, and the Congress were represented on that committee. The academic world was also represented. . . ." Reuther was the labor representative. Other members were Whitney Young, executive director of the National Urban League and a national Negro leader, Ben W. Heineman, president of the Chicago and Northwestern Railroad, Edgar Kaiser, president of Kaiser Industries, Senator Abraham Ribicoff (D., Conn.), Kermit Gordon, president of the Brookings Institution, William L. Rafsky, an economist who had served as program coordinator of the Philadelphia city government, and Charles M. Haar, a Harvard Law School professor who had written on city planning. Apart from the last three and Wood himself, none had any special knowledge of urban affairs.

This time there was to be no liaison with the Bureau of the Budget. The task force would get technical advice from its own professional staff, drawn from persons outside the government. Perhaps the differences between this task force and its predecessor reflected the president's belief that "big" and "fresh" ideas practical enough to be "exploited" would not come from scholars or career civil servants. As he explained later in *The*

Vantage Point, he considered task forces better than the standard method of generating legislative proposals, which consisted of taking them from the departments and agencies and filtering them through the Bureau of the Budget and the White House staffs. He believed the bureaucracy was preoccupied with day-to-day operations, dedicated to the status quo, and not equipped to solve complex problems that cut across departmental jurisdictions. Scholars, in his view, had a different but equally serious limitation—that of impracticality.

In seeking to avoid these disadvantages, the president ran the risk of incurring others. For example, leaving agency interests out of account in the design of a new program might mean that the program would be sabotaged by them later on. Apparently he was prepared to take such risks. From his standpoint, the crucial thing seems to have been to present Congress and the electorate with a program that they would regard as a bold and promising response to "the urban crisis." If this was the president's intention, it must have been enormously strengthened in August 1965, when—after the decision to set up another task force had been made—the black enclave of Watts in Los Angeles erupted in a long and destructive riot.

The terms of reference that the president gave the task force were very general. They did, however, include one particular: "Pick up on the demonstration idea."

Picking Up on the Idea

The task force was not fully constituted until early October 1965. Like its predecessor, it would have to do the best it could in weekend meetings over a period of about 2 months. Its proceedings (again like those of its predecessor) would have to be carefully hidden from the press. (The president's insistence that his advisers work without publicity resulted, his critics said, from his desire to monopolize the limelight. His own,explanation, given later in his book, was at least as plausible: Advisers tend to be more candid and critical as well as less cautious when they work on a confidential basis; moreover, when plans leak, opposition is given time to form.)

To preserve confidentiality and to avoid the bureaucratic interests which the president so much distrusted, the task force avoided contact with the agencies concerned. Even Robert D. Weaver, who seemed likely to head the soon-to-be-created Department of Housing and Urban Development (HUD), was not officially informed of what was going on. (As will appear, he managed nevertheless to find out.)

The professional staff of the task force wrote some two dozen background papers, all of high quality (they cost somewhat more than $70,000), but little or no use was made of them. The policy alternatives discussed in the papers were not considered sufficiently practical. It was all very well to document the need for metropolitan area governments, for example, but creating such governments was beyond the power of Congress and the president. Consolidating the 200 or more categorical grant-in-aid programs into a relatively few would doubtless (as the previous task force had stressed) improve coordination, but there was no point in studying this either, for Congress could not be persuaded to allow consolidations and, anyway, the press and public would not be much impressed by that sort of achievement. Califano stressed that the president wanted ideas that would yield spectacular results and yield them *while he was still in office.*

The members of the task force soon found out that they differed on important matters. Reuther wanted to bulldoze slum districts out of existence and replace them with "model communities." Young was opposed to this. Slum clearance, he pointed out, generally turned out to be Negro clearance; he favored tearing down or rebuilding housing where absolutely necessary, but he insisted that the emphasis go on measures like improvement of schools, provision of health services, job training, and protection of civil rights. Kaiser shared Young's preference for the "social and psychological" rather than the "bricks and mortar" approach.

Wood thought of the new program as having the purpose (among others) of coordinating existing programs; he saw it as a way of exerting leverage on the federal agencies that administered the categorical grants as well as on state and local agencies. In this way vastly more resources would be brought to bear on the causes of urban poverty and distress. (This, it will be recalled, had been the main thrust of the previous year's report.) Gordon, who recently had been director of the Bureau of the Budget and who had served with Wood on the other task force, was also much concerned with achieving coordination.

The differences were mostly of emphasis (no one envisioned a program *solely* to clear slums or *solely* to improve coordination), but they were important because they entailed further differences. For example, the "social and psychological" approach implied giving the residents of slum and blighted neighborhoods a large measure of control over programs, for only in this way, it was supposed, could the morale and self-confidence of the poor be improved. "Coordination," however, implied putting control firmly into the hands of elected officials. Wood was as irked as anyone by the arrogance urban renewal officials had often shown in their dealings with local people, and he had no doubt that residents of affected neighborhoods should be consulted. But to give them *control*—that was out of the question.

The task force received a memorandum from the director of the Bureau of the Budget, Charles L. Schultze, which impressed it deeply. (As one of the president's staff, he was not subject to the ban against consultation with operating agencies.) He suggested that there might be a threshold below which public investment in poverty areas yielded little or no return. He had a hunch, he said, that by spending at a "saturation" level the net return might be increased by several orders of magnitude. But since this was only a hunch he favored trying "saturation" in no more than five or ten cities while making careful studies of the results. What he had in mind was an experiment, he told an interviewer later, not a national program, still less a national crusade.

Schultze's "hunch" was one that a first-rate economist might be expected to have. It is worth noting, however, that in 1963, as assistant director of the Bureau of the Budget, he had welcomed essentially the same ideas when he presided over the group which worked up the proposal for demonstration programs in several cities that Heller carried to President Johnson. He himself had then suggested appointing a "federal czar" in each area to open doors to Washington decision makers and to "knock heads together when necessary to get cooperation" from local agencies. This idea also impressed the task force favorably.

The task force considered briefly giving one city "the complete treatment," but then decided not to, partly from fear that the administration would be charged with "tokenism" and partly because it would be impossible to choose between Detroit, Cavanagh's and Reuther's city, and Chicago, the city of the even more powerful Mayor Daley. Perhaps five cities should be chosen, someone said. Senator Ribicoff answered that five would not be nearly enough. Members of Congress would not vote large sums for a program which they knew in advance would not benefit their constituents. It was therefore a political necessity that enough cities be chosen to assure majorities in both Houses.

The task force began its report with a ringing declaration: 1966 could be the year of the urban turnabout in American history. For this to occur a dramatic new approach embodying three principles was required: *concentration* of available and special resources in sufficient magnitude to demonstrate swiftly what qualified urban communities could do and could become, *coordination* of all available talent and aid in a way impossible where assistance was provided across the board and men and money had to be spread thin, and *mobilization* of local leadership and initiative to assure that the key decisions were made by the citizens living in the cities affected. These principles were to be applied through a national program of city building in which specially qualified communities executed plans of such size and scale as to transform existing urban complexes into new cities, by tying together physical and human resource programs, by developing and testing methods and programs, and by bringing to bear all the techniques of which technology was capable.

The task force proposed that all cities be invited to propose action programs designed to have a major impact on the living conditions of their citizens. After the most promising of these proposals were identified by a special presidential commission, the qualified communities were to prepare more detailed proposals. Each was to establish an appropriate administrative mechanism, not necessarily a formal unit of government, to assemble leadership and resources both public and private. A federal coordinator, the task force said, should be assigned to each city to bring all relevant federal aids together. Once selected as qualified, a city would receive two types of federal assistance: (1) the complete array of existing grants to the maximum extent authorized by law and on a priority basis, and (2) supplemental grants (at a ratio of 80% federal, 20% local) to make up any difference between what was available under existing programs and what the demonstration would cost.

The report recommended that there be 66 demonstration cities: 6 of over 500,000 population, 10 of between 250,000 and 500,000, and 50 of fewer than 250,000. In the largest cities the typical program should build or rebuild about 24,000 units of housing, in the medium-sized ones about 7500, and in the smaller ones about 3000. In all cases the objective should be to eliminate blight completely in the designated area and to replace it with attractive, economical shelter in a neighborhood with amenities essential to a full life.

If there was anything new in these proposals it was the supplemental grants. Wood referred to these as "bait" and "glue" because they would attract federal grants to the cities and also bind them together in workable programs. (These images, incidentally, had been used in 1963 by the Bureau of the Budget officials who worked up the proposal that, much altered, became OEO.) In private, out of earshot of department and agency heads, the supplementals were also spoken of as "clubs," and this indeed was the principal function they were intended to serve and what made this proposal different from earlier ones. A demonstration city, knowing that it would get from HUD any funds that might be lacking to carry out its approved plan, would be in a position to bargain with the other federal agencies and to compel them to accept coordination on the basis of its locally made, HUD-approved plan on pain of being left out altogether from the biggest and most glamorous undertakings. Thus city governments, in partnership with HUD, would bring about the coordination that had so far proved unachievable. The result of all this, Wood hoped, would be to "suck the system together."

Hurry to the Hopper

The task force's proposals did not get the close scrutiny from affected agencies, the Bureau of the Budget, and the White House staff that is usually given to policy proposals before they are publicly endorsed by the president. LBJ met with the task force once to say that they had his wholehearted backing, but it was well understood that he did not want to be bothered with specifics. That was the job of Califano mainly, and he, of course, had countless other matters to attend to. Without much deliberation, then, the president committed himself in the State of the Union Address (January 26, 1966) to "a program to rebuild completely, on a scale never before attempted, entire central and slum areas of several of our cities. . . ." The next day he swore in Weaver and Wood as secretary and undersecretary of HUD, and a few days later he sent to Congress a special 4000-word message on city development which began with words strikingly like those of the task force report: "Nineteen-sixty-six can be the year of rebirth for American cities." He went on to promise "an effort larger in scope, more comprehensive, and more concentrated than any before." The following day, the Cities Demonstration bill was introduced in both the House and the Senate.[2]

The bill followed the task force report very closely. It declared improving the quality of urban life to be the nation's most critical domestic problem; its purposes were to enable cities "both large and small" to plan and carry out programs to rebuild or revitalize large slum and blighted areas and to improve public services in those areas, to assist cities' demonstration agencies to develop and carry out programs of sufficient magnitude "in both physical and social dimensions," "to remove or arrest blight and decay in entire sections or neighborhoods," substantially to increase the supply of low and moderate cost housing, "make marked progress" in "reducing educational disadvantages, disease and enforced idleness," and "make a substantial impact on the sound development of the entire city."

Demonstration programs were to be "locally prepared" and approved by the local governing body and by any local agencies whose cooperation was necessary to their success; they were to provide for "widespread citizen participation," "counteract the segregation of housing by race or income," and meet "such additional requirements as the Secretary may establish."

[2]A second bill, implementing other recommendations of the task force, was introduced at the same time; it provided "incentives for planned metropolitan development." Eventually the two bills were combined, becoming different titles of an omnibus bill. For present purposes this development, as well as the substance of the metropolitan planning measure, can be ignored.

The secretary was authorized to make grants covering 90% of the cost of planning demonstration programs and 80% of that of administering them and, when a city's program was approved, to make grants ("supplementals"), amounting to 80% of the nonfederal contributions to the program, for the support of any or all of the projects in a city's program. In each demonstration city, an office of the federal coordinator was to be established with a director designated by the secretary. This gave HUD no authority over other departments, however, and the bill required it to consult each affected federal agency before making a demonstration grant. The bill did not say how many cities were to have demonstration programs, what the mix of city sizes was to be, or how funds were to be apportioned. Appropriations were to be authorized in "such sums as may be necessary" and the program was to terminate in six years.

Despite the speed with which the task force's recommendations moved into the legislative hoppers, they did not escape *all* high-level review. Weaver had arranged, doubtless with Wood's assistance, to have one of the task force's professional staff "leak" its doings to him, so that, when finally he was appointed secretary, he knew enough about the new program to be sure that (as he put it later) he "could live with it." HUD lawyers drafted the bill and this gave him a chance to go over it in detail and even to add a declaration that the new program would not supersede urban renewal. He was sure that without some such language, the bill would have no chance of passage.

Another cabinet member who was given an opportunity to express his views was Willard Wirtz, the secretary of labor. He told Califano that he did not think that the program would work. Concentrating federal spending in certain cities for purposes decided upon by the local officials might be desirable, but the hard fact was that practically all appropriations had to be allocated as Congress specified in statutes. Moreover, as a practical matter, department and agency heads had to exercise what little discretion the laws left them in ways acceptable to the congressmen and the interest groups upon whose good will they depended.

Hearings, and a Forecast

Hearings began at the end of February 1966 before the Subcommittee on Housing of the House Committee on Banking and Currency. Secretary Weaver was the first of some 75 witnesses whose testimony (not all of it concerning the bill) took four weeks and filled 1100 pages.

When he entered the hearing room, Weaver believed that the president had in mind five to ten demonstration cities. (This, incidentally, was also the understanding of Schultze.) Before the session was called to order, however, it became apparent to him that congressmen expected there would be about seventy. After hasty consultation with Wood, he let that figure go unchallenged. He could see, he said later, that some of the congressmen would not discuss, let alone support, a program involving only five or ten cities.

After describing the provisions of the bill ("the most important proposal in the president's program for rebuilding America's cities"), Weaver responded to questions. He assured the chairman that many cities had indicated interest in the program, that its creation would not lead to any decrease of urban renewal funds for any city, that the federal coordinator's function was merely "to sort of lubricate the process" of reaching into the existing federal grant programs. When the ranking minority member expressed fear that the coordinator would leave local officials no discretion, Weaver explained that the demonstration program would be developed by the locality *before* the coordinator entered the picture. Spending decisions, he emphasized, would be made by the local government in accordance with a plan made by it.

A subcommittee member pointed out that a city's program had to meet "such additional requirements as the Secretary may establish. . . ."

"Do we have to have that type of criteria?" he asked.

That provision, Weaver replied, would be used "very, very lightly" and "no major criteria will be added which is not in the substantive statute."

The witnesses who followed Weaver were mayors. Addonizio of Newark was first, then Cavanagh of Detroit, Lindsay of New York, Daley of Chicago and (eventually) a dozen others. The mayors, of course, were enthusiastic at the prospect of getting more federal money for their cities, but they thought the sum proposed much too small. Lindsay said that as a rough guess the program to be "really meaningful" in New York would cost $1 billion for the "bare bones" on the physical side and another $1 billion on the human side. He proposed that the entire $2.3 billion for the 6-year program be appropriated at once so that the cities could enter into long-term contracts right away. Chicago, Daley estimated, needed between $1.5 and $2 billion. Cavanagh's hopes ("dreams," he called them) were by far the most extravagant ("grand," he said). He envisioned building "a town within a town." "If we think," he told the subcommittee, "of a nation with a population of India by the end of the century and if we think of most of us living in cities, then we must not only dream grand dreams but we must also make them come true."

Opposition to the bill came chiefly from the National Association of Real Estate Boards, the U.S. Chamber of Commerce, the Mortgage Bankers Association of America and the National Association of Manufacturers. The chamber of commerce man remarked that with huge subsidies a few favored cities would show that they could get certain things done. What, he asked, would this demonstrate to cities in general? Other opponents doubted that the federal agencies could be induced to coordinate their programs, and one said that there were not enough skilled workers to rebuild the cities within a few years on the scale contemplated.

Although the bill seemed to be faring well in the hearings (in his opening remarks, the chairman termed the president's special message "inspiring" and declared that "our job is to give the Administration the legislative authority it needs to get the job done"), afterward the chairman and the ranking minority member agreed to report the bill out amended so as to authorize grants only for planning. Such a move would have amounted to killing the bill. Their decision cannot be accounted for by the weight of the testimony they had heard. Perhaps it reflected distress at the rising costs of the Vietnam war or a feeling that the administration should be satisfied with the many programs for the cities that had already been enacted. Wood, however, suspected a more particular cause: A committee staff man, miffed at not having been given a high post in HUD, had persuaded the chairman to scuttle the bill. Whatever the reasons, the outlook was now bleak. "All signs on Capitol Hill," the *New York Times* reported in mid-May 1966, "suggest that the program is dead."

The Prophecy Proves Self-Defeating

When he read that in the *Times*, the president was furious. Calling in Vice President Hubert Humphrey and his assistant for congressional relations, Lawrence O'Brien, he told them to find a way to save the bill. If the most important item in his urban program could be dumped by a House subcommittee, his prestige would suffer and the rest of his legislative program would be in great danger.

O'Brien telephoned the chairman of the subcommittee and told him that the president's bill would have to be reported out intact—"or else." This was unusual language to use, but O'Brien considered it necessary and justified. In due course (on June 23, 1966), the bill was reported with only two amendments of importance. One, which Weaver had proposed, authorized an additional $600 million to be earmarked for urban renewal within demonstration city areas (the renewal "add-on," this was called); the other eliminated the office of federal coordinator.

Reproached in private by the ranking minority member of the subcommittee for having failed to abide by their agreement, the chairman replied as one politician to another. "There are times," he said, "when a man changes his mind and there are times when he has it changed for him. . . . I had mine changed for me."

The full committee reported the bill favorably with other minor changes 5 days later. "Metropolitan expediters" were provided in place of the coordinators. The committee report said that they were to have a "clearinghouse" function and were not to pass upon applications. "This," it declared, "is to be a local program. . . ." It also declared that the new program would not "in any way change the flow of funds, as among cities, under existing grant-in-aid programs." This could be taken as a mere statement of fact—the fact Wirtz had pointed out to Califano—or as a warning to federal administrators not to use what little discretion they had in such matters to bring about the concentration of effort that, in the opinion of some—Budget Director Schultze, for example—was the program's main justification.

Despite this progress, the bill now was stymied. It could not reach the floor of the House without clearance from the Rules Committee, seven members of which were strongly for it and seven strongly against. The swing vote was that of a southerner who objected to the provision requiring that demonstration programs promote racial integration.

Meanwhile, the vice president and O'Brien had been rounding up support for the bill. They got the AFL–CIO to lobby energetically for it. They organized a committee of 22 business leaders, including David Rockefeller and Henry Ford II, to issue a statement calling for its passage. With other high figures in the administration, they had scores of private meetings with members of Congress to make explanations, listen to objections, and, when absolutely necessary, offer assurances that a place would not be overlooked when the time came to select the "winning" cities. By the end of the summer, this promise had been made to more than 100 legislators, which was less than a third of those who asked for it.

By late summer, the Senate hearings had long since been completed (they began April 19 and lasted only a few days); the bill would by now have been brought to the Senate floor but for the fact that the senators who normally managed housing legislation were not willing to manage it.

Senator John Sparkman (D., Ala.), the chairman of the Subcommittee on Housing of the Banking and Currency Committee, although surprised that after passage in the previous session of (as he described it) "one of the most comprehensive housing bills of all times" the president was proposing important new legislation, had said when he opened the hearings that his first reaction to the bill was favorable. The objective—coordination of federal programs—was one he approved. He was up for reelection, however, and therefore too busy to lead the fight. Senator Paul Douglas (D., Ill.), who stood next to him in seniority, would not lead it either; he also was busy campaigning and, besides, his staff was critical of the bill.

O'Brien then turned to Senator Edmund Muskie (D., Me.), who was much interested in intergovernmental relations, and found him reluctant.

He, too, had received a critical report on the bill from his staff (among other things, it was badly drafted and did not provide adequately for "institutional change"). Moreover, Maine, having no large cities, could not expect much benefit from it. After an all-night session with Muskie's legislative assistant, in the course of which representatives of the White House, HUD, and the Bureau of the Budget accepted certain modifications in the bill, the senator agreed to be its floor manager. On August 9 the full committee reported the bill favorably.

Because of concessions that had been made to Muskie and others, the Senate bill differed considerably from the one bottled up in the House Rules Committee. The Senate bill reduced the term of the program from six years to three, authorized smaller amounts for supplemental grants and the renewal "add-on," did not require cities to plan for racial and economic integration, emphasized the importance of local initiative and instructed HUD to give "equal regard to the problems of small as well as large cities." During the all-night session in Muskie's office, it had been agreed that supplemental grants would be distributed according to a formula based on population, amount of substandard housing, percentage of families with income below $3000 and percentage of adults with less than eight grades of schooling. This enabled three Maine cities—Bangor, Augusta, and Portland—to qualify. The formula was not written into the bill, however.

The committee bill reached the floor of the Senate on August 19. In the ensuing debate (which took parts of two days) it was made unmistakably clear that the small cities were to get their share of benefits.

George McGovern (D., S.D.): Do I understand the Senator correctly that in his judgment some reasonable consideration will be given to the allocation of funds to our smaller cities, and that not all the funds will go to a few great metropolitan centers?

Edmund Muskie (D., Me.): I would say to the Senator that I would expect that we would get demonstration city programs in these small areas, and I would be disappointed if we did not.

After the defeat of several threatening amendments, the Senate passed the bill by a roll call vote, 53–22. Under the threat of a procedure (passage of a resolution for which 21 days' notice had been given) that would bypass it, the House Rules Committee finally (21 days after the filing of such a resolution) granted a rule. After acrimonious debate in the course of which 17 amendments were voted down and 20 others (all agreed to by the administration) were adopted, the bill was passed by a vote of 178–141 in a late-night session on October 14, 1966. (The lightness of the vote is accounted for by the fact that the 14th was a Friday not many days before an election; many members had left for their constituencies before the vote was called.) The conference committee report favored the Senate version, although conceding some details to the House. The Senate accepted it quickly on a voice vote. In the House, there were moments of uncertainty, but in the end it was approved by a margin of 14 votes.

The president must have been well satisfied when on November 3, 1966, he called the chief actors to his office to witness the signing of the bill and to receive the souvenir pens that are distributed on such occasions. In all essentials and in most details, he had got what he had asked for. What was more, he had got it at the right time—election day was only a week away.

By Words We Are Governed

If anyone had hoped that the hearings and debates would resolve, or even call attention to, the contradictions in the program proposed by the task force, he would have been disappointed. Some penetrating questions had been raised: Could the agencies administering the categorical programs concentrate on the demonstration cities? Would they if they could? Was it possible to have both "citizen participation" and control by elected officials? Could there be a "partnership" between HUD and local governments?

The matters that had been of most interest to the few congressmen who had familiarized themselves with the specifics of the bill were mainly of symbolic importance, however. What did it matter whether an official was called a "coordinator" or an "expediter"? (That provision had been put in the bill in the first place as a "loss leader" to attract support from the "good government" movement, Wood later told an interviewer.) Actually, the secretary needed no special authorization to employ assistants to try to bring about coordination. Dropping the requirement that city programs "counteract the segregation of housing by race or income" was also of purely symbolic significance. Cities were still free to counteract racial segregation if they wished, and no one had ever supposed that a city making only a perfunctory gesture in this direction would be denied funds on that account.

In its final form the bill authorized only $900 million to be used over 2 years rather than $2.3 billion to be used over 6 years. This also made no practical difference; HUD had assured the subcommittees that it could not use more than that amount in the first 2 years anyway.

A few minutes before the president reached for the first of the pens with which he would sign the bill, Weaver told him of a congressman's objecting to the name Demonstration Cities on the grounds ". . . we got enough demonstrations already . . . we don't need any more"—a reference, of course, to the riots of the summer before. The president took the point seriously. As he signed the Demonstration Cities and Metropolitan Development Act of 1966 into Public Law 89–754, he referred to the new program as Model Cities. It would, he said, "spell the difference between despair and the good life."

THE PROGRAM'S FIRST YEARS

An Administrator's Impress

H. Ralph Taylor, the man chosen to administer the new program, had been the first executive director of the New Haven Redevelopment Agency (New Haven, it will be recalled, was widely regarded as having led the way in urban renewal) and had later worked for AID in Latin America. As assistant secretary of HUD for Demonstrations and Intergovernmental Relations, the Model Cities program would be his main but by no means his only responsibility. As his principal subordinate, he chose Walter Farr, a young lawyer who had also been with AID in Latin America. Farr was to be the operating head of the Model Cities Administration (MCA).

The staff was small by the standards of the government—about 40 professionals in Washington and 70 in regional offices—but it had an unusually high proportion of its personnel in the upper salary ranges. Morale was high. Taylor and Farr got along well and conferred often, and relations between them and their subordinates were easy and cordial. As a new agency, MCA was regarded with apprehension by the long-established housing and renewal agencies of HUD. Farr and the young men around him were dubbed "Taylor's Green Berets" by the stand-patters in these agencies.

Although he had to spend most of his time in the first hectic months haggling with HUD administrative officers and the Civil Service Commission and meeting with mayors and others who were impatient for decisions, Taylor nevertheless managed to put the impress of his views on the program. The task force report could not, in his opinion, be taken seriously: Its authors "did not understand housing." No one who *did* understand it would talk of rebuilding whole districts of the large cities: There were not enough carpenters, plumbers, and electricians to do the job and, anyway, it was obvious that Congress would not appropriate the scores of billions of dollars that would be required.

What Model Cities *could* do, Taylor thought, was, first, to document the vast extent of the cities' needs so that, when the Vietnam war ended, the nation might be persuaded to make a commitment on the scale required, and, second, to prepare local governments for effective action when the nation finally made that commitment.

His experience in New Haven had convinced him that excessive fragmentation of governmental structure was the major obstacle to getting things done. This was being made steadily worse by the almost daily increase in federal efforts—most conspicuously OEO's Community Action Program—which bypassed local governments. He was determined that Model Cities should not add to the governmental confusion. It would help the cities plan, but not impose plans on them. As one of his Green Berets wrote later,

> We had a great deal of faith at first in the latent power of the people "out there" in the cities, in their ability to come up with innovative solutions that could be replicated throughout the country if they were left alone with a nice piece of federal change. We saw them as coworkers in an urban problems laboratory. Our job was to furnish equipment, assistance, support and occasionally a tube of catalyst. Theirs was to innovate.

For Taylor, at least, the people "out there" were not primarily the residents of the slum and blighted neighborhoods. Model Cities, he told his staff, was to be "a mayors' and planners' program."

When the Model Cities bill was still before Congress, HUD had set up a committee under the chairmanship of William Rafsky (a member, it will be recalled, of the task force) to advise on policies to be followed when it passed. In the committee's recommendations, Taylor found much to support his views. It urged HUD to insist upon high-quality programs. Before receiving a planning grant, a city should be required to describe and analyze the physical and social problems of its poor areas, lay out 5-year goals for dealing with them, and tell how it proposed to attain the goals. In addition, it should answer a long list of questions about its government and related matters. If its application did not meet HUD's stringent standards—if, for example, its projects were not innovative—HUD should demand something better. The cities making the best applications would receive grants for a year's further planning. An "action program" involving supplemental grants could begin only after satisfactory completion of "the planning phase."

The decision to require a 1-year "planning phase" had been made at a very early stage: Weaver had mentioned it in his testimony to the House subcommittee. (For that matter, the planners of the 1963 antipoverty proposals had intended to have the "pilot" cities spend a year planning and, as they put it, "tooling up.") Taylor, by following the recommendations of the Rafsky Committee and establishing an application process that might require several weeks or months, was in effect delaying the "action phase" still further. When the mayors realized how much delay there would be, they could be expected to protest vigorously. This would be awkward from a public relations standpoint, but Taylor was willing to pay the price in order to get information to document the extent of the cities' needs. With this in view, he established what he called a "high sights" policy: applications were to be made on the assumption that *all* of a city's problems were to be dealt with *within a few years.*

Fearful lest support for his agency in Congress melt away if more than a year passed without *any* "action," Taylor considered giving the cities small supplemental grants for "immediate impact projects," such as improved street cleaning, as soon as their applications were approved. Against the public relations advantages of this there were, however, two offsetting disadvantages: first, such "cosmetic" grants would do nothing to cure the cities' fundamental ills, and, second, they would distract the cities from the "in depth" planning that was crucial. Reluctantly, Taylor decided to withhold the supplementals until planning had been done properly. Somewhat to his surprise, Weaver and Wood, who would have to bear the brunt of any criticism, agreed enthusiastically to these decisions.

In December 1966, MCA mailed out 3000 copies of its program guide, a 60-page brochure entitled "Improving the Quality of Urban Life." This explained that although Model Cities programs were to reflect local initiative, they had to conform to certain statutory requirements. The programs had to be of sufficient magnitude to (among other things) "make marked progress in serving the poor and disadvantaged people living in slum and blighted areas . . ." and make "a substantial impact on the sound development of the entire city." Therefore the programs would have to deal with "all of the deep-rooted social and environmental problems of a neighborhood" and "make concentrated and coordinated use of all available federal aids. . . ."

The guide emphasized another standard which, although not derived from the statute, was in Taylor's opinion fully consistent with it—namely, innovation. "Cities," it said, "should look upon this program as an opportunity to experiment, to become laboratories for testing and refining new and better methods for improving the quality of urban living."

The guide was soon followed by *CDA Letter No. 1,* "Model Cities Planning Requirements," which was the first of many formal instructions from MCA to city demonstration agencies. This letter made the "high sights" policy explicit.

> . . . cities must set their sights and their goals high. Model cities programs should aim at the solution of all critical neighborhood problems which it is within the power of the city to solve, and should be designed to make as much progress as possible toward solutions within five years. In most cases, it should be possible within five years to make all necessary institutional and legal changes at the state and local level and to initiate all

necessary projects and activities which will, when carried to completion, achieve the long-range goals set by the city.

Applications, the instructions said, should describe and analyze each major problem, explain how and why each developed, and give a preliminary judgment as to what should be done about them. Cities were to decide for themselves what to do, but they must show that they followed proper procedures in making their decisions. "Program analysis," MCA stated, "is the foundation on which the entire Model Cities undertaking rests."

"Program analysis" was fashionable in Washington at this time. In fact, the president had in 1965 instructed all agencies to institute PPBS—the Planning, Programming, Budgeting System—a procedure for analyzing and evaluating program alternatives that had been used in the Defense Department and much acclaimed by the press. The popularity of PPBS had little or nothing to do with MCA's enthusiasm for planning, however. Some of the principal Green Berets were graduates of city planning schools and, as such, products of a different planning tradition, one that derived from the city beautification movement rather than from economics. Taylor seems to have accepted on faith their claims to having skills that, if given scope, would cure the ills of the cities. Moreover, he saw in comprehensive planning a means of collecting information that would impress the country with the extent and seriousness of its ills.

Knowing that there would not be funds to support the full programs proposed by 75 cities (it had been decided to choose this number from a "first round" of applications; a "second round" would follow shortly), Taylor decided that the cities would have to concentrate their efforts on a single model neighborhood of not more than 15,000 persons or 10% of the city's population, whichever was larger; New York and a few other of the largest cities were to have more than one model neighborhood.

This decision left city officials wondering why they were required to describe and analyze the problems of *all* poor neighborhoods. It also raised the question why huge sums should be poured into one neighborhood while others nearby and equally poor got nothing. And it reduced whatever possibilities there were for collaboration between Model Cities and those federal and other agencies whose programs operated citywide. But Taylor really had no alternative. Given that there had to be 75 cities to begin with and more very soon, to make a "substantial impact" on a unit even as large as a neighborhood was hardly possible.

The essential decisions having been made, Taylor and some of his assistants set out in January 1967 as a "flying circus" to explain the program to local officials, answer their questions, offer help in filling out applications, and urge that applications be made early. "Analyze yourselves and your cities," Taylor told his audiences. "Walk the alleys and the streets and talk to people and get to the roots of the problem."

Needed: New Standards

Applications soon poured in, but Taylor and his assistants were disappointed when they read them. One Green Beret thought that less than a dozen showed any understanding of the experimental nature of the program. The projects proposed were not innovative, they did not constitute comprehensive or coordinated programs, and it was evident that they had been made with little or no consultation with the residents of the affected neighborhoods or even, in some instances, with the mayor and city council. "Our lab partners," he wrote, "didn't seem to get the hang of it."

With a view to improving the quality of future applications (the "second round" would begin within a few months) as well as of the first year's planning by the "winning cities," Farr brought his staff into a conference with consultant specialists. (Dr. Duhl, the psychiatrist who with Mrs. Chayes had written the 1964 memorandum proposing Demonstration Cities, was one.) The result of these and other deliberations was revision of the instructions on planning and citizen participation.

The new planning instructions reflected the staff's conviction that most cities were incapable of "real" ("comprehensive") planning. Accordingly, the Five-Year Plan was deemphasized, becoming a "five-year forecast." City programs were henceforth to be based on analysis of *not quite* everything:

CDA Letter #1 (the original version, October 1967)
Each city's program should be based on a systematic analysis of all relevant social, economic, and physical problems which describes and measures the nature and extent of the problems, identifies their basic underlying causes, examines the inter-relationship between problems, and indicates the critical changes which must be made in order to overcome these problems.

CDA Letter #4 (the revised version, July 1968)
The problem analysis should cover all significant problems but the depth of the analysis can vary according to the significance of the problem and data available. High priority problems should receive the most attention the first year. Future planning should direct attention to these significant problems not adequately covered during the first year of planning. Although this section and its contents will vary according to local conditions and according to local understanding of problems, it should not avoid significant and historical causes of deprivation and inequality.

In a foreword by Taylor and in several footnotes, the new instruction described itself as "guidelines" which were to be interpreted "flexibly."

The main purpose of the letter ("40 pages of agonized noncommunication," one of its authors—the Green Beret already quoted—called it) was to *explain* the nature of planning, not to tell the cities what they must do.

A revised statement of policy on citizen participation was issued in order to keep peace within the staff. In the spring of 1967 Taylor had agreed to substitute "meaningful citizen participation" for "widespread" in a revision of the program guide. Later, when the first planning grant application began arriving, it was evident that in most places citizens were not being consulted. The citizen participation specialists of MCA, OEO, and HEW then jointly wrote Taylor and Farr, the heads of MCA, proposing that the residents of model neighborhoods be given the right to choose their own representatives, have a "genuine" policy role, be provided a budget from which they could hire technical assistance of their own choice, and be compensated for their time and travel.

Farr knew that there would be trouble if these recommendations were not accepted. Citizen participation, however, was one of the few matters Weaver insisted on having brought to him for decision. Weaver believed that the recommended changes went far beyond what Congress had intended by the phrase "widespread citizen participation," but he recognized that concessions were necessary to mollify a part of the staff. Accordingly *CDA Letter No. 3* (it was dated November 30, 1967, but distributed to the cities about a month before) informed applicants that in order to build "self esteem, competence and a desire to participate effectively" on the part of neighborhood residents, there would have to be "some form of organizational structure . . . embodying [the residents] in the process of policy and program planning and program implementation and operation." The leadership of such a structure "must consist of persons whom neighborhood residents accept as representing their interests," and these must have "clear and direct access" to the CDA's decision-making. Cities were to provide the residents' representatives with technical assistance "in some form" and were to compensate them when (but only when) doing so would remove barriers to their participation.

The compromise did not please the community participation specialist, who resigned before it was issued, but the rest of the staff was apparently satisfied.

The Case of Compton, California

One of the cities to file an application was Compton (population 56,000), a predominantly Negro suburb of Los Angeles. Following the common practice of small cities, the city manager engaged a firm of planning consultants to prepare the application. This cost $5000 and assured its failure. A city could not learn about its problems by employing outsiders, MCA wrote. The rejection came to a new manager, James Johnson, who put everything else aside in order to draw up a new application himself. The task took three weeks.

When he had accumulated 300 pages ("I put everything I could think of in it"), he sent the application to Washington. After several months' wait, he was surprised and elated to learn that Compton had been granted $110,000 for further planning. His elation faded somewhat, however, when he found that he might not use the money to work out the details of the projects that he had outlined in the application. His 300-page document, MCA told him, was not a plan, but a "plan to plan." He would now have to set in motion a planning process that would be carried on for a year by the City Demonstration Agency (CDA) and in which the residents of the model neighborhood would be "meaningfully" involved. Only when this was done and Compton's problems had been analyzed in depth, its goals defined, a 5-year forecast made, and a first-year action program derived from it could he hope for an "action grant."

The action grant—assuming the city eventually qualified for one—would not necessarily be in an amount sufficient to support more than a fraction of the first-year action program. At best, Compton could get only its pro rata share of whatever supplemental grant funds Congress appropriated.

To Johnson it appeared that MCA was requiring that the planning grant be used to prepare a rewrite of the 300 pages that he had already submitted: He doubted that the CDA and the citizens' advisory board could find much of anything to say about Compton's problems that he had not said in his application. It displeased him also that the further planning would have to be done by the CDA. This would tend to cut him, the city manager, off from a process which, if it were to lead to action, required his intimate participation. Perhaps in a large city such participation by a chief executive was impossible or undesirable, but why not let a city decide such matters for itself?

Johnson was also dubious about the citizen participation requirements. As in other black communities, politics in Compton was in a state of ferment; people who had had little or no experience in public affairs, many of them young and militant, were searching for leadership. In these circumstances, "citizen participation" was likely to mean endless talk at best. It was exasperating, too, Johnson thought, that the program could operate in only one neighborhood. Anyone could see that Compton's problems were citywide—indeed, *more* than citywide.

Choosing the "Winners"

The "first round" applications were read by the MCA staff in Washington; it prepared brief appraisals of each. These included summary information about each city's political leadership, administrative capability, and understanding of its problems, along with a judgment as to the innovativeness of its proposals. These appraisals were read by an interagency committee of which Taylor was chairman. It found some applicants clearly unsuitable. The others were given an "advanced" review. After considering a proposal for assigning numerical weights to a long list of sharply defined criteria, the interagency committee fell back upon an unsystematic "commonsense" procedure.

A list of 63 cities recommended by the committee was forwarded to Weaver in June in the expectation that it would be quickly approved. It was not, however. A month or two before, Weaver had spent a bad morning answering questions before an appropriations subcommittee which was considering MCA along with other HUD items. It was evident that the congressmen did not like the idea of appropriating $650 million without knowing where the money would be spent or (except in very general terms) for what purposes. When they were told that only eight cities had so far submitted completed applications, some of them were surprised and annoyed. Recalling their attitudes, Weaver decided not to announce the "winning" cities until the bill had been passed. This, he supposed, would be fairly soon: appropriations bills were normally passed before the start of a fiscal year, July 1. This time, however, there was disagreement over many items in the bill and, although passage seemed likely from week to week, it did not actually occur until November.

The delay in announcing the "winning" cities, the reasons for which could not be made public, caused the backers of some promising projects to lose interest in them. The MCA staff, however, thought that on the whole the effect of the delay was beneficial because most cities had not yet developed accounting procedures that met its standards.

All but 9 of the 63 "winners" were in Democratic congressional districts. This was not surprising, since most sizable cities were Democratic. Asked by the press how much politics there had been in the selections, Weaver said, "As little as possible."

This was undoubtedly true. Taylor had resisted political interference because he knew both that his staff would lose respect for him if he "went too far," and that the prestige of the program—perhaps even its existence—would be threatened by including cities whose projects were ill conceived or certain to fail for other reasons, such as administrative incapacity. In some instances, however, political influences could not be withstood. The White House was sure that Eagle Pass and Laredo, Texas met all possible criteria. Smithfield, Tennessee was the home town of the chairman of the House subcommittee that passed on HUD appropriations, and Pikesville, Kentucky was the abode of another chairman. Montana, the Senate majority leader's state, had two especially deserving cities. Maine, Muskie's state, had three.

Some voices—Republican ones, of course—had been saying all along that Model Cities was just another Democratic pork barrel. To prove them wrong, at least one large city represented in Congress by a Republican had to be on the list. Happily, one—Columbus, Ohio—was found. A few cities that could not have qualified by nonpolitical standards were on the list (Laredo had not even submitted an application). In general, however, the "political musts" met MCA's standards as well or better than other applicants. Of the 150 cities eventually chosen, fewer than a dozen, Taylor said later, were accepted solely because of political pressure. If he had succumbed to it very often "the pressure would never have stopped . . . and the program would have been ruined from the start."

When he was asked how much politics there had been in the selections Weaver might have said as truthfully, "Less than necessary." For, despite his precautions, Congress in late 1967 gave Model Cities less than half what had been asked for—$200 million for supplemental grants and $100 million for the renewal add-on. The only item *not* cut was for additional planning grants—$12 million.

This meant that Congress was ready for a "second round" of applications, bringing the number of Model Cities to 150. By halving the appropriations and doubling the number of cities, it was making ridiculous Wood's continued declaration that the purpose of the program was "to determine the 'critical mass' for real change in the problems of human and physical deterioration in our cities."

More Disappointments

The first-year programs, which began to reach MCA in the fall of 1968, nearly 2 years after the passage of the act, were found to be even worse than the applications had been. This at least was the judgment of the Green Beret who had helped write the "40 pages of agonized noncommunication" that was *CDA Letter No. 4.* The cities, this man wrote later, were "willing to play our silly little game for money," but they did not understand that MCA was trying to get them to experiment and innovate; they found it easier to accept regulation than to make use of freedom.

Very likely he was right. The CDA planners, however, worked under certain constraints that should be noted. For one thing, the amount of the planning grant ($150,000 for most cities) was not nearly enough for "in depth" fact-gathering and analysis of a great many problems. It was inevitable, too, that careful analysis would sometimes knock the props out from under proposals of the sort that the planners were expected to bring forward. In Binghamton, New York, for example, one survey of opinion in a model neighborhood revealed that more than 75% of blacks considered their housing either "good" or "excellent," and another survey showed that 78% of those polled (black and white) were satisfied with the public schools.

However hard they might have tried, the cities would have found it remarkably difficult to devise programs that were "innovative," "comprehensive," or "coordinative," and perhaps impossible to devise ones that were all three simultaneously. The words themselves were ambiguous in the extreme. (In Atlanta, researchers asked 70 local officials what they understood by "coordination" and got 7 distinctly different replies.) Even if the objectives had been made perfectly clear, the cities might not have been able to devise programs to achieve them because of the inherent difficulty of the task. Innovation, for example—devising measures that are new, not unreasonably expensive, acceptable to the public, and that produce the effects intended—is not as easy as Washington seemed to think. (In Boston, where the Ford Foundation created a committee of "experts" to find "new ideas" for helping the poor, a long effort yielded next to nothing.)

It was probably impossible to achieve simultaneously and in a high degree all the standards MCA set because, however they might be interpreted, there were tensions if not incompatibilities among them. The more "comprehensive" a program, the less "innovative" it was likely to be; to the extent that it was "innovative" it would probably make "coordination" more difficult. (Taylor's determination not to worsen the fragmentation of local government led him to insist that projects be administered through *existing* agencies, but innovation, sometimes if not generally, required creation of new ones.) And the more "innovative" a project the less its chance of making a "substantial impact," for new efforts usually have to start small. Similarly with citizen participation: The more seriously MCA took it, the more it had to sacrifice in terms of its other goals.

CDA directors seized different horns of these dilemmas. Some bore down hard on "comprehensiveness," appointing dozens, or even scores, of task forces that produced hundreds of projects which were offered as a "program," although they were really a sort of civic laundry list. Others emphasized "coordination" and drew up schemes for exchanging information among agencies by means of committees, conferences, and the distribution of memoranda. Those who placed their bets on "innovation" usually hired consultants to think up ideas for them.

Whichever way they turned, the CDAs had to take account of something that *CDA Letter No. 4* overlooked: local politics. As perceived from Washington, a city government was an entity capable, if sufficiently prodded and when provided with a grant, of making decisions in a rational manner, that is, of comprehensive planning. City officials, including of course CDA members, knew, however, that only in a rather limited sense did such a thing as a city government exist; for them the reality was bits and pieces of power and authority, the focuses of which were constantly changing. Bringing the bits and pieces together long enough to carry out an undertaking was a delicate and precarious operation requiring skills and statuses that few persons possessed. To those who saw governing from this perspective, MCA's rigamarole about program analysis, goals statement, and strategy statement did indeed appear a silly game. "If the Feds tell us to jump through hoops for their money," a CDA director said, "we'll jump through hoops."

Interagency Relations

After 2 years of trying, MCA could not claim much success in "sucking the system together." When the act was passed, there had been in the larger cities a rush by local bodies to offer cooperation in the spending of the large sums that Model Cities was expected to control, but this enthusiasm faded fast. Some mayors (and city managers) used the CDA to strengthen their management. Others, however, more or less deliberately let their Model Cities program become the preserve, or playground, of persons who claimed to speak for the poor. The CDA letter strengthening citizen participation requirements, which appeared at the end of the second summer of urban riots (1966), made such mayors all the more inclined to (as an MCA official put it later) "turn the whole thing over to the noisiest citizens' group in order to keep them quiet." It is probably safe to say that where mayors *tried* to use the program to improve coordination, they found it useful, and where they did *not* try the result was confusion worse confounded.

Supplemental grants, it will be recalled, were intended by the task force to serve as both "bait" and "glue—"bait" in that they would enable a city to attract categorical grants from federal agencies anxious to try things that they could not try elsewhere; "glue" in that they could be used to bring diverse projects (federal, state, and local) into internally consistent wholes. In this way, MCA and the city governments, working in partnership, were expected to bring about coordination.

To establish the relationships with federal agencies required for this, Taylor had sent them drafts of the program guide for review and comment. Except for OEO, which urged MCA to adopt its "confrontation" tactics in dealing with city agencies, their responses had been perfunctory. He had persisted, however. When the time came to select the first round cities, he created regional interagency committees to make recommendations. These played little or no part in the selection process, probably for lack of time to give them training, but (as has been explained) a Washington interagency committee *did* pass upon the applications.

After the selections had been made, the interagency committees, both regional and Washington, were given the task of reviewing the cities' plans and giving them technical assistance. Since the funds for model cities' projects would presumably come mainly from departments and agencies other than HUD, it was necessary to bring these units into close contact with the CDAs, the local bodies making the plans.

That these arrangements sometimes did not work as they were supposed to is evident from the experience (perhaps not typical) of the Texarkana, Arkansas, CDA when it asked its regional interagency committee for advice. "We expected a dialogue on the purpose and potential impact of individual projects and groups of projects," a CDA official wrote. Instead, the federal agency representatives met first in a session from which the local people were excluded; later the local people found themselves answering questions about budgetary and other details of particular projects. It was apparent that most of the "Feds" had not read the city's 5-year plan; they were interested only in its first-year action program and only in those parts of it that related to their agencies' programs. "Federal employees," the Texarkana official concluded, "are generally limited to specific project categories." This, of course, was one of the very conditions that the Model Cities program had been created to correct.

It is not surprising that the interagency committee members were not interested in Texarkana's 5-year plan: Each was there primarily to protect and promote the interest of *his* agency. It was all very well for MCA, which had cast itself in the role of coordinator, to preach the virtues of coordination. The other agencies did not have the same interest in the matter: On the contrary, they had reason to view coordination with some suspicion; its success would tend to subordinate them to MCA.

Relations between MCA and OEO were always difficult. In theory, CDAs did planning, whereas CAAs (Community Action Agencies of OEO) operated programs. Naturally, CDAs contended that *all* programs in model neighborhoods should fit harmoniously into their plans; naturally, too, CAAs insisted that they had a right—indeed a responsibility—to extend any of their programs to the *whole* of any city.

What most concerned Weaver, Wood, and Taylor was the failure of supplemental grants to serve as "bait," "glue," or "clubs." "Supplemental" soon proved to be a misnomer. Most CDAs made little or no effort to get categorical grants; instead they asked for supplementals to finance projects that could have been financed with categoricals.

There were several reasons for this. CDAs found it less trouble to use supplementals because they did not have to find out about, and adapt to, the detailed restrictions with which Congress had loaded the categoricals, and also because they were more used to dealing with MCA, their parent agency, than with others. The administrators of the categorical programs thought—or claimed to think—that model cities (the "winners" in the national competition) would be generously funded by MCA and that therefore their own grants should be given to less-favored places. Thus when the Seattle CDA allocated $35,000 in supplemental funds to expand an OEO legal services program, OEO at once reduced its contribution to the project by that amount. From OEO's standpoint, this was the sensible thing to do: Since the legal services program was now going to be supported at what it (OEO) deemed an adequate level, it could put its $35,000 into something else.

As Secretary of Labor Wirtz had pointed out to Califano (special assistant to LBJ), administrators of categorical grants had very little discretion in the allocation of them. For example, HEW, the department most disposed to cooperate with model cities, had appropriations of $6.4 billion in 1968 but only $181 million of this—roughly 3%—was not committed by statute or otherwise.

By the spring of 1968, it was evident that vigorous intervention from the White House would be required to establish MCA in a coordinating role. The president's prestige was now very low (he had announced that he would not be a candidate); even so, a few well-chosen words from him would greatly strengthen MCA's influence with the other agencies. Getting him to say the words was a problem, however. Only Weaver, the cabinet member, was in a position to approach him on the subject, and he sensed that to do so might irritate him and do MCA's cause more harm than good.

Accordingly, Weaver, with Wood, Taylor, and Farr in tow, went to see Califano and Schultze, the White House assistants most responsible for such matters. Both of them readily agreed to request in the president's name that the relevant departments and agencies earmark part of their discretionary funds for use in model cities neighborhoods.

Taylor meanwhile was doing what he could to get state governments to give the model cities neighborhoods more of what they got in federal grants as well as more from their other revenues. At his suggestion, Weaver invited nine states (later others as well) to participate in the review of "second round" applications. These efforts, however, yielded little. State agencies had not much more freedom of action than did federal ones, and, besides, they too had their own axes to grind.

The Pre-Inauguration Day Rush

Two years after the passage of the Model Cities Act, Richard Nixon was elected as president, and Weaver, Wood, and Farr made ready to leave the program to successors who, it seemed likely, would liquidate it. As matters stood on Election Day, this would have been easy. As yet only planning grants had been made, and not as many of these as intended. The first round cities were now approaching the end of their "planning year," but none had submitted its first-year program. Consequently, not a dollar of supplemental grants had been obligated.

To make liquidation of the program awkward for the new administration, MCA put the first round cities under pressure to make program submissions by December 1 so that funds could be committed to them before Inauguration Day. Sixteen cities met the deadline, and the programs of nine were approved. Selecting the remaining second round cities was easier, and the quota was filled by the end of December.

The Nixon administration would be in office for 6 months before the beginning of the new fiscal year, but, unless great inconvenience and confusion were to ensue, the Johnson administration had to prepare a tentative budget proposal for fiscal 1970. In the previous 2 years, Congress had appropriated nearly $1 billion for Model Cities grants. Only a few million of this could be obligated, for lack of cities whose submissions were ready, or almost ready, to be approved. Nevertheless, the Johnson administration's 1970 budget proposed another $750 million for Model Cities. It was, of course, good politics to put the Nixon administration in the position of appearing unsympathetic to the poor and blacks by trimming from the Johnson budget funds that could not possibly be spent.

Weaver, Wood, Taylor, and Farr, although loyal members of the Johnson "team," were, it is safe to say, less interested than the White House in creating embarrassments for the next administration. They did, however, want to do what they could to assure the continuance, growth, and success of the Model Cities program. Taylor approved only 9 of the 16 program submissions because he depended upon a normal bureaucratic evaluation process, which took a certain amount of time and turned up only 9 submissions that met the established standards. (One partial exception may be noted: Seattle's submission was taken out of turn because it was thought expedient to show West Coast Republicans that they had a stake in the continuance of the program.)

This was in fact a time when politics receded further into the background than usual. "We were leaving office," one of those most concerned said later, "therefore we had nothing to lose by being *not* political."

Two Voices of Experience

Before they emptied their desks, Taylor and Farr wrote memoranda to be read by their successors.

Farr said that substantial progress had been made in strengthening local governments and in creating a federal organization that could respond quickly to the cities' needs. But so much time had been required to develop workable relations between city governments and neighborhood groups that little had been left for planning. Innovation had been hard to "pull off," both for lack of money and because of the commitment not to increase the fragmentation of local government. Coordination, when it occurred, had more often been information sharing than program integration, and the federal agencies (except those in HUD itself) had made only nominal efforts to help the cities develop high-quality programs.

The promise of the program, Farr said, could not be realized unless there was a "quantum leap" in the amount of technical assistance given the cities and in the attention given to the evaluation of their results. The likelihood of MCAs ever having enough personnel to do these things adequately was, he judged, zero. But without vast expansion and improvement along these lines the Model Cities program would amount to little more than block grants. This might be valid and appropriate, but it was not what Congress intended.

Taylor, in his memorandum, revealed that 2 years of trying had left him convinced that local governments could not be "tooled up" from Washington: The federal government simply did not have the capacity. The categorical programs, he said, were too many and too diverse to be managed, even by a "super-department" that some would like to see created. Moreover, the categorical system was an impediment to local planning: Except as they had latitude to make choices, local governments were without incentives to plan. The number of categorical programs, he thought, should be reduced by at least one-half through consolidation; HUD should be made a "Department of Urban Affairs" with authority to coordinate federal efforts in urban areas, and revenue sharing (an arrangement by which the federal government would pass regularly a fixed percentage of its revenue on to the states and cities to use as they saw fit) should be instituted.

The role Taylor envisioned for Model Cities was a limited one, and it was based upon assumptions that the rest of his memorandum seemed to contradict. MCA, he thought, should be the Department of Urban Affairs' instrument for developing and testing new techniques for improving local public services; in particular it should try to discover whether, by the use of block grants and the concentration of resources, local officials could be induced to take responsibility for the solution of local problems.

CONCLUDING OBSERVATIONS

There was not in 1965, when the second task force did its work, the slightest possibility of a federal program being brought into existence which could accomplish any of the various large purposes that Model Cities was supposed to serve. The president and his advisers, including the members of the task force, knew perfectly well that the boundaries of political possibility precluded measures that would change the situation fundamentally. Block grants, not to mention revenue sharing, were out of the question. (As Wood remarked later, "Congress was not about to collect taxes and then let the states and cities spend them with no strings attached.") Bringing the more than 200 categorical programs under central control was equally unfeasible.

It was also politically impossible to concentrate federal funds and efforts in a few large cities, let alone to "saturate" a few. Even if there had been no Vietnam war, the scores of billions that would have been required to make a "substantial impact" on the physical slum in the dozen or so largest cities would not have been appropriated, and, even if it were, men could not have been found to do the work. Even to *stop* doing things that manifestly did not work—urban renewal, for example—was beyond the bounds of possibility; one had to expand what did not work as the price of trying something that *might*.

These constraints were all apparent to the designers of the Model Cities program. There were other constraints which a charitable reader may suppose were *not* apparent to them and are visible now only by the light of hindsight. That local political arrangements in the United States preclude anything remotely resembling "comprehensive" or "rational" planning is a fact familiar to all practical men and documented repeatedly by journalists and even by scholars. That inventing social reforms that are likely to work and that voters are willing to have tried is very difficult to do anywhere (and almost impossible to do in an American city where "veto groups" abound) is a fact hardly less obvious. As for citizen participation, very little judgment or experience was needed to see that this would be costly in terms of other goals—planning, coordination, and innovation.

Even if these constraints had not existed, the new program would have been the product of (at best) the "educated guesses" of persons with experience and judgment but without any sort of technical expertise on the basis of which they could answer the really important questions. That the "social and psychological" approach would achieve worthwhile results, for example, was mere conjecture. No "facts" or "tested theories" existed from which a remedy for any of the ailments of the cities could have been derived.

There *did* exist, however, a fairly good example of the very program that the designers of Model Cities were trying to create, one which, had they examined it closely (time did not permit) would have revealed the futility of what they were about to attempt. New Haven (as was remarked above) was a model city before Model Cities was invented. Its circumstances were peculiarly favorable: small (population 150,000) and without much poverty, it had (what was most unusual) a mayor who not only won elections but surrounded himself with able assistants, some of whom were unusually talented at devising innovative measures to improve the lot of those for whom poverty had become a way of life. While the Wood task force was at work, New Haven had more than 25 agencies, public and private, participating in about 60 programs that were coordinated by a special body. Federal and other spending there was close to a "saturation" level, amounting in 1965 to nearly $7000 for each family with an income under $4000.

If Wood and his associates had studied this ready-made "pilot program," they would not have found evidence that it was making a "substantial impact" on the "quality of life" in the city. But even if they *had* found convincing evidence of this, the significance of the finding for other cities would have been questionable. Weaver was optimistic, to say the least, when he told the House subcommittee that successful demonstrations in a few cities would be copied by thousands of others. This might happen if the demonstrations were of new methods that could be applied easily, although political or other circumstances might stand in the way even then. But if the nature of a demonstration were such as to preclude its general application—if, for example, it required extraordinary political or administrative skills—then Weaver's hope could not be realized. It was more than likely that any measures that could make a "substantial impact" would be so costly in money and other resources (e.g., political leadership) as to preclude their being generalized. To invest as much per capita in *all* cities as had been invested in New Haven was fiscally impossible.

Supposing, however, that from the example of New Haven or otherwise the task force had devised a simple and highly effective method for bringing about complete coordination of federal, state, and local efforts, public and private, while realizing simultaneously and to the full the ideals of comprehensive planning, citizen participation, and innovation. Is it likely that this would have "solved," or much alleviated, the problems of the cities? There is very little reason to think so. Conceivably, the result might have been the more effective pursuit of courses of action that in the long run would have made matters worse. (Suppose, for example, that such successes had, by making life in the poorest parts of the city less dismal, reduced the pressure to move to the suburban areas where job opportunities would certainly be better in the long run.)

However this may be, President Johnson's prediction that the Model Cities Act would "spell the difference between despair and the good life" was farfetched in the extreme. Possibly, however, his rhetoric and the act itself were not intended to be taken at face value but rather were gestures intended to help create confidence in government and (what may have been the same in the president's eyes) in himself as a leader. If this is taken as the "real" purpose of the program, one may well wonder what was the nature and extent of the gains that accrued from holding out such promises and whether they were later offset—perhaps more than offset—by a loss of confidence when the promises proved unrealizable.

These questions will never be fully answerable and it is probably fruitless even to speculate about them now. The forces that converged in the making of the Model Cities program are still at work and what they will lead to eventually is anyone's guess.

ACKNOWLEDGMENTS

The following were kind enough to read an earlier version of the case in its entirety: Jay Janis, Marshall Kaplan, William L. Rafsky, H. Ralph Taylor, Robert C. Weaver, and Robert C. Wood. Others who were helpful on particular matters were: Antonia Chayes, William Cannon, James Johnson, Martin Meyerson, and Charles L. Schultze. It goes without saying that some of these may disagree with my interpretations.

SOURCES AND READINGS

The reader is asked to bear in mind that this account does not carry the Model Cities program beyond January 1968. It should not be assumed that the program and the conditions affecting it have remained unchanged.

The work is based largely upon interviews by the author with participants. He has also drawn upon interviews by Christopher DeMuth, for which privilege he is grateful. He is grateful also for much stimulating comment and criticism from Mr. DeMuth and from Lawrence D. Brown.

Only such source material is cited as is easily available in published form. This includes especially the hearings held in 1966 by the housing subcommittees of the Committees on

Banking and Currency of both House and Senate. The House hearings are entitled *Hearings on Demonstration Cities, Housing and Urban Development and Urban Transit*. The Senate ones are entitled *Hearings, Housing Legislation of 1966*. President Johnson's special message on demonstration cities may be found in *Public Papers of the Presidents*, 1966, Vol. I. For the reaction of academic specialists to the president's message the student should read the symposium of comment in the November 1966 issue of *The Journal of the American Institute of Planners*. In the writer's judgment, Professor James Q. Wilson was particularly prescient in his contribution to that symposium.

The debates on the bill are to be found in the *Congressional Record*. The Senate debates were on August 18 and 19 (Vol. 112, Part 5) and the House debates on October 13 and 14 (Vol. 112, Part 20).

For the ideas and efforts that preceded and presumably influenced the planning of the Model Cities program the student is referred to Richard Blumenthal's chapter "The Bureaucracy: Antipoverty and the Community Action Program," in Allan P. Sindler (ed.), *American Political Institutions and Public Policy*, Boston: Little, Brown, 1969, Peter Marris and Martin Rein, *Dilemmas of Social Reform: Poverty and Community Action in the United States*, New York: Atherton Press, 1967, and D. P. Moynihan, *Maximum Feasible Misunderstanding*, New York: Free Press, 1966. For a full and careful account of what was done in New Haven, consult Russell D. Murphy, *Political Entrepreneurs and Urban Poverty*, Lexington, Mass.: Heath Lexington Books, 1971. Former President Johnson's (retrospective) account of his administration (which is quoted or paraphrased several times in the case study) is of course of unique interest and value; his book is *The Vantage Point* (New York: Holt, Rinehart and Winston, 1971).

Some who played active roles in the Model Cities program or who observed its beginnings at close range have written about it. One short but valuable article is by Fred Jordan (the "Green Beret" much quoted in the text above): "The Confessions of a Former Grantsman," in *City*, Summer 1971. Planning in three model cities is described at length by the members of a firm of consultants employed by MCA to evaluate its efforts; see Marshall Kaplan, Sheldon P. Gans, and Howard M. Kahn, *The Model Cities Program: The Planning Process in Atlanta, Seattle and Dayton*, New York: Praeger, 1970.

The Model Cities program has been described as a "coordinating structure" in one chapter of a study of coordination in the federal system by James L. Sundquist with the collaboration of David W. David; their book is *Making Federalism Work*, Washington, D.C.: The Brookings Institution, 1969.

10

WASHINGTON:
ANGRY CITIZENS AND
AN AMBITIOUS PLAN*

Martha Derthick

The President today requested Secretary Weaver, Administrator Lawson Knott of the General Services Administration, and Walter Tobriner, Chairman of the District of Columbia Board of Commissioners, to "move at once to develop a new community within the Washington city limits."

The new development will be built on the 335-acre site in Northeast Washington formerly occupied by the National Training School for Boys. . . .

"This spacious open tract," the President said, "can become a new, attractive, and well-balanced community at a major gateway to the Nation's Capital. It can provide comfortable and urgently needed housing. . . . But it should be more than a housing project. Washington needs and deserves the best in community planning—and this new development can be the best of communities."

White House News Release, August 30, 1967

*Reprinted by permission from *New Towns In-Town: Why a Federal Program Failed*, by Martha Derthick. Copyright © 1972, The Urban Institute, Washington, D.C. This material includes the Washington case study and the final portion of the concluding chapter of *New Towns In-Town* (pp. 25–40, 93–102).

The President wanted to get off to a fast start in the District of Columbia.[1] This would give the program momentum and show a skeptical public that the government really meant to act. The symbolic purpose of the program—to act for action's sake—had a high priority at the White House, and in any case suited the President's nature. Once seized with an idea for improving his country, he was not a patient man. Effort in the District of Columbia therefore took two forms—constructing "Project One," to consist of 400 housing units on a 20-acre parcel; and planning the "Fort Lincoln New Town," the complex new community, named for a Civil War fort, that would occupy the full site.

Both undertakings came as a test for the District's new government—a mayor-commissioner and nine-man city council—which the President had proposed to Congress early in 1967 to replace a board of three commissioners. That the city government was undergoing reorganization might have been a serious disadvantage except that the reorganization itself was meant to increase the local capacity for action. The White House expected that one executive would be more effective than three. And it expected that the new government, as a creature of the President, would be more responsive to the federal executive branch than the old, which was more the creature of Congress. In the new government as in the old, the President would appoint the leading local officials.

The action plan that federal and local officials prepared for the President called for construction of Project One to begin July 1, 1968, to be completed a year later; the first tenants would move in by May 1, 1969. This project would consist of 250 units of public housing for the elderly and large families, and 120 to 150 units of 221(d)(3) housing. Planning for the rest of the development would be done by June 30, 1968; construction would take 5 to 7 years.

GETTING STARTED WITH PROJECT ONE

Project One soon ran into opposition from neighboring residents, most of whom were middle-class blacks. If the training school site were to be redeveloped at all, they preferred a use that would secure the middle-class character of their neighborhood. In 1965–66 they had objected to a proposal for building a Government Printing Office plant at the site. Now they objected to public housing. In early October 1967, a group of them protested Project One at a public hearing of the District commissioners. Kenneth Kennedy, chairman of the Northeast Neighborhood Planning

[1]For a more detailed description of this case, see Martha Derthick, "Defeat at Fort Lincoln," *The Public Interest*, Summer 1970, pp. 3–39.

Council, demanded that the hearing be postponed until the new city government could conduct it, and then led a walkout.

Local officials responded to opposition with offers of "participation." These offers, however, were not simply a response to citizen action. Thomas Appleby, the executive director of RLA, the urban renewal agency for the District, wanted to achieve citizen participation.

Appleby had frequently affirmed a commitment to citizen participation since coming to the District from New Haven in 1965. As proof of this commitment, in the spring of 1967 RLA agreed to give the Model Inner City Community Organization (MICCO), founded by a black minister and civil rights leader, $200,000 a year to help plan the Shaw urban renewal project in the center of the city. Before neighborhood opposition to Project One arose, but knowing that it was likely, Appleby sought to arrange participation in planning for Fort Lincoln. Among other things, he suggested to other local officials that Kennedy be notified "of all our proposals and plans, inasmuch as he appears to be the leading spokesman in the neighborhood." The appearance of opposition and Kennedy's walkout did not deter Appleby.

After the new mayor, Walter Washington, took office, he too strongly supported citizen participation. The new government, whose sponsors thought of it as a compromise step toward home rule for the District, was generally expected to be more sensitive than its predecessor to citizen opinion, black opinion especially. Mayor Washington and a majority of the council were blacks. Late in November, when the mayor announced receipt of a large ($887,000) survey and planning grant from HUD, he promised "maximum citizen involvement in all phases" of Fort Lincoln's development. At the mayor's invitation, Kennedy sat beside him as he made the announcement.

With this encouragement, Kennedy submitted to local officials a request for funds for the Model Outer City Community Organization (MOCCO), which he had founded as a counterpart to MICCO. Early in December he began to negotiate a contract with local renewal and planning officials. However, before they could reach agreement, RLA got a letter from the president of a community association in the northeast, Jesse Jackson, denying that MOCCO existed and challenging Kennedy's right to speak for the neighborhood. Jackson promptly formed his own imitation of MICCO and submitted a prospectus to RLA. A dispute over citizen participation in the project was beginning to overshadow citizen opposition to it.

Confronted with this new claimant, RLA declined to give a contract to either. It told Kennedy and Jackson that they must resolve their differences. Before long a third citizen group, led by white and black clergymen, arose in the northeast to mediate between them, but when that effort failed, it too applied to RLA for funds and recognition.

By the end of February, then, RLA was confronted with three claimants whereas in November there had been only one. They were unable to settle their differences independently, and Kennedy—who was bitter at the government's failure to recognize him after its initial encouragement— grew hostile and threatening. "You have not kept faith," he wrote Appleby in early February. "The RLA does not wish to involve citizens." And again, 2 weeks later, "Your inaction compels us to no longer request, but to demand meaningful participation."

Both the dispute over citizen participation, which was highly visible and much publicized, and the initial problem of citizen opposition, which was still latent, could hamper the public agencies' work on Project One. For reasons having nothing to do with local politics, however, work was not advancing fast.

At HUD's urging, Appleby in January agreed to use Project One to demonstrate new housing technology. To HUD officials, Project One was the pilot development in the pilot project for a nationwide model communities program. As such it should serve the objective of innovation. Appleby divided the project into three parcels and assigned each to an architect chosen for his work with a new technology. The three were Moshe Safdie, Paul Rudolph, and Harry Weese; respectively, they were working with concrete boxes, mobile home cores, and concrete panels. RLA signed contracts with them in March.

Innovation—HUD's dominant objective—conflicted with speed, which had been the President's. The architects soon encountered problems with building code specifications, and Deputy Mayor Thomas W. Fletcher decided to set up a task force to study changes in the code. It was late May. Construction could not possibly start in July, as the President had been told. Technical and political problems would have to be resolved first.

PLANNING THE NEW TOWN

In January RLA hired Edward J. Logue to take charge of planning the new community. As development administrator in New Haven and Boston, Logue had built a national reputation as an urban expert and man of action. Having recently lost a campaign for mayor of Boston, he was available for the Fort Lincoln project.

As principal development consultant, he was to oversee the work of other specialized consultants (for planning and design, engineering, transportation, etc.), prepare a statement of objectives, set up an advisory panel to help define objectives, review plans for Project One, and prepare a report, in preliminary and final versions, that would cover all aspects of the plan for Fort Lincoln. He would be paid $295,000, of which approximately $235,000 would be for subcontracts to other consultants.

Within the government, responsibility for planning was lodged in a staff committee consisting of the executive director of the National Capital Planning Commission (Charles H. Conrad) as chairman, the deputy mayor of the District (Fletcher), the executive director of RLA (Appleby), and the deputy assistant secretary for renewal assistance of HUD (McCabe), who was added to the committee at HUD's request. Logue was to receive guidance from this committee and report to it. He also had HUD's development standards for guidance.

Logue believed, as did the authors of HUD's development standards, that race and class integration should be the overriding goal. By mid-April, he concluded that this goal could not be achieved with the housing mix described in the President's announcement (1500 public housing units, 2200 units of 221(d)(3) housing, and 800 conventionally financed units). The proportion of the poor, nearly all of whom would be blacks, was too high. It would not be possible to draw middle-income whites to the community; over the long run, middle-income blacks might not stay. The staff committee agreed, but was reluctant to change figures that the President had announced. Only after soliciting Secretary Weaver's approval did it tell Logue he could change the housing mix.

Logue also feared that Project One would jeopardize the entire Fort Lincoln community. With 250 low-income units and 150 moderate-income units, it would contain a disproportion of the poor and give Fort Lincoln an unfavorable reputation. Thus Logue sided with neighborhood residents who wanted to delay construction of Project One, and he also sided with them in asking the local government to build a new school at the same time it built family housing. The advisory panel of experts that Logue set up, most of whom were middle-class blacks, became a sounding board for the neighborhood's complaints about Project One. The panel's report, submitted in June, asked that it be cancelled as a separate project.

Again, the staff committee agreed with the substance of Logue's analysis. Officials in both HUD and RLA feared that Project One would kill any chance of achieving the model balanced community. But again they feared to change a commitment to the President, whose desire for a fast start had produced Project One.

In June the secretary and undersecretary of HUD and the District's mayor and deputy mayor considered how to meet the objections to the project yet keep their promise of prompt action to the White House. They decided that all of Project One might be deferred except for some public housing for the elderly, which would be less offensive to the neighborhood and less damaging to the reputation of Fort Lincoln than would family housing, and would not add a single pupil to the schools. They agreed that work on the housing for the elderly should start the earliest possible moment in order to achieve a groundbreaking before November. They also agreed to build community facilities, especially schools, as promptly as housing.

In mid-July, Logue submitted a report to the staff committee that outlined objectives and a preliminary plan for the entire project. In keeping with HUD's guidance to the staff committee, he limited low-income units to 20% of the total. He recommended a mix of 900 low-income units, half of which would be for elderly; 2250 moderate-income units; and 1350 middle-income units.

Meanwhile, local officials had acted to settle the dispute over citizen participation, which had troubled Logue's planning effort as well as Project One. After repeated pleas for action from Appleby, Mayor Washington in early June set up the Citizens' Planning Council for the Fort Lincoln Project, composed of 15 residents of the northeast (5 from each of the 3 rival groups) and 8 citywide members. Henceforth, public officials hoped, planning could proceed with the cooperation of this organization.

IN PURSUIT OF ACTION

Progress depended on achieving satisfactory designs for Project One, but in late summer, RLA and HUD officials appraised the work of the three architects with discouraging results.

Safdie's design was not feasible and had to be abandoned. Rudolph's design was not feasible either, though it came near enough to justify more work. The principal problem in both cases was cost. The District government was prepared to make building code revisions to accommodate the new technology, but the costs of the technology, at least as applied on the limited scale that Project One permitted, would not come within HUD's limits for public and 221(d)(3) housing. Of the three preliminary designs, only Weese's was feasible.

In addition to this, citizen participation problems recurred. Local officials had hoped that by bringing the rival neighborhood groups together in one organization, they would put an end to delay. This assumed that the new organization would cooperate with the government. In fact the council was extremely hostile. The eight citywide members, who were meant by the mayor to be a moderating and disinterested force, soon tired of the meetings and left them to the neighborhood members. These members, though still plagued by differences of interest, nevertheless had one opinion in common: that RLA had unfairly excluded them from a share in planning.

Before it would consider plans, the council wished to define its power and secure funds. Early in July it delivered to Appleby a list of 17 demands that in essence called on RLA to surrender the planning function to it. Having been invited by local officials to submit a budget request, the council at the end of July asked for $820,000, virtually the entire amount of HUD's survey and planning grant to RLA. And in September, it sued the District government and RLA, asking a federal district court to enjoin planning for Fort Lincoln until local officials permitted "meaningful" citizen participation and developed "adequate plans . . . to protect residents in the affected area."

A groundbreaking before November, which Undersecretary Wood had decreed in June, seemed impossible. As of September there were no finished architects' drawings and only one set was in prospect. The government had created a vehicle for citizen participation, but the citizens had gone to court in an attempt to halt planning altogether. This situation precipitated another round of official decision-making.

The White House was determined to have a groundbreaking. The President and his staff continued to want action for action's sake. Beyond that, both the White House and HUD wished to get far enough along with the new community that another administration could not turn back. After a meeting on September 20 with Califano, Wood set November 25 as the date for a groundbreaking. Construction was to start with 120 units of high-rise public housing for the elderly designed by Weese. To Appleby's relief, Califano had vetoed a tentative suggestion from HUD to transplant finished designs from an urban renewal project elsewhere in the country.

To get the project ready for construction by November would require the public agencies to make extraordinary effort and hard choices. Within HUD, for example, the Housing Assistance Administration had to give approval hastily, on the basis of incomplete plans and uncertain cost estimates. It balked, not wanting to risk "adverse audit findings," but went ahead after eliciting an explicit memorandum of justification from Undersecretary Wood.

The bureaucrats proved willing to bend their rules, but the mayor was unwilling to ignore the citizens' council. He would not go ahead until it had approved Project One, and it was unwilling even to consider the subject. When, on October 14, it finally did begin consideration, it objected that Project One contained too much public housing. By the end of October it was clear that there would be no groundbreaking by December 7 (the latest choice for a date), and maybe none before President Johnson left office.

Clinton wrote Wood on October 30 that "unless the Mayor is instructed by next week to proceed with or without the citizens, this Administration will not have a groundbreaking ceremony."

HUD and the White House pressed the mayor to act. HUD drafted a letter threatening to withdraw funds from Fort Lincoln, and although the letter was not sent, its message reached city hall. Simultaneously, the citizens' council for the first time was showing signs of cooperation. In mid-November it sent Appleby comments on Project One that at least laid a basis for negotiation. The council asked, for example, that the government limit public housing construction to the 120 units for the elderly and that it promise in writing that a new school would be finished before any family housing.

The council had changed its position in response to a change of opinion in the neighborhood, which in turn resulted from the public agencies' offer to build a new school there. In July the District government had decided that it would build a permanent school right away rather than the demountable classrooms to which the neighborhood and Logue had objected. As of early October, the House Appropriations Committee had approved funds and local officials were looking for an architect. In this situation, for the citizens' council to obstruct Project One was to deprive the neighborhood of a benefit to which it attached a very high value.

It was still necessary to get the council to go along with the groundbreaking. To do this, local officials agreed to build a school before family housing, and they reduced to 25 the number of low-income family housing units planned for Project One—which was 25 more than the council wished, but, as Appleby told its president, "the minimum we think is necessary to fulfill our public responsibility." They also sought to reach agreement on the council's funding, which had been at issue since July.

In response to the council's request for $820,000, Appleby had offered $36,500 for a 1-year period. In mid-November he raised this to $60,000. The council, which had reduced its request to $316,000, thereupon appealed to the mayor, who doubled Appleby's offer. For its part, the council acquiesced in a start on construction. Because RLA could not or would not spend as much as Mayor Washington had offered, he had to appeal to HUD for the money. HUD found the funds—a grant of $60,000 for a 6-month period—in its Office of Urban Research and Technology, which administers urban renewal demonstration grants. Fort Lincoln, HUD decided, would be an appropriate place in which to "demonstrate" the citizen participation process.

The groundbreaking finally occurred on January 15, less than a week before the inauguration of President Nixon. More even than most groundbreakings, this was merely a symbolic event. The architect had finished drawings only for the foundation, and construction did not actually start until May 5.

THE LOGUE PLAN

After the Nixon Administration took office, the burden of initiative shifted to the local agencies. Formerly under federal pressure to act, they now had to solicit federal support. This meant that they had to come to grips with the Logue plan. Presumably, they would use it as the basis for grant applications to HUD.

Fort Lincoln, Logue had told the staff committee in July, "must travel 'first class'." In order to achieve the ambitious goals of class and race integration, it must have "an exceptionally high level of public services" and make use of "new approaches in both planning and development." With approval from the staff committee, Logue had proceeded during the fall to elaborate the more ambitious of two preliminary plans. His strategy, which was wholly faithful to HUD's guidelines, was to attract a balanced population to Fort Lincoln with the promise of "community," and he sought to assure community through a series of measures that would both differentiate Fort Lincoln from its environment, the rest of the District, and integrate it internally.

Logue finished the plan in December. Federal and local agencies reviewed it in January and February, and by early March RLA's Fort Lincoln project director, Arnold Mays, had distilled the results of the review for the staff committee. In a series of memoranda, Mays analyzed the problems that had been revealed, some of which seemed very serious.

One problem was economic. To provide a large amount of open space, the plan called for extensive use of structured parking, which would raise the cost of housing development well above what HUD could legally subsidize. Mays concluded that it was "highly unlikely that the plan, as presently proposed, could be developed." The economic dilemma was made worse by the failure of GSA and RLA to agree on a price for the land. In August 1967, when the project was conceived, officials from HUD and RLA had understood that GSA would sell the land for its reuse value, but in the summer of 1968, when RLA began negotiations, GSA asked fair market value. It said then that it had no legal authority to sell at a lower price. According to a GSA official who took part in the initial planning session, HUD had misunderstood what was said—GSA had made no commitment to sell at reuse value.

Another major problem arose from Logue's proposal for transportation. Again in order to obtain open space, he proposed use of a minirail, which would consume less land than a street-and-parking system. But neither the cost nor the technical feasibility of such a system had even been established. In December HUD and the Department of Transportation had agreed to finance more studies of feasibility, but they and RLA had been unable to agree on how to proceed. Besides, more studies could not answer all of the economic, administrative, and technical questions that needed answering.

A third set of questions concerned the schools. Logue had hired as educational consultant Mario Fantini of the Ford Foundation, who had recently helped lead an effort to decentralize New York City's public schools. Along with Milton Young of the Travelers Research Center, he developed "a design for a new and relevant system of education" that Logue incorporated into his plan. In the spring of 1969 the District Board of Education was preparing to sign a $420,000 contract with the General Learning Corporation of New York to elaborate the plan, but Mays was appalled by the vagueness and vacuity of the contract language ("a rehash of the educational mish-mash that has been discussed for months"), and thought the Fantini–Young report inadequate as guidance. He urged the staff committee to develop its own guidelines for the Fort Lincoln school system after consulting with the Board of Education.

Like other elements of the Logue plan, the proposal for education raised serious questions of feasibility. It called for Fort Lincoln's schools to be administered independently of the rest of the city system. The new-town system would consist of a series of "dispersed but interrelated" general learning centers, which would serve as the "home rooms" and fulfill "general academic functions," and special learning centers, which would "provide specialized instruction in the arts, sciences, and practical arts, with an emphasis on 'real life' experience—relating the school curriculum to actual social and economic enterprises on the site." Since this system would cost more than the conventional system in the rest of the city, it would be contrary to a federal district court decision of 1967 (*Hobson v. Hansen*) that prohibited inequality in per-pupil expenditure in the District's public schools.

Because the survey and planning grant from HUD expired on June 30, the staff committee hoped to have a plan ready by then, but the Logue plan posed so many problems that Mays recommended against submitting it to HUD. Instead he urged the staff committee to carry out Fort Lincoln under the newly enacted neighborhood development program (NDP), a course that would—if HUD agreed—enable the District to construct Project One with federal urban renewal funds while continuing to plan the rest of the project. With more time Mays hoped to resolve the problems in the Logue plan. In April, following his recommendation, the NCPC instructed its staff to prepare an NDP plan for submission to HUD.

The local agencies also grappled in the spring with two questions of procedure—how to manage construction of Fort Lincoln, and how to manage the intractable problem of citizen participation, which threatened to make a farce of the whole undertaking.

Logue believed that Fort Lincoln should be developed by a corporation with comprehensive powers, and hired a Washington lawyer to show how this could be done. However, lawyers in the District's public agencies were not convinced. The assistant general counsel of the NCPC wrote that the many contractual and informal agreements required were "legally questionable" and "practically untested"; that there was no legal way to avoid the complex series of approval and review steps involved in a project like Fort Lincoln; that it was doubtful that the corporation could be created without legislation, and legislation would take too much time; and that its financial feasibility had not been demonstrated. The staff committee rejected the development corporation and began in April to explore an alternative—a development agency, to be made up of representatives of existing agencies and endowed by delegation with some of their executive powers and a staff.

After HUD agreed to finance citizen participation with a demonstration grant, RLA opened negotiations with the citizens' council over a contract, but in 2 months had been unable to reach agreement. One issue was HUD's insistence that the council withdraw its suit against the government. Another was a provision that the hiring of personnel have RLA approval. On April 15 the staff committee decided to cease doing business with the council (it had received a petition from northeast residents, including many of the council members' wives, urging it to do so), and began to consider other ways of consulting citizen opinion. With the backing of the mayor, it decided to hold meetings throughout the city at which plans for Fort Lincoln would be presented to civic organizations.

By May the local agencies were ready to take their case to the administration. Though a formal NDP application could not be ready before fall, it was none too soon to seek federal support informally.

THE FEDERAL RESPONSE

The local officials took their plea to the White House and to HUD. In view of the amount and variety of federal support it required, Fort Lincoln was unlikely to survive except as a presidential project. RLA had identified nearly a dozen federal "concerns," matters in which federal agencies must act favorably if Fort Lincoln were to be built. The Departments of Transportation, Interior, and Health, Education, and Welfare were involved, as well as HUD and GSA. In particular, local officials hoped that by getting support from the White House they could put pressure on HUD, the department with primary concern. It would bear $40.4 million of the $51.65 million in federal expenditures that RLA estimated Fort Lincoln would need.

In May and June, local officials made their case, led by Fletcher and Melvin Mister, Appleby's successor as RLA director. (Appleby left when the administrations changed, but Washington and Fletcher, having been reappointed by President Nixon, remained as mayor and deputy mayor.) They briefed HUD officials late in May and then responded to HUD's questions with two long letters that set forth objectives and cost estimates. In mid-June they briefed Daniel P. Moynihan, director of the newly created Urban Affairs Council and President Nixon's advisor on District affairs.

They found HUD skeptical and resistant. HUD officials doubted, as did local agencies, the feasibility of the Logue plan. They lacked confidence in the local government's capacity to execute so ambitious a project, and the longer the citizen participation dispute persisted, the less confidence they had. (An attempt by the mayor's office in June to explain Fort Lincoln to civic organizations was a "disaster," according to an observer from HUD. Leaders of the citizens' council and other black activists broke up the meeting.) Finally, they objected to the cost. In urban renewal funds alone, the District was asking $36.4 million for Fort Lincoln, three times the capital grant reservation that HUD had made in 1967.

The high cost threatened to distort the new administration's priorities, which called for using urban renewal funds to rebuild riot areas—starting in Washington. The Nixon Administration had been in office scarcely more than a week when the President visited the riot areas with Mayor Washington and announced a large grant. Like the Johnson Administration, it was using the capital as a "demonstration city," a place in which to symbolize a commitment to the cure of urban problems.

When the District's request for funds to rebuild the riot areas, which President Nixon had inspired, was combined with its request for Fort Lincoln, which President Johnson had inspired, the total for Fiscal Year 1970 was more than $134 million. That was nearly a sixth of the urban renewal appropriation of $850 million that HUD expected Congress to provide for the whole country. HUD balked.

It sought to avoid commitment to any particular development plan. Especially, it did not want to get committed to the Logue plan, and it tried to forestall action by either local officials or Moynihan's office that would lead to such a commitment. In any case, Moynihan shared HUD's doubts about the District government's administrative capacity. HUD ceased to participate in meetings of the staff committee except as an observer, and it explicitly released local officials from any obligation imposed by the Johnson Administration to go ahead with Project One.

Despite repeated signs of discouragement from HUD, the local agencies continued work on a preliminary plan and an NDP application, a strategy that HUD feared would commit it to the Logue plan or something similar. The NCPC was scheduled to approve a preliminary plan on September 11. On September 30, it got a letter from Undersecretary Richard C. Van Dusen saying that "it would be premature" for HUD to commit funds for Fort Lincoln or encourage a start on development activity. Specifically, it would not grant money for Project One beyond what was needed to finish the 120 units of public housing for the elderly.

HUD had not killed the project. A departmental task force, after several months' review of Fort Lincoln and consideration of various alternatives—including disposition of the land by GSA in the normal way—chose to retain the site for housing. Accordingly, HUD agreed to give the local agencies money for more planning and feasibility studies.

THE FUTURE OF FORT LINCOLN

In the summer of 1970, RLA and HUD agreed to seek a private planner–developer for Fort Lincoln. Unable themselves to resolve the problems of design and finance, they invited a private organization to try, specifying that it must adhere to "the primary objective of . . . a well designed socially, racially, economically, and functionally balanced community."

Following a competition, RLA awarded a contract in November for a feasibility study to the Westinghouse Electric Corporation, in combination with Building Systems International, an industrial housing producer. In effect, Westinghouse was given a license to revise the Logue plan, with a promise of a development contract if its revision satisfied RLA and HUD. Nixon Administration officials in HUD seemed determined to insist on a showing of feasibility, and to avoid a major commitment of public funds until such a showing had been made.

Sooner or later, the Fort Lincoln site will be developed somehow. More than 300 acres of prime land in the nation's capital will not lie vacant forever. But whatever happens there, the Fort Lincoln New Town is not likely to be remembered as an example of "the best in community planning." No doubt, that was what Washington needed and deserved, as President Johnson had said, but it was not what it got.

FEDERAL DISABILITIES: THE CENTRAL
GOVERNMENT AS SOCIAL ACTIVIST*

In summary, the surplus lands program failed both because the federal government had limited influence at the local level and because it set impossibly high objectives. Its goals exceeded by far its capacity to achieve them.

These causes of failure cannot be dismissed as peculiarities of the program. To be sure, it was peculiar in its impulsive origin and improvised character, but it arose because President Johnson and his aides in the White House believed that other federal programs, especially public housing, were failing. It was designed to make them work better. Very probably, its own failure reveals something about them too.

Fundamentally, the program failed because of characteristics of the federal government that are associated with, and to a degree are inherent in, its central position in the governmental system. These characteristics are the scale of its jurisdiction and its separation from the actual execution of domestic programs. Separation, in turn, results from the division of authority among governments in a federal system and the distance between the "top" and the "bottom" level of government hierarchy in a large, complex society.

These characteristics make it hard for federal policymakers to know what must be done to achieve their objectives locally, and for administrators to bring federal resources, however scarce or plentiful, effectively to bear in local settings. The same characteristics largely account also for the federal tendency to set unrealizable objectives. The second point, because it is less obvious, requires more elaboration.

Why, in this case, did the idea of a model balanced community find expression in a federal project? Or, why should a federal project begun as an effort to build housing for the poor turn so quickly into an effort to create a model community? The surplus lands program was but one example of a general phenomenon that requires explanation—the tendency of the federal government to be the innovator in American public policy and the source of ideal definitions of the public good.

The division of authority in the federal system has tended to cast the central government in the role of a reformer of local affairs. The fact that the federal government is formally distinct from local governments, yet can be used to influence their conduct, has generated political and administrative activity at the federal level to bring about local change. The federal

---

*Editors' note: This material is reprinted from Derthick's final chapter entitled "The Limits of Centralization." That chapter follows seven case studies, of which Washington is the first.

government is available as an instrument of local reform for interests that wish to use it in that way. It is an especially tempting instrument because it can be used to bring about local change on a wide scale.

Secondly, separation from local politics and administration gives federal policymakers a license to formulate ideal, innovative objectives, because the political and administrative burdens of the innovations they conceive will be borne locally. They are free, much freer than local officials, to stand publicly for progress and high principle. Not having ordinarily to decide concrete cases, they do not have to make the compromises that such cases require. The farther removed they are from the cases, the more principled they are able to be.

Even had the planners of the surplus lands program been more concerned with accommodating to local realities, they would have found this very difficult. The scale and social heterogeneity of the nation, which was the object of their policymaking, were so great that they could not possibly take detailed account of the variety of local circumstances that the program might encounter. Guidelines would have to be founded on social theories presumed to be universally applicable and embody values that, from the planners' view at least, were universally desirable.

Having the opportunity to express ideal, progressive objectives, federal policy makers tend to believe that they have the duty. Theirs are the obligations of leadership. And, believing that they have the duty to show other governments what ought to be done, federal officials have developed the strategy of the "demonstration," the single project or program that can be put forth as a model for governmental conduct generally. Though the tangible benefits are restricted to a particular locale, if the project is conceived of as a demonstration the intangible benefits of it can be distributed universally: Everyone can share in the symbolic returns from a showing of what the public good requires.

If the federal government did not conceive of its objectives in ideal terms, it could not rely on the demonstration strategy; but the strategy gives further impetus to the striving for the ideal. It might not be possible to build Utopia at Fort Lincoln, but once the federal government became committed to a national demonstration project there, Fort Lincoln's planners could do no less than try. Thus, the strategy of federal conduct as well as the structure of the federal system contributes to the inflation of federal goals.[2]

[2]A full explanation of the federal government's role as reformer and innovator would take account of many other factors, including, for example, its superior revenue-raising capacity, the greater professionalism of its civil service, the activism of its chief executive, and features of its party system. The analysis here emphasizes the one factor that most obviously shapes the federal government's role vis-à-vis local governments—the formal structure of the federal system itself.

If the flaws described here are inherent in the federal government, it may be asked why all federal domestic programs do not fail. How do any survive and achieve their purposes? What distinguished the surplus lands program from those that succeed?

One answer is that the degree of federal dependence on local government varies from one domestic function to another. Community development is extremely dependent on local initiative and thus extremely vulnerable to the vicissitudes of local politics.

The peculiar origins of the surplus lands program did handicap it. More than most federal programs, it was centrally conceived. Not only did it originate exclusively at the federal level, but even within the federal government, it received no consideration from the legislature, where local interests are formally represented. Within the executive branch, federal officials at the regional level did not participate in the planning of it, nor were local officials invited to do so. Those officials in the White House and HUD who did plan it did so in great haste, without themselves making a careful attempt to take local interests into account.

The usual case is characterized by greater representation of local interests. The President's proposal may be inspired by the demands of such interests. In the case of federal aid to education, for example, although the Johnson Administration in 1965 worked out details of a feasible program, locally based school organizations had for years been demanding federal legislation.[3] The typical proposal is submitted to Congress, where local interests again have an opportunity to make their positions known. And the formulation of administrative goals or guidelines is likely to follow consultation with local officials. In these various ways, local interests are more or less systematically taken into account as the federal government formulates a program. No doubt, the trend in federal policymaking is toward greater centralization. Increasingly, federal programs are conceived by the President in his search for campaign issues or legislative program material, and they are planned by his executive office or special task forces and commissions that he has appointed.[4] The surplus lands program illustrates this trend carried to an extreme.

In the usual case, too, federal programs generate their own local

[3]Frank J. Munger and Richard F. Fenno, Jr., *National Politics and Federal Aid to Education,* Syracuse University Press, Syracuse, 1962, and Eugene Eidenberg and Roy D. Morey, *An Act of Congress: The Legislative Process and the Making of Education Policy,* W. W. Norton and Company, New York, 1969.

[4]For example, see Thomas E. Cronin and Sanford D. Greenberg, eds., *The Presidential Advisory System,* Harper & Row, New York, 1969. The origins of the anti-poverty program illustrate the point. See Richard Blumenthal, "The Bureaucracy: Anti-poverty and The Community Action Program," in Allan P. Sindler, ed., *American Political Institutions and Public Policy,* Little, Brown and Company, Boston, 1969.

support by creating organizational allies. When the federal government undertakes a new grant-in-aid program, it specifies that the local government shall designate an agency to receive funds and carry out the program. Such agencies tend to become advocates of the federal purpose at the local level, especially if they are created anew in response to the federal program and have no other function than to execute it.[5] They also become focal points of activity around which local pressure-group supporters of the federal program can rally. The federal antipoverty program, for example, although centrally conceived, created its own local support by requiring the formation of community action agencies. More or less by chance, it also "found" a constituency among upwardly mobile blacks whom the civil rights movement had elevated to new heights of political awareness.

Again, the surplus lands program contrasts with the usual case. The federal government took no formal steps to create local allies: It did not require the formation of "model new communities" agencies or agencies for the development of federal surplus lands. Nor was it fortunate enough to find locally a group with enough political awareness and capacity for organization to promote the program.

Federal programs often "work" at the local level—that is, they survive and make progress toward federal goals—because in the usual case an adjustment between the federal program and local interests is worked out. This is an elaborate process, beginning when a federal legislative proposal is formulated and continuing as it gets enacted and administered. Often it is a very time-consuming process. Some federal programs—urban renewal, for example—start very slowly, and pick up momentum only after the original enactment has been amended many times to make it of use to local interests. Years may pass before the program develops a local constituency whose supporting activity will help it to flourish.

No federal programs succeed totally. In the process of adjustment to local interests, purely "federal" purposes are compromised: Ideals expressed at the federal level are revised to suit local realities. Yet the adaptation is not on the federal government's part alone. Federal action does influence what happens on the local level, with the net result that domestic programs are neither "federal" nor "local," but a blend of the two.

The surplus lands program failed because it was too centralized; it did not incorporate the necessary adjustments to local interests. Perhaps no

[5] For an analysis of the role of the federal "counterpart" agency, see Martha Derthick, *The Influence of Federal Grants: Public Assistance in Massachusetts,* Harvard University Press, Cambridge, Massachusetts, 1970, pp. 202ff. The case of public assistance in Massachusetts, by contrast with the surplus lands program, illustrates the effectiveness of federal influence at the local level.

federal program that seeks to build housing for the poor through the agency of local governments can succeed on a large scale. The federal purpose in this case may be so at odds with the prevailing local interests that no compromise can be worked out that will satisfy the federal purpose very well.[6]

Granting that the surplus lands program suffered from federal disabilities at the local level and from inflated objectives, it might be argued—contrary to the position taken here—that these handicaps are not inherent in federal action. For instance, some might say that the failings were those of the federal chief executive or of a progressive administration. Still others might say that failure occurred not because the program was too centralized, but because it was not centralized enough.

Within the federal government the program was purely presidential, and it suffered from the inability of the President to elicit the necessary support from other elements of the government—Congress and the executive agencies—and then to coordinate them so as to make federal action as effective as possible at the local level. If these other parts of the government had been more responsive to the President's direction (Congress, of course, was not even asked to respond) the program would have had a better chance.

It also suffered from the personality and mode of action of the particular President who started it. Had President Johnson been a more patient and methodical man, the program could have been planned more carefully and would have had a better chance of being founded on workable assumptions. (To be sure, if the President had been a different kind of person, there probably would not have been a program at all.) It seems clear in retrospect that the federal executive agencies initially misled the President as to what they could do, but it is equally clear that the White House invited this error with its demand for instant planning.

Even if the President had been more successful in directing federal action, however, the problems of articulating federal and local action would have remained as a serious handicap. In this case, a distinction between the federal government and the federal chief executive is artificial. He has handicaps of his own within the federal government, but when trying to get something done in the cities he suffers as well, and more fundamentally, from the handicaps of the government he leads.

As an effort to house the poor and, even more, as an effort to build model communities, the program was more likely to have come from a

[6]The failure of the public housing program should not be exaggerated. Though it has fallen far short of goals, since 1937 it has produced 750,000 units. For recent appraisals of housing programs, see the spring 1970 issue of *The Public Interest*.

liberal than a conservative administration. It is arguable that at least one of the disabilities it revealed—the tendency to set ideal, innovative objectives—is characteristic not of federal administrations generally, but only of those that are "progressive." Crudely put, the failure of the surplus lands program was of a kind that could happen only to the Democrats. Other kinds of failure, those that come from doing too little rather than trying to do too much, presumably afflict the Republicans.

The history of the program does not have very much to say on this point, since it deals almost entirely with a Democratic administration, but what it does say suggests that the differences between federal administrations are differences of degree rather than kind. The Nixon Administration, despite its many reservations, did not repudiate Fort Lincoln. Although this was a hastily conceived personal project of a president of the opposite party and although the goals stated for it were of very doubtful feasibility, the Nixon Administration did not say that it would abandon them. Moreover, that it failed fully to commit itself to Fort Lincoln is in part to be accounted for by the fact that it was engaged in a more or less analogous undertaking of its own. Rebuilding the riot areas in Washington, if less "innovative" or "idealistic" than building a model new community, was equally an expression of the federal propensity to undertake symbolic demonstrations in local affairs.[7]

If the federal government is to achieve its domestic aims, perhaps it should pursue them independently, without relying on local governments. If it had centralized the surplus lands program altogether and tried to develop the land itself, it might have accomplished more. Given the present state of constitutional law, there would have been no constitutional barrier to its doing so. There are several reasons why the President and HUD did not take this approach.

The federal government would have had to start afresh as an administrator of community development. The President would have had to ask new authority and appropriations from Congress, and he would have had to enlarge HUD very much or create a new federal administrative agency. Local agencies for community development were already organized, and it seemed faster and cheaper to rely on them than to contrive a means of direct federal action. At least in Washington, where the program was

---

[7]The Nixon Administration did find a politically feasible, even profitable, use for surplus land. Early in 1970 it launched the Legacy of Parks program, intended to transfer federal land to state and local governments for recreation. As of the fall of 1971, 57 tracts totalling 15,400 acres and worth nearly $70 million had been or were about to be conveyed (*Wall Street Journal*, September 13, 1971, p. 32). According to the *Journal*, President Nixon got the idea for the program while strolling along a federally owned beach near the Western White House at San Clemente.

formed, the local redevelopment agency was eager to take the initiative. In summary, direct federal action, even in the national capital, would have been a major departure from the usual way of carrying out community development, requiring a radical revision of custom and existing arrangements.

Relying on local agencies seemed so much the natural thing to do that the federal administration did not make a serious effort to do otherwise. It did consider a compromise form of direct action—bypassing the local government to deal with a private developer—but no such arrangement was concluded. In Clinton Township, MDCDA was technically an agent of the local government. Though HUD's surplus lands project office sought to carry out development in San Antonio without support from the local government, it soon gave up. Within HUD it had encountered resistance from the budget office, which rightly saw the effort as a major departure from existing policy and practice in intergovernmental relations.

Even if direct federal action were practicable, it might not be effective. Obstacles to achievement of federal goals are internal to the federal government as well as external; and if the federal administration grew much bigger and more complex, problems of coordination and control *within* the federal government—which are serious already—would be increased manyfold. Beyond this, as the federal government supplanted local governments in the performance of domestic functions, it would have to assume the political burdens that they now bear and that are often the principal obstacle to accomplishment. Citizen demands that now are addressed to local governments would be addressed to it.[8] If it responded, it would be no more able to act on controversial matters than local governments are. If it did not respond, democracy would be ill served.

Presently the federal government shares most domestic functions with local governments, and in respect to financing and administration, there is an obvious logic to the sharing. The federal government, better able to raise revenue than local governments, helps them with financial aid. Local governments, better organized collectively to execute programs, help the federal government with administration. The "logic," if any, of the sharing of political functions in the federal system is more obscure, but such a logic may exist.

In shared programs, both the federal government and local governments have a political function: both play a part in defining the objectives of public action and in responding to differences of value, interest, and

---

[8]As the Nixon Administration was aware. It considered direct federal action for development of Fort Lincoln, but as one memorandum noted, "HUD would be put in the position of dealing directly with Fort Lincoln citizen participation groups, a precedent which may not be wise."

opinion. The federal government, being removed from particular and parochial conflicts, is better able to express idealistic and progressive objectives. Local governments, more deeply engaged in these conflicts, are better able to respond to the actual preferences of active political interests.

In this system, the accomplishments of government constantly fall short of the objectives expressed at the federal level, and disillusionment follows among both the public and public officials. Such a system may nevertheless be fairly well adapted to the governing of a very large and diverse society—providing, as it does, for the expression both of abstract ideals and of particular, tangible interests. In the process of governing, the two have to be reconciled. Tension between the federal and local governments in the American system may be one sign that such reconciliation is occurring.

IV

TRANSFER PAYMENT PROGRAMS

11

THE IMPLEMENTATION OF SSI: GUARANTEED INCOME OR WELFARE?*

Beryl A. Radin

It is rare to find a commentary concerning the Supplemental Security Income (SSI) program that does not emphasize the "sleeper" quality of the legislation which federalized the adult assistance programs of aid to the aged, blind, and disabled. During the planning and early implementation phases of the program, social welfare planners and practitioners dealt with the substantive as well as administrative nuances of SSI, acknowledging that the minimal congressional debate on the measure did not reflect the magnitude of change which it mandated. An extremely sparse legislative history exists around SSI, reflecting the program's entrapment in the rhetoric of the congressional debate centered around the Family Assistance Plan (FAP). But the thinnest part of that sparse legislative history revolves around questions dealing with the *implementation* of SSI.

To a large extent, the SSI program was sold to some doubtful members of Congress as a program which was amenable to a highly centralized and automated implementation effort. As a nationally administered check-writing process, few agencies could be as well equipped (both in

*Reprinted with permission of the American Public Welfare Association from *Public Welfare*, Fall 1974, Vol. 32, No. 4. Revised by the author.

personnel and in hardware) to handle the job as the Social Security Administration (SSA), the agency given the responsibility for administering the legislation.

Between the passage of the SSI legislation in 1972 and its effective date of implementation in January 1974, the program was amended substantively twice. Because both amendments occurred prior to the date of implementation, they provoked an underlying sense of uncertainty for the implementors. While, as some noted, SSI "may well be considered landmark legislation in the sense that it breaks out of traditional welfare concepts,"[1] it was difficult for members of Congress, committee staff members, agency officials, and those in the attentive public to draw a coherent blueprint for the construction of that landmark. Indeed, although the substantive aspects of the program became more sophisticated and complex through the amending procedures, officials in HEW—especially in the Social Security Administration—approached the conversion date of January 1, 1974 with a number of administrative unknowns.

The implementation strategy for any policy is important. But the implementation effort for SSI involved logistics for the conversion to the unified national Social Security system of some 3.3 million individuals on state or county welfare rolls, governed by more than 1350 governmental units. In addition, more than 3 million other individuals were thought to be potentially eligible for SSI payments. While a sizable number of those newly eligible for SSI were already receiving a small check under one or another of existing Social Security programs,[2] the inclusion of a "welfare" population in its jurisdiction constituted a new responsibility for SSA.

At the same time that the implementation requirements of SSI presented a series of problems due to the scale of the effort, the policy also posed questions involving the overriding style or philosophy of policy implementation. Despite some of the progressive elements in the legislation (such as standardized eligibility, nationally financed and administered systems), in a number of other ways the SSI program did not constitute a radical substantive departure from the pre-January 1 state- or county-administered programs of aid to the aged, blind, and disabled.

The Social Security Administration was thus charged with the implementation of a program that contained a number of ambiguous elements. SSI continued some of the elements of the past state- or county-administered welfare programs; eligibility was dependent on the estab-

---

[1]Martha N. Ozawa, "SSI: Progress or Retreat?", *Public Welfare,* Spring 1974, pp. 33–40.

[2]It has been estimated that approximately 70% of the SSI recipients transferred from the aged categories were already receiving a small SSA payment. According to SSA, more than 90% of those newly eligible for SSI will also be receiving an old age survivors payment.

lishment of individually based need. Unlike the annuity-based programs also administered by SSA,[3] SSI eligibility was established only after a complicated process of verification of need.

At the same time, however, the implementation of SSI was given to an agency that prided itself on an administrative style of predictability, consistency, and minimal exercise of discretion. This administrative style was one which some welfare reform advocates associated with a guaranteed income approach; that is, a matter of fact, nonmanipulative bureaucratic mode that simply certified eligibility and proceeded to make a regular payment. With such an approach, no attempt would be made to exert influence or control over the life style of the recipient—an orientation often associated with the traditional, helping, welfare philosophy.

Although the substantive content of the legislation certainly circumscribes the implementation effort,[4] administrative decisions were taken within SSA and in other parts of HEW that illustrate the problems faced during the process of absorbing a welfare system into a uniform standard formula.

This author has been working with faculty colleagues and graduate students at the LBJ School of Public Affairs on a study of issues related to the early stages of the SSI implementation. Although most of the field work for this study has been located in Texas, the study has been viewed as a microcosmic look at the national implementation effort. The Texas experience has been the porthole through which have been viewed interactions among state welfare agencies, other state service agencies, the regional offices of SRS and Social Security, and national offices of Social Security and other parts of the Department of Health, Education, and Welfare (HEW). This chapter will attempt to describe some aspects of the implementation effort, scrutinizing the activity of a number of actors, analyzing the impact of SSI on other programs, and reviewing some of the administrative problems which affected the policy process.

A Two-Tiered Implementation Strategy

The SSI policy called for the development of a single, consistent, nationally applied standard for eligibility, and a national payment floor; the

[3]Inflation and growing SSA rolls have meant that the annuity contribution basis of the Social Security Fund is already stretched. In a sense, a form of guaranteed income is operating, since the size of individual contributions does not entirely determine the size of the Social Security payment.

[4]See Ozaka; also Gary W. Bickel and David Wilcock, *The Supplemental Security Income Program: Estimated Impact, by State,* Bureau of Social Science Research, Inc., Washington, D.C., January 1974.

implementation of the policy required two quite distinct and separate strategy levels. The first level of implementation involved the *conversion* effort: the tedious and complicated job of converting three million recipients of state and local adult assistance payment programs to the federal program. The second strategy level for SSI involved the establishment of an *ongoing system* within the Social Security Administration that would deal with the policy and integrate it into the agency operations. The first level of implementation had to be in place at the date of the actual conversion since the first checks were sent to recipients on January 1, 1974. The ongoing phase, however, had a less defined time constraint; it reflected the long-term response of the agency to the absorption of SSI into the rest of its activities.

The planning and strategizing for the two phases of implementation provoked separate and often conflicting responses from the agencies and actors involved. The differing response reflected the extent to which an agency was directly involved in the phase, the level of "publicness" of the activity, and—often at a symbolic level—the degree to which an agency or group perceived itself threatened by the SSA action.

SSA IMPLEMENTATION STRATEGY

Until the enactment of SSI, the Social Security Administration had no direct involvement with the administration of the three programs of aid to the aged, blind, and disabled poor.[5] The agency and various staff members had been parties to the welfare reform conversations of the late 1960s as well as to those of the early 1970s. SSA staff were assigned to the welfare reform task force organized during the early years of the Nixon administration, and agency officials were involved in both executive level and legislative policy discussions of federalization of the nation's welfare programs.

During the early stages of the welfare reform debate, SSA put together an internal task force to design a scenario for the administration of a federalized program of assistance to the aged, blind and disabled. The draft proposals that were circulated inside SSA in February 1971 spelled out an implementation scheme that bore a skeletal resemblance to the proposal that actually was put in place several years later. Soon after the proposal was circulated, SSA established an official internal planning effort for the

---

[5]However, the disability program administered by SSA did involve the state rehabilitation agencies; state agencies were responsible, by contract, for disability determination for SSA.

conversion. An Adult Assistance[6] Planning Task Force was made up of staff from established bureaus of the agency, reflecting SSA's view that administration of the adult programs would necessitate an agency-wide effort.

The internal attention to this program and the agency's legislative activity during the same period are evidence of an extremely important posture inside SSA. The agency sought the SSI implementation—top officials of SSA clearly wanted a role in the administration of welfare reform. This desire was not officially supported in the administration's welfare proposals. The Nixon administration's draft bill did establish a minimum income level for the adult categories, but it left the administration of the programs to the states. In the Senate, the powerful Finance Committee originally supported the administration's proposal. On the House side, however, the Ways and Means Committee argued that the state-run program be replaced by a federally financed *and* administered effort in which SSA would have a major role.

When HR 1 emerged from the House and was sent to the Senate including the provision for federal administration of the adult assistance programs, Senate Finance Committee members supported the House version. The argument most convincing to the members was that if the federal government was going to fund fully the program, it should be federally administered. When Nixon signed the legislation, he noted: "This entire program will be fully funded by the Federal Government and efficiently executed with a minimum of paperwork by the Social Security Administration."

Conversion in SSA

Although SSA had anticipated the general contours of the conversion demands before the enactment of SSI in October 1972, the specific requirements of a complex information system could not be set in place as long as the program was in flux. The effect of the two amending processes to the original SSI legislation was that questions dealing with eligibility and payment levels—major issues in the conversion process—were changing up to a few months before the January 1974 date of conversion.

The changing signals posed administrative difficulties for SSA. The development of a new federal information and payment system for more than three million new recipients is a monumental task. But in addition, it was necessary to transmit the changing signals to the 1350 state and local

[6]The original proposals for the federalization of the adult programs were known as the Adult Assistance Programs; the name was later changed to Supplemental Security Income. Some children, however, are included in the program through the disability category.

public welfare units responsible for feeding the conversion information to SSA. The modified stipulations for information transfer from state and county welfare rolls reflected the following provisions that changed the original legislation:

1. States were required to make supplementary payments to all December 1973 recipients who received higher payments under the old state-administered programs, in order to prevent a reduction in income under SSI;

2. SSI recipients transferred from state rolls who had received payments for "essential persons" (individuals in their homes to help care for them) were entitled to increased federal payment amounts;

3. SSI benefits levels were increased effective in January; another increase in SSI payment was enacted payable in July 1974;

4. Only those individuals who had been on the disabled rolls of the state in a month prior to July 1973 were to be automatically transferred to SSI.

Each of these changes affected the development of an information series in the data transfer process and, in some cases, required that state legislatures act to facilitate compliance with the stipulations.

The complications that resulted from the amending process in Congress meant that the timetable which had been devised within SSA for the conversion could not be followed. The entire SSA apparatus, from the level of the commissioner to that of the district office claims representative, was involved in the transfer. Regional office SSA staff spent considerable time working with state and local welfare officials arranging for the staggering job of the transfer of information.

New Relationships

Because SSA had minimal contact with state or county welfare offices prior to the enactment of the SSI program, the agency could not rely on a formal set of relationships with these agencies to facilitate the conversion of the rolls. As a result, SSA devised a new network of contacts; formal contracts were drawn up with 72 state and local public welfare jurisdictions covering the costs of the SSI conversion and outlining shared responsibilities in the changeover. In addition, SSA also developed a formal contractual relationship with the American Public Welfare Association, utilizing the organization's ability to maintain contact with a broad span of public welfare officials.

The frequent shift in policies did not allow SSA to make a dry run of the payment system. The actual issuance of checks in January was the first full scale test of the system. SSA estimates that the error rate was in the range of about 5 to 6%. Most of the errors involved either nonpayment altogether to someone who should have been converted from state or county rolls or payment of an incorrect amount because of errors in picking up information from the individual's record or problems with change of address. SSA estimated that about 60,000 persons reported not receiving a January check. In those cases where the record for an individual was incomplete, the agency decided to err on the side of overpayment for January and, when in doubt, paid the full amount of $140 for an individual and $210 for a couple.

A few of the problems at conversion time received extensive publicity. The most publicized problem occurred at the Social Security district office on 125th Street in New York City when a large group of disabled Vietnam veterans confronted Social Security officials with nonreceipt of checks.[7] The chaos experienced in that district office (as well as district offices in other parts of New York and in California) reflected problems related to the size of the population to be served and, in addition, difficulties which stemmed from the conversion of county-administered welfare programs to the federal rolls.

Despite these problems, most observers of the transfer gave SSA passing marks for the conversion effort. Given the magnitude of the job and the constraints which SSA faced, the federal conversion process developed relatively smoothly. While many bugs in the system continue to plague SSA, to frustrate state welfare departments and state legislatures, and to affect the lives of recipients, there is a general sense that the skeleton of the system is in place and—assuming that the postal service operates—the checks will be delivered regularly.

SSA: Long-term Implications of SSI

Although the conversion represented a monumental demand on the resources of the Social Security Administration, the tasks involved in the transfer were basically of a technical sort and did not depart drastically in style from past SSA experience. The conversion of recipients who formerly received state or county payments was a process of paper and record change; if performed accurately, each recipient would continue to receive a payment no smaller than the one received in the past.

The effects of the conversion and the process of developing administrative and organizational responses to a new clientele, however, represent

[7]See *The New York Times*, Saturday, January 12, 1974, p. 32, editorial, "The Long Line."

a sharp shift in operations for the Social Security Administration. Since its birth in the 1930s, the agency had emphasized the difference between Social Security and welfare. The insurance-annuity argument underlying Social Security had some fiscal limitations, but the fact of worker contributions to the Social Security Trust Fund provided agency leaders with sufficient evidence to justify the belief that through contributions SSA beneficiaries had a *right* to their payments. With SSI, for the first time SSA was faced with the responsibility of developing policies and supportive administrative practices for a needy clientele with a legislative right to benefits toward which they made no contribution. That responsibility included the development of a wide range of new organizational as well as political contacts on behalf of a group of citizens who were peripheral to the mainstream of power in American society.

Despite the reality that about half of the SSI recipients had previous contact with SSA offices (receiving a small Social Security payment under the old age survivor or disability stipulations), reports from some Social Security district offices indicated that the new clientele was greeted with some uneasiness. Some staff members in district offices, according to reports, were uncomfortable with the new client population coming through the doors. The discomfort took a number of forms; some staff—particularly individuals who have been long-time SSA employees—found it personally uncomfortable to deal with individuals who were a part of the category of "those welfare people." Others were uneasy about the ability of the Social Security Administration to respond to the needs of the SSI clientele—that is, individuals with service and counseling needs that are more immediate and intensive than those of many others previously receiving SSA payments. Still others were disturbed about the tendencies within the agency to develop an administrative structure that assumes two classes of citizens—the SSI recipients and the other SSA clientele. Although there was a significant overlap between the two groups of clients, the SSI population did include a number of individuals who had a desperate need not only for cash assistance but also for the full range of other available services and assistance. As such, they did present a new problem for the SSA staff.

While SSA made an attempt to deal with each of these issues, they continued to present problems for the agency. Staff training for the SSI takeover was intensified. Although limited, some recognition was given to the service and counseling needs of the new population through attention to information and referral practices in the district offices. The agency attempted to minimize the two-class recipient problem by establishing a system that rewarded claims representatives and service representatives in the district offices who worked as generalists; that is, representatives who were able to deal with anyone who walked in the district office door regardless of the specific program inquiry. There was little, if any, external manifestation of the difference between an SSI recipient and an SSA claimant in the *formal* day-to-day operations of the district office, although differences have been noted in the *informal* operations.

One of the few aspects of the program that offered evidence of a two-class citizenry in the Social Security clientele was found in the differentiation in color of the check received in the mail. If someone was covered by the old age survivor or disability programs, the check received in the mail was green. If one received payment from SSI, the check was yellow. And, in nearly half the cases, if someone received payments from both programs, two checks were received in the mail—one yellow and one green. Whether or not to issue separate checks provoked a controversy in SSA. According to some officials, the final decision rested on efficiency considerations advanced by the Treasury Department; it was argued that the presence of a separate SSI check allowed faster replacement since it was more easily distinguished from the regular check. However, the communications system did not ask for the color of the check when replacements were requested.

Administrative Structure

The question of separate treatment for the SSI population was also raised in the decisions related to organizational structure in SSA. If SSI were to be absorbed into SSA in a "normal" fashion, a separate bureau dealing with the substantive requirements of the program would be created. Thus a bureau of SSI (BSSI) would take its place in the SSA family, along with a Bureau of Disability Insurance, a Bureau of Retirement and Survivors Insurance, a Bureau of Health Insurance. Staff in such a bureau would be given status to act as the program's specialists and the other operating bureaus would defer to these individuals for the determination of policy for the program. Instructions to the district offices, through entries in the claims manual, would percolate through the SSA structure but would emanate from the SSI bureau. Such a bureau would have staff not only at headquarters in Baltimore, but in the regional offices of SSA around the country.

The formal structural response by SSA to the SSI authority did follow the "normal" pattern. On an organization chart, BSSI did not appear to function differently from the other bureaus. In reality, however, the picture was more complex. When SSA developed its original planning task force for the implementation of the adult programs, the membership of that group was drawn from the ongoing bureaus of the agency, reflecting SSA's view that administration of the program would require an agency-wide effort. Although the official organizational response of SSA to the new program involved the creation of a new bureau, the planning task force for the SSI program did not completely dissolve; it continued to operate both formally and informally during the conversion and after.

On one hand, the continuation of a network reflected SSA's concern that the program be implemented in a forthright fashion and be absorbed as quickly as possible into the regular operations of the agency. But in order to achieve this, the agency leaders used a process that was extraordinary. To some extent, the special process undercut the ability of a separate bureau to develop a program that would become an institutionalized part of the agency. When, for example, a number of problems arose in the implementation of SSI, the strategy of the agency was to appoint in the spring of 1974 a "strike force," operating out of the commissioner's office, to clean up the log jams in the system.[8] The "strike force" operated in the name of an executive level, three-person committee, and had the unusual ability to override line responsibility within the agency. The strike force was later dissolved when a reorganization in the agency placed all operating bureaus under a single Office of Program Operations.

Although it may be too early to evaluate the impact of the special treatment accorded the SSI program on the long-term ability of the program to survive as an equal within SSA, the special considerations do create a sense of uncertainty for staff members within BSSI both in Baltimore and in the regional offices. Any bureau in any agency such as SSA must anticipate natural struggles and competition with other bureaus and offices in the agency. Normal interbureau rivalry includes competition for budget, allocation of staff, training time, as well as natural tension between field operations and policy units. As the newest member of the bureaucratic family, BSSI would enter the allocation struggle with fewer resources, less-defined relationships, and no seniority to use in trade-off negotiations. When the newness combines with the unusual agency-wide activities, it provides a somewhat unstable condition for those charged specifically with SSI policy implementation.

At a symbolic level, at least, the organization questions reflect the larger problem of meshing an income maintenance–welfare program with a contributions or wage-related approach. The agency, for some time, will be faced with a dilemma. Should it develop separate administrative rules for the SSI program, responding to specific and special needs of the SSI

[8]The major attention of the strike force has been given to the simplification of procedures in the eligibility determination process. These procedures include the shortening of turn-around time of cases that are returned to the district office for additional information, and the simplification of the computer system in those areas that are particularly troublesome.

clientele? Or should the agency attempt to minimize any difference in treatment between the SSI population and other SSA recipients, and, as a result, be placed in a possible position of ignoring some needs of the SSI population? The choices become especially important during periods when resources are limited by department and OMB actions.

THE IMPACT OF SSI ON OTHER PARTS OF HEW

Although the Social Security Administration was a strong advocate of the administrative form which SSI eventually took, other parts of HEW were less enthusiastic about the federalized administration of the adult programs by SSA. The welfare reform conversations that developed throughout the administration during Nixon's first term represented a conflict between two opposing forces. One group, most usually represented by White House domestic counselor Daniel Patrick Moynihan, advocated a federalized guaranteed income—a strategy that took legislative shape through the proposals for the Family Assistance Plan (FAP) and the federalized adult programs. The other force represented the viewpoint of a number of Republican governors—most notably California governor Ronald Reagan—who argued that states should be given greater control over their own welfare programs.

While the Moynihan forces initially prevailed, advocates of the state-control position were never completely muted, and their arguments continued to be heard inside HEW. For example, former California welfare director Robert Carleson, who held the formal title of U.S. Commissioner of Welfare during this period but had no line authority over the welfare programs, argued publicly against the SSI program.[9] Others were less willing to attack SSI directly but emphasized the program's problems with implementation, using that experience as evidence for opposition to further federalization of welfare.

The advocates of federalization of the welfare programs also presented diverse views regarding the administration of such an effort inside HEW. Although many in Social and Rehabilitation Services (SRS) were ideologically committed to the movement toward guaranteed income, the emergence of the Social Security Administration on the scene was greeted with mixed responses. For the most part, however, the tension between administrative units within HEW did not surface until the legislation was passed and the struggle for bureaucratic turf became more apparent. As

[9]Carleson presented this argument at a meeting of the 1974 National Conference on Public Administration, Syracuse, N.Y. May 6, 1964, during a panel entitled, "Whither Welfare Reform in Our Time?".

long as FAP was alive, administration leaders (including those in HEW) were more interested in the impact of that program than in the SSI effort.

Conversion in HEW

When the smoke cleared from Congress in October 1972 and as the months progressed toward the date of SSI implementation, it became increasingly apparent to administration officials that the SSI program had a more far-reaching impact than was originally assumed. The Social Security Administration was assigned the responsibility under HR 1 (PL 92–603) for the implementation of the payment system. However, HEW officials began to realize that the conversion of the adult assistance rolls to SSA affected other programs in the Department. Especially affected were SRS agencies: the Medical Services Administration, the Community Services Administration, and the Rehabilitation Services Administration (since moved to the Office of Human Development). As long as the income maintenance programs were also in the jurisdiction of SRS, under the administrative direction of the Assistance Payments Administration, the specification of eligibility and referral mechanisms could come out of the department with some semblance of consistency. With the conversion, new eligibility requirements were developed; not only did these requirements represent a change from past practices in their substantive form, but they also reflected an administrative arrangement in which income provision was severed from service provision.

By March 1973—less than a year before the January 1974 conversion—the Office of the Secretary of HEW began to respond to the broader implications of the new program. A unified strategy for implementation of HR 1 was laid out in a memorandum from the secretary requiring *each* of the agencies in HEW affected by HR 1 to develop their implementation "in a comprehensive, coordinated way."[10] Agencies that had traditionally operated with a strong sense of independence were now being asked to submit their proposals for review. The review process included not only the review of the secretary, but that other agencies—including traditional rivals—be asked to comment on implementation plans.

The memorandum regarding the implementation strategy represented an attempt to "meet people's needs more efficiently with better quality service and with greater cost effectiveness."[11] But the request for coordinated activity was not received in a vacuum. The ongoing power

[10]Memorandum from the Secretary of HEW, Casper Weinberger, to Assistant Secretaries, Agency Heads and Heads of Staff Offices, "HR 1 Implementation," Department of HEW, Office of the Secretary, March 27, 1973.
[11]Ibid.

battles among elements within HEW and between agencies and the Office of the Secretary made the request for a uniform departmental policy tension provoking. The Social Security Administration had viewed itself as a nonpolitical agency, subject to minimal controls over most aspects of its program, which it viewed as technical and specialized. Some within the agency perceived the move by the secretary for coordinated activity as a method of politicizing the work of SSA—that is, expanding the sphere of interests involved in the decisionmaking and, hence, exposing it to a range of pressures otherwise avoided by SSA.

The SRS agencies that were included in the coordinated activity demand responded with a different set of perceptions. For the most part, the proposals for welfare reform had emerged from the administration at a level which bypassed the officials charged with the implementation of the old welfare programs. The Assistance Payments Administration (APA)— the agency most directly involved in the SSI conversion—was also the agency already vulnerable to departmental and administration criticism. If FAP had been enacted, a new administrative agency would have been created to bypass APA; thus, if HR 1 had emerged intact, APA would have been decimated. Two other agencies within SRS were also uneasy with the coordination requests. The Community Services Administration (CSA), charged with the implementation of social service programs, was engaged in a controversy within HEW regarding the extent to which the "feds" would enforce requirements for state-run social services. A similar controversy was underway within HEW regarding the Medicaid program; the Medical Services Administration (MSA) was caught in the middle between pressures from some states for state control of medical services and pressures from SRS and the department for tighter controls.

The drive for coordination that emanated from the Office of the Secretary was closely tied to the movement inside the Department to use a fiscal knife on the HEW budget. Independent bureaus and agencies, supported by intensive and long-term relationships with Congress, were difficult to hold in place long enough for a secretary to wield the knife. Thus the move for coordinated, department-wide activity to implement HR 1, constraining the latitude of the bureaus and agencies to operate independently, could be interpreted as a limitation on their power as well as on their financial independence.

Whether or not agency officials in CSA or MSA welcomed the intrusion of SSA on the scene, the arrival of SSI did require changes in the social service and Medicaid programs. Not only were changes required at a national level of policy establishment, but the shifts in eligibility and referral processes had to be worked out on a state-by-state basis. In most states, before SSI adult assistance programs, Medicaid and social services were under the authority of a single state agency. Eligibility requirements for the programs could be coordinated and a single mechanism devised for the establishment of eligibility for these programs. With SSI, however, a new administrative tier appeared on the scene, and a new set of eligibility standards and referral mechanisms was operating.

This new mixture of agency jurisdiction and program responsibility was not left dangling prior to the SSI conversion. Social Security Administration regional officials and SRS staff were charged with the negotiation of memorandums of understanding with state agencies affected by the SSI implementation, attempting to work out an arrangement that was responsive to the specific needs within each state. The response to this charge varied greatly across the country. In the Dallas region, for example, teams of officials representing the Social Security Administration and the various SRS agencies travelled to each state in the region working out agreements for service referral and eligibility establishment. The balance of responsibilities depended on the specific program affected as well as on the desires of the state. For Medicaid, the department established an incentive for the states to defer to eligibility determination by SSA; if the state wished to provide medicaid coverage to everyone who received SSI, the federal government would supply eligibility information and hence allow the state to save the administrative costs of a separate eligibility determination. Referral mechanisms for social services, however, were included in the memoranda of understanding but were a less formal enterprise. States informed the Social Security regional office and district offices of the availability of specific services for SSI recipients, and attempts were made to devise systematic information and referral practices for SSI recipients. Because the states were given the initiative in these conversations, the response varied greatly across the country.

Long-Term Effects of SSI on HEW

The conversion activities throughout HEW—both in Washington and in the regional offices—indicated that the seemingly simple transfer of three million recipients from state or county rolls to a federal payment system had ramifications that extended far beyond the immediate agencies involved.

The extent of change provoked by SSI in the administrative and organizational relationships around the public welfare policy area remains unclear. A number of unanswered questions revolve around the role of the federal government in the welfare area. One question deals with the posture assumed by the federal government toward the states: Will the federal government (through SSI and any other efforts which flow from it) continue to defer to the states for the determination and administration of services and other programs for the welfare population? (The 1975 Title XX social service program moves in that direction.) Or will the federal posture be prescriptive and, with enforcement of such prescriptions, represent a change from the past grants-in-aid stance of relationships with the states? If the move is toward tighter federal control, it will require a radical departure in administrative style for many SRS national and regional officials. Individuals who have been rewarded for their ability to respond to state-defined needs will be asked to assume a different and quite difficult role.

Although the present administration has tied the prescriptive federal posture to a budget-cutting strategy, the two goals are not intrinsically related. A prescriptive posture could just as easily be used as the method by which service provision is intensified around the country, reaching toward the development of consistent service provision. The present system does allow states with a high level of commitment to provide additional services to recipients through the federal matching formulae. It does not, however, place enforceable demands on those states that take minimal service money but provide less than adequate services.

The relationship between the federal government and the states is of particular importance to the SSI program because of the current uncertainty about the general direction of American welfare policy and the relationship between cash payments and services. While some changes have occurred during the past few years, deference to the states has been the traditional political and organizational framework for welfare policy. With the federalization of SSI, SSI recipients are placed in a policy world where the federal government administers the cash payment while the states provide services. The effect of that shared responsibility on the quality of treatment is unknown.[12] Some critics have argued that the shared responsibility will push SSA closer to the development of a two-class clientele by accentuating the differences between SSI recipients and other SSA recipients through state-controlled variability in service provision. On the other hand, a more consistent and controlled federal posture— including services as well as payments, administered with a commitment to adequate funding and liberalized eligibility requirements—may support the push to link SSI to the rest of the SSA programs, toward a guaranteed-income philosophy.

[12]The impact of the supplementation program, according to some critics, has been to push the program away from a standardized stance (necessary for the guaranteed income posture) to a variable stance (related to welfare).

SSI AND THE STATES

Although some state welfare officials were among the original advocates of the federalization of at least a part of the welfare package, the implementation activities involving SSI have had a mixed reception on the state level. During the early debate on the program, the basic thrust of SSI as a part of a federalization of welfare was supported by many welfare officials because of its financial appeal. Rising welfare costs were distressing for many states; while the major rise in costs had come from the Aid For Dependent Children (AFDC) program, states were looking to the federal government to take over an increased share of the costs of welfare. The federalization of AFDC, as proposed through FAP, would have relieved states of a program that was both costly and politically unpopular; the federalization of the three adult programs, on the other hand, meant that states would lose control over programs that often had political appeal within the state and, as well, had stable or decreasing recipient rolls.

When the original proposals for the federalization of the adult programs were advanced, the states were offered fiscal relief through the federal government's assumption of the costs. At the same time, however, states were left with administrative control over the programs—a situation that allowed the states to maintain visibility in the policy area. This stipulation was particularly important in those states where a heavy political investment had been made in the adult programs, particularly for the aged. The final version of SSI, however, shifted that possibility. Visibility was possible for the states only in two more minor ways: first, through supplementation and second, through the delivery of services.

The original legislation did not require states to supplement ("supplementation" is the term given to the requirement that states with a payment level higher than that to be paid under SSI make up the difference between the payment levels). But the first amending round in July 1973 mandated that such a payment be made. States were required to make that payment only to individuals who had been grandfathered into the SSI program, that is, to individuals who had been receiving state or county payments prior to the SSI conversion. It was still the prerogative of the state to devise an optional supplemental payment, providing newly eligible SSI recipients as well as those grandfathered with additional payments themselves (thus maintaining visibility to the recipients) or of taking advantage of financial incentives offered if they chose to have the federal government administer the payments.

States were also left with responsibility for the delivery of services; Congress did not formally mandate any change in that responsibility. However, at the same time that the SSI program was in the formative implementation stage, other elements of HEW were in flux. This affected the SSI population and the service delivery in several ways. State welfare departments were being squeezed by HEW over social services; the controversy over federally mandated requirements was in full debate during the implementation period. State welfare departments also were anticipating new requirements from the federal government in the Medicaid area; utilization review procedures were being developed to clamp down on expenditures and the professional standards review organization requirements were on the horizon.

The States and Conversion

Uneasiness about the loss of control over aspects of the adult programs was exacerbated during the conversion period. States and SSA had very little contact prior to the enactment of the SSI program, and although attempts to reach out to state and local officials were made during the conversion to maintain communication at all points in the SSA organization, the shifting policies involved with SSI made stable relationships difficult. State welfare departments could not make time and resource allocation plans for the conversion.[13] The changes in the legislative authority were followed by changes in administrative requirements; many of the formal requirements by SSA for the conversion were in a state of flux beyond the date of implementation.

In addition to the administrative uncertainties prior to the conversion, state and county welfare departments found that their local offices became the point of reference for individuals with inquiries or complaints about SSI. Individuals who had no previous contact with Social Security did not seek out information from their local district office; rather, they continued to query the local welfare official for information dealing with questions about the amount of the check or some other detail of the SSI payment system.

Despite these problems, reports from around the country indicate that state and county officials—sometimes somewhat grudgingly—generally admit that the conversion was a success.

Long-Term Effects of SSI on State Policies

The long-run effects of the federalization of the adult programs, however, involve more far reaching ramifications. The style of operation of

[13]See, for example, Sidney E. Bernard, "Implementing the Supplemental Security Income Program: A Michigan Case Study," paper presented at Conference on Policy Implementation in the Human Services, College of Human Development, Pennsylvania State University, June 12–15, 1974.

SSA is quite alien to the procedures and ideology of many welfare departments. The helping philosophy of the social work profession assumes a role quite different from the efficient but friendly, matter-of-fact orientation of the Social Security Administration.[14] And whether or not the level of effectiveness of the two styles is appreciably different, the difference in approach is obvious and, from some reports, appears to distress some state and local welfare officials who argue that SSA is not able to meet the needs of the SSI population.

States also react to the SSI program because of the changes that the program has provoked in the medical area. When a state chooses to allow SSA to establish Medicaid eligibility on the basis of SSI eligibility, it loses control over its medical services expenditures even though it saves money on the administrative costs. In Texas, for example, the Medicaid state expenditures have jumped from about $133 million per year to $190 million; most of that increase comes from the expanded SSI coverage. This situation puts SSA in an uncomfortable position; serious and thorough outreach programs to find potentially eligible SSI recipients will cost the state money. Federal action creates state costs.

The process of administering the Medicaid program also creates problems for many states. If SSA establishes eligibility for Medicaid on the basis of SSI eligibility, states are dependent on SSA for the lists of those eligible. These lists provide the basis for the state issuance of Medicaid cards. The system of communication for this process is called SDX—the state data exchange. Theoretically, the state gets the information from SSA on these tapes and then proceeds with its own programs. Despite the preplanning of the system by SSA, SDX has been full of problems. The system has not remitted tapes on a regular basis, and states have felt that their control over the system is ineffectual.

Supplementation requirements also have established a new set of ground rules for state programs. The current structure of the supplementation program does not create any incentive for low-paying welfare states to make supplemental payments above the SSI level. But in those states where supplementation is required, a state agency must determine whether it is politically feasible to administer a two-tiered program: higher payments for grandfathered individuals and smaller, if any, supplementation for newly eligible individuals. Political ground rules for AFDC may also be affected by the development of SSI. Over the years in Texas, for example, according to state officials, the state, operating under a constitutionally established welfare ceiling, had underbudgeted for AFDC and over-

---

[14]An interesting discussion of this issue is found in Murray Edelman, *The Political Language of the Helping Professions*, Discussion Paper, Institute for Research on Poverty, The University of Wisconsin, Madison, February 1974.

budgeted for the adult categories. This process was established to protect the already low AFDC payment level from further legislative cuts. As the year progressed, within legal authority, the funds were transferred from one category to another. With the federalization of the adult categories, the welfare department will have to confront the actual expenditure under AFDC.

SSI implementation also coincided with a new examination of the social service programs provided by states. Some states provide few services for adult citizens, and some individuals are questioning the eligibility criteria underlying services for adults. If the adult population under SSI is not administratively distinguishable from other individuals served by SSA, should services be provided for only a part of the SSA population? And, if so, what is the state role in the service provision?

If the ideological characterization of SSI moves toward a noncategorical, more universal posture, the state role in the ancillary areas—especially involving services—may be eroded. This erosion may affect only programs that are based on categorical definitions of eligibility, that is, predicated upon an income or status definition of a client population.

The Political Overlay

Although a number of problems and tensions involved with the SSI implementation were intrinsic to the effort, there were other problems which resulted from the political climate of the early 1970s. The fiscal knife wielded by the Nixon administration was also a political weapon, aimed at the agencies and bureaus within HEW in which a heavy concentration of Democrats could be found. Informed observers have viewed the removal of Robert Ball, long-time head of Social Security, as a result of political pressure.

The period of planning for SSI coincided with these attacks.[15] Negotiations about SSI policy as well as requests for staff and financial resources for the implementation could not be separated from the political overlay. Several policy questions illustrate this problem. Staffing questions, for one, reflected the political climate. In the past, SSA had a strong tradition of promoting from within; new programs usually were absorbed into the ongoing operations through the appointment of top administrators from other parts of the agency. In the case of the Bureau of Supplemental Security Income, however, both of the two top officials came from outside the agency. While both of these individuals had prior related experience, in

[15] By the time of the conversion, however, some of the uncertainty was resolved and the agency had a new Commissioner, Bruce Cardwell, former Comptroller of HEW.

the context of internal SSA politics, the nontraditional appointment route did appear to work against the development of a strong bureau.

The flow of information and policy development also illustrates the effect of the political overlay on the program. Substantive policy changes and, more importantly, delay resulted from the negotiations that took place between the Social Security Administration in Baltimore and the Secretary's office in Washington. One example of those difficulties related to outreach. Almost a year before the January 1, 1974 federalization, officials in SSA wanted to embark on an outreach/public information campaign, aimed at contacting the individuals who were potentially eligible for SSI but were not on the state rolls. The plan was vetoed by the secretary, and a very small public relations campaign for outreach was devised. That program was of minimal effectiveness[16] and, during the summer of 1974, the original plan was revived. System-wide staffing limits and freezes, imposed across the federal agencies by OMB, also created problems for SSA as it attempted to gear up for the new program.

Because of the intensive political cast given to the program, the implementation efforts within SSA were not devised with a fallback strategy, which would operate if problems arose with the first-line system. As one Social Security official noted, the entire implementation effort was constructed as if waste or error would not occur at any point in the system. When that system broke down—as it did in the operation of the SDX and in the underestimation of the walk-in volume in District Offices—SSA did not have the resources to bring in to meet the emerging difficulties. Although some part of the noncontingency planning can be attributed to bad planning inside SSA, it is hard to overestimate the effect of the political pressures on the agency from the Office of the Secretary or from the Office of Management and Budgeting.

The Future of SSI

The implementation of the SSI program is an ongoing process. The continual change which characterized the program before it was officially implemented on January 1, 1974 continues. Debates are heard in Congress over the relationship of the food stamps program to SSI, payment levels, and the future of supplementation. Reports from around the country evaluating the implementation are extremely varied. Some observers have noted that the SSI program has brought increased payments to individuals and, as well, respectful and nonpunitive treatment in Social Security Dis-

---

[16]The estimates of new recipients of SSI were generally inflated; it is not known whether the estimates are incorrect or the outreach visibility was so low as to miss the potentially eligible.

trict Offices. Others, such as the New York State Assembly Committee on Social Services, argue that recipients must now contend with "the frequently insensitive attitudes of two bureaucracies"—the state or local welfare department as well as the SSA.[17]

The variation in perceptions of success or failure may be attributed to a number of issues: (1) While SSA is a national, unified organization, discretion is delegated to regional offices and district offices for a number of areas. Some of these discretionary policy areas appear to have affected the SSI implementation and set the scene for variation; (2) Although SSA did carve out a new set of relationships with state agencies during the SSI implementation planning phase, the agency could not drastically depart from past relationships between other parts of HEW and the state agencies. The quality of these past relationships varied greatly across the country; (3) The pre-SSI level of payments within a state may have affected the perception of success or failure of SSI. Recipients in a state like New York may have been more likely to feel that they *might* lose benefits and services under SSI since the levels prior to the conversion were high. In a state like Texas, on the other hand, many recipients immediately benefited from the conversion.

The first year of the SSI implementation tended to focus on the variations and complications implicit in the conversion. The original intent of the legislation—the development of a "clean system" of payments—has often been obscured in the morass of conversion. The complexities of a national income maintenance program are much clearer to policy planners in both the Congress and in the administration as a result of the first year of SSI implementation.

While it is too early to make a total assessment of the success or failure of SSI, it is not too early to recognize that this program raised many more questions than were originally envisioned. As policies related to welfare and income maintenance are debated during the coming years, a number of problems are more sharply focused as a result of the SSI efforts. Among them are:

1. Responsiveness to individual needs (whether determined by a case worker, a county welfare agency or a state welfare agency) constitutes a philosophical break from "clean" programs that emphasize predictability and uniformity. Thus the question of supplementation policy becomes more and more crucial.

2. Determination of levels of payment is very complex. Not only must the determination decision contend with variations in cost of living

[17]See *The New York Times*, Sunday, August 11, 1974, "Supplemental Aid to Poor Assailed," p. 53.

across the country and general cost of living problems, it must also be sensitive to the relationships between SSI (or other future programs) and other SSA payments. When the average SSA payment is $175 and is based on worker contributions, a $166 SSI payment, made without contributions, is difficult to justify in the political world.

3. Finally, although the movement of the past decade has been toward the separation of cash payments and services, the SSI experience has indicated that the two cannot be totally divorced from one another. As long as payment levels are at a subsistence level, planners must deal with the interrelationships and interdependencies between cash payments and services. Food stamps and medical service provision are of particular importance in this area. In addition, a definition of social services becomes more essential for future policy planning.

Before the implementation of SSI, the divisions between policies called "guaranteed income" and those called "welfare" were viewed as rather straightforward differences. As a result of SSI, however, those differences are much more difficult to determine, and the question—"The Implementation of SSI: Guaranteed Income or Welfare?"—is currently not answerable.

V

IMPLEMENTATION ANALYSIS
AND ASSESSMENT EFFORTS

12

IMPLEMENTATION ANALYSIS
AND ASSESSMENT*

Walter Williams

The underlying theme of this book is that the lack of concern for implementation is currently *the* crucial impediment to improving complex operating programs, policy analysis, and experimentation in social policy areas. The preceding chapters have given sharp dimension to key elements of this theme. Several have explored the politics of implementation, showing the almost overwhelming complexity that arises from an implementation effort involving many actors at several different layers of government. Moreover, they have shown how political and bureaucratic factors interact with technique, often making it difficult to apply current methods and producing problems that our techniques cannot begin to handle.

*The chapter is revised from an earlier paper of the same title that appeared in *Policy Analysis*, Volume 1, No. 3, pp. 531–566 (Copyright by The Regents of the University of California), and the portions used from the earlier work are included with the permission of The Regents of the University of California. Work on the paper was supported by a grant from the National Science Foundation. A number of individuals commented on earlier drafts: Richard Elmore, Lucille Fuller, Eleanor Holmes, Laura Kemp, and Jeanette Veasey, all at the time at the University of Washington; Robert Levine, Congressional Budget Office, and Arnold J. Meltsner, University of California, Berkeley. The author, however, is solely responsible for the views expressed.

Nothing comes across more strongly than the great naiveté about implementation. We must learn that the implementation period for complex social programs is not a brief interlude between a bright idea and opening the door for service. Thus, because implementation was viewed that way in the performance-contracting experiment, we still do not know whether performance contracting in education will or will not work. What we do know is that haste and a simplistic belief in the forces of the market are not compatible with a true test of the idea. Another point that emerges so strikingly from the volume is the requirement for some specificity in the treatment packages to be implemented. For example, we need more than just a catchy title reflecting a few hunches about how to educate disadvantaged children. And even where program details are put down on paper, the translation into useful field concepts often demands long, hard work.

The recent experience with experimental efforts puts into sharp focus the same implementation problems of politics and bureaucracy, timing and specification, that plague the regular programmatic activities of social agencies. However, the problems for the agency are even more complicated, embedded as they are in the many layers of an organizational hierarchy. This chapter looks at implementation primarily in the context of a large social agency and through the eyes of a policy analyst. My introductory chapter pointed out that the major problem for policy analysis is not in developing relatively sound policy alternatives but in failing to consider the feasibility of implementing these alternatives. The aims of this chapter are to provide a framework for investigating what the policy analyst must do to treat implementation issues more effectively, and then to develop some ideas about moving in that desired direction.

Figure 1 provides a basis for considering more fully the scope of this chapter. Someone else, for expository purposes, might well have fewer or more stages than those depicted; however, the six stages shown do characterize what ought to occur when major social policy decisions are made or when a large and complex social experiment is undertaken. In either the policy or experimentation process there should be movement from speculation to a more orderly formulation of ideas, and then to some decision on what to do. Implementation, the stage between a decision and operations, starts with the development of program guidelines or design specifications; moves to what may be a quite lengthy stage of trying to work through a myriad of technical, administrative, staff, and institutional problems that confront a new activity; and ends when the experiment is deemed ready to test or when the nonexperimental activity is judged fully operational. At some point an assessment of the effectiveness of the operation may provide information that will start the process again.

	DECISION-MAKING			IMPLEMENTATION		OPERATIONS
POLICY	Search for information and theory; formulation of policy ideas	Development of policy alternatives	Policy decisions	Policy specification	Field implementation	Operations
	1	2	3	4	5	6
EXPERIMENT	Search for information and theory; theorizing	Development of alternative hypotheses	Decisions on experimental hypotheses	Experimental design and specification	Field implementation	Operations
		Implementation analysis		Specification assessment	Intermediate and final implementation assessment	Outcome assessment

Figure 1. Stages and analytic assessment activities in the policy and experimentation processes.

Of particular importance are the analytic and assessment activities shown at the bottom of panels 2, 4, and 5 in Figure 1:

Implementation Analysis: Scrutiny of (1) the preliminary policy specifications, to determine their clarity, precision, and reasonableness; and (2) staff, organizational, and managerial capabilities and implementation strategies, to determine the degree to which the proposed policy alternative can be specified and implemented in its bureaucratic/political setting.

Specification Assessment: Assessment of the final policy or design specifications and measurement procedures, including interim feedback devices, to ascertain the degree to which the specifications correspond to decisions, are amenable to successful implementation, and are measurable.

Intermediate Implementation Assessment: Assessment of the degree to which a field activity is moving toward successful implementation and is providing useful feedback information to improve the implementation effort.

Final Implementation Assessment: Assessment of (1) the degree to which a field activity corresponds to the design specifications, and (2) the level of bureaucratic/political functioning, to determine whether or not there is a valid basis for testing a theory or for deeming a field activity fully operational.

Timing is crucial in these activities. Thus, if implementation analysis is to have any value, it must be performed *before* a decision is made, and its results must be available at the same time that the policy or experimental recommendations are. Surely policymakers at the time of choice ought to have reasonable estimates of the organizational capacity to carry out alternative proposals. But however obvious that may be, few people have ever thought in terms of analyzing implementation during the decision-making stages!

Experience shows that the field implementation period (stage 5 in Figure 1) often stretches over several years, only to end in failure. Hence, early assessment can be critical. At the end of stage 4, even before the effort is made to move into the field, there should be a specification assessment to determine whether the final design corresponds to the decisions reached at the end of stage 3, provides sufficient program information and operational detail, and is amenable to measurement. Why is such an obviously necessary determination almost never made? Mainly because different organizational levels in an agency are responsible for a decision and its specification, and their efforts are not coordinated. Poor or improper specification is only discovered at the gloomy point of blaming someone for the failure or rationalizing it.

Before any program or project is deemed operational and its outcome ready to assess, there should be some opportunity to work out initial kinks and to make some adjustments for problems that could not be foreseen on the drawing board. But how much time should be taken for this? How long can one wait before getting an idea off the ground—or before deciding that it is never going to get off the ground? If a great deal of time is involved, intermediate implementation measures must be taken in stage 5 to provide feedback information for improvement or for an early decision either that the project will never become operational or that, even if it does, it looks in practice like a bad idea. At some later point, for the project that does get the go-ahead, there should be a final assessment to determine that the policy or experiment is actually in place and ready to move into operations and toward outcome assessment.

But a word of caution: The orderliness of the stages in Figure 1 and the rigor of the definitions are heuristic devices used to facilitate exposition. Implementation is too complicated, and too little is known about it to expect either orderliness or rigor when analysis and assessment are actually undertaken. Indeed, the study of implementation carries us into social science's weakest area—dynamics. The determination of whether or not a social program or policy can be implemented cannot be based on a static checklist. Rather, it must involve an analysis of whether technical, bureaucratic, staff, and institutional/political elements can be blended into a viable process. Implementation analysis must ask whether the organization can do what is desired in technical terms, whether it can function well in a bureaucratic sense (which involves micro-organizational issues), and whether it can operate successfully in its larger environment (macro-organizational/political issues). Questions of this type push into relatively uncharted research terrain. As Levine has observed, "much (probably most) public policy will continue to be carried out by public bureaucracies, and the manipulation of such bureaucracies is a vast unexplored area, resembling the continent of Africa during mid-nineteenth century."[1]

It would be nice if this paper could lay out strategies for analyzing and assessing implementation, not in the abstract but in terms of specific instruments and techniques that could now be applied with reasonable rigor; and it would be equally nice to be able to spell out the precise kinds of technical skills needed to carry out these strategies, and to pinpoint the organizational mechanisms that would be likely to move a decision effectively through the bureaucratic/political environment. Alas, this paper will be long on issues, short on solutions. Moreover, the implementation questions are so complex and subtle that one hardly knows where to begin; or, perhaps more accurately, one feels the need to do the impossible task of starting simultaneously down several paths.

[1]Robert A. Levine, *Public Planning: Failure and Redirection,* New York: Basic Books, 1972, p. 192.

All this makes organization of the paper difficult, but we must start somewhere and proceed in some sort of orderly sequence. The first section that follows considers briefly some key terms and distinctions and then discusses four overlapping sets of issues that cut across later discussion—the issues of (1) theory, specification, and implementation; (2) programmatic objectives; (3) detailed packaging of programs versus broad directional guides; and (4) implementation success. The next section provides an overview of techniques and strategies for the analysis and assessment of implementation. The focus is on broad approaches that might be taken rather than on a detailed critique of existing methodologies or strategies. After that, there is a consideration of past research on implementation and the potential contributions that several scholarly disciplines might make. Finally, a brief section presents some concluding observations.

Given the complexity of implementation and the paucity of knowledge about it, it is clear that we will not be able to solve most of the problems set forth in this paper at the present time. But surely we can move to more desirable ground, somewhere between ignoring implementation completely and achieving a level of sophistication that would permit us to treat most contingencies in a reasonable way. At the very least, simply recognizing the need to do something about the problem will have a salutary effect. In my previous experience with social programs for the disadvantaged, I have often wondered whether the programs would have been started quite differently, or in some cases not started at all, had there been systematic efforts by reasonable people to judge the capacity for implementation by considering the organization, techniques, and people in the field, as well as the strategy for implementation or lack thereof. The weaknesses were often so obvious, had people only taken a look and asked a few simple questions. The first need in implementation is not for disciplinary giants to make breakthroughs in dynamic social theory, but for sensible persons with knowledge of program areas to ask if the people in the field really can do what is being proposed. We do have techniques for detecting gross defects in the implementation process, and this should be kept in mind as we struggle with the extraordinarily complex issues discussed below.

KEY TERMS AND CROSSCUTTING ISSUES

Some Key Terms and Distinctions

Differences in the way some common words like "project," "program," and "inputs" are used necessitate a discussion of key terms. The usual distinction between a "program" and a "project" is that a project is a single operating activity while a program comprises many such activities bearing the same general title. For example, there may be a national Head Start program, a Head Start program in the city of Chicago, and many individual Head Start projects in these programs.

The term "input" is employed in this paper to describe an element or characteristic of a program, or of a project, or of the treatment package(s) that comprise a project or program. Inputs may include both nonhuman elements (such as a new reading curriculum's text and test material and scheduling routine) and the human elements involved in their use (e.g., reading specialists and teacher's aides). The term "output" is used to describe organizational change deriving from changes in inputs or other factors. Organizational change may be physical (for example, the rearranging of a classroom) or behavioral (less lecturing by the teacher). The term "outcome" describes change in the status and/or behavior of participants in a program or project. Outputs speak to the issue of whether or not an organization is doing things differently; outcomes have to do with whether or not participants are better off.[2]

Implementation has to do with inputs and outputs. Inputs are basically static; outputs are more dynamic. In trying to determine whether or not an innovation has been implemented successfully, it makes sense to have a checklist that asks whether the project has certain specified elements. However, a far more important task is to determine whether or not implementation has taken place by assessing the degree of correspondence between expected and actual outputs.

Beyond drawing a sharp distinction between a decision and its implementation, as is done in Figure 1, it is useful in discussing policymaking in a complex organization to distinguish between decisionmakers and implementors. At the top of a federal agency there will be a group concerned mainly with major policy decisions, while at lower levels there will be others concerned mainly with putting programs in place. However, decisionmaking and implementation each involve a series of points at which decisions must be made and subsequently implemented.

It also will be true that, from different organizational perspectives, an actor may be viewed by some as primarily a decisionmaker and by others as primarily an implementor. An agency head will consider a bureau head responsible for implementing agency decisions. However, organizations in the field that are funded by the bureau will see the bureau generally and the

---

[2]A word of caution against becoming overly concerned with these definitions: I recognize that a discussion of terms is likely to be disruptive to the reader who disagrees with my definitions, but that a lack of discussion may mislead the reader who is unsure of my usage. So the discussion should be viewed as a means of laying out some ground rules about the jargon in an emerging area where terminology is still likely to be a problem.

bureau head in particular as a key decisionmaker. These distinctions fit well with our commonsense image of the world, since we are talking about the quite general phenomenon of somebody deciding something and that something having to be carried out. When the situation involves a decisionmaker and an implementor who are different persons or organizations, a *series* of decisions are likely to be made and implemented before the primary decision becomes implemented or fails to become implemented. Moreover, in the process of implementation it will almost always be necessary for the implementors to make decisions that may modify the primary decision and other decisions. In essence, there will be a number of decisionmakers and implementors all along the way on a major decision/implementation path. Again, this notion is quite straightforward. Problems arise not in trying to appreciate it in some abstract conceptual way but in following the many trails that repeated decision/implementation points may produce.

Crosscutting Concepts and Issues

Theory, Specification, and Implementation

Any new program or project may be thought of as representing a theory or hypothesis in that—to use experimental terminology—the decisionmaker wants to put in place a treatment expected to *cause* certain predicted effects or outcomes. If the program or project is unsuccessful, the explanation may be that it "did not activate the 'causal process' that would have culminated in the intended goals (this is a failure of program), or it may have set the presumed 'causal process' in motion but the process did not 'cause' the desired effects (this is a failure of theory)."[3] That is, it is useful to distinguish between an idea that was put in place properly and did not work and an idea that was not tested because it was not actually implemented properly. However, whether the program was implemented can become an almost meaningless, or at least unmeasurable, notion when the underlying theory is little more than a catchy label with a few hunches attached. Besides looking out for theory and implementation failure, then, it is important to recognize the possibility of specification failure.

The concept of specification is quite broad. Specification may include what is to be done (the elements of the treatment), how it is to be done (guides for implementation and operation), what organizational changes (outputs) are expected, and what the specific, measurable objectives are. It

[3]Carol H. Weiss, *Evaluation Research*, Englewood Cliffs, N.J., Prentice Hall, Inc., 1972, p. 38.

is the key link between a theory and its implementation. In the policy process, specification determines whether a decision with imprecise operational language can be translated into a set of useful guidelines for action in the field.

Program Objectives

At the core of policy planning and policy analysis has been the notion that program objectives can be clearly defined in measurable terms, accepted by the various parties involved, and distinguished from input and environmental factors. But what we are finding over and over again is that program objectives are often so illusive as to be difficult to determine at all, much less define rigorously. Moreover, as we move from broad objectives that are subject to many interpretations to rigorous ones that are not, the likelihood of disagreement rapidly increases. For example, few would disagree with the goals of a program "intended to enhance learning and improve life opportunities," but this is hardly true of objectives defined in terms of cognitive increments measured by specific standardized educational tests.

The tentativeness of program objectives and their potential interrelationship with inputs and environmental factors is gaining currency in recent discussions.[4] The points are well made by John Pincus in discussing educational research and development (R&D) policy:

> *If* [educational] *goals are in some sense undefinable, it is inappropriate to adopt the standard rationalist approach of first defining goals, then seeking means appropriate to achieve them efficiently. Instead, R&D strategy should be based at least in part on the converse approach.* If the present situation is unsatisfactory, then it may be wiser to try out systematic innovations and assess their consequences than to continue to pursue uncertain goals with unclear technologies.[5]

Separating objectives under actual field conditions from inputs and environmental factors is difficult. It is not that inputs, outputs, and outcomes cannot be distinguished conceptually, but that in the field the subtle interplay and feedback among inputs, the institutional environment, partial outputs, and partial outcomes are so complicated that they are likely to

[4]For an important early discussion, see Robert S. Weiss and Martin Rein, "The Evaluation of Broad-Aim Programs: A Cautionary Case and a Moral," *Annals of the American Academy of Political and Social Science*, September 1969, pp. 133–42. A useful paper in thinking about program goals and with an extensive bibliography is Irwin Deutscher's "Toward Avoiding the Goal-Trap in Evaluation Research," mimeographed, Department of Sociology, Case Western Reserve University, May 1974.

[5]John Pincus, "Incentives for Innovation in the Public Schools," this volume, p. 60.

defy our ability to separate out independent effects. Hence, the path to developing more meaningful outcome measurement is through the study of inputs and outputs. Moreover, it is likely that the conceptualization of outcomes will change as we gain a better understanding of the subtle interrelationships among outcomes, program inputs, and the institutional/political environment.

Detailed Packaging of Programs versus Broad Directional Guides

Thus far, at least implicitly, I have cast implementation in terms of a specific treatment package—for example, a new classroom approach—that must move down a process from decision to field operations with a number of people in different layers of an organization or in different organizations becoming involved. In this case the success of implementation depends heavily both on the clarity and specificity of the package and on the capability of the people taking part in the implementation process. Here detailed instructions and a firm guiding hand throughout could be needed.

But there have been difficulties with the detailed-package, guiding-hand approach, and Robert Levine draws upon them to advance an alternative. He observes that

> we are forced willy-nilly to look for broad-brush programs, self-applied and incentive-guided, as exemplified by the market systems. . . .[6]

> . . . the contention here is that we need a new sort of planning. Rather than selecting desirable future states and laying out courses over deceptive terrain, both policy-making and policy planning should be directional. That is, policy-makers should decide what general sort of future would be better than an alternative, and policy planners should lay out steps that show a probability of moving in that general direction.[7]

The driving forces that will move people toward the broad directional goals set out by policymakers are competition, incentives, and self-interest—the forces of the marketplace, Adam Smith's unseen hand.

At their extremes the detailed-package, guiding-hand approach and the broad-direction, unseen-hand alternative seem to be 180 degrees apart. Yet these two approaches are much more similar than they appear: Assume, for purposes of exposition, a hierarchical organization such as a social agency. First, under both approaches decisionmakers at the top of the organization will determine objectives and expect these objectives to be accomplished through the operation of some entity, such as a local school, that is not necessarily a part of their organization. Second,

[6]Levine, *Public Planning*, p. 135.
[7]*Ibid.*, pp. 164–65.

under both approaches higher echelons (such as policy planners) will seek means of moving the operators toward the desired objectives. Third, the two approaches do not necessarily differ in terms of the *final* specificity of the treatment package at the point of delivery—both may lead to individual projects of equally detailed specification.[8] What distinguishes one approach from the other are (1) the mechanics of determining the treatment and its degree of specificity, and (2) the bureaucratic levels at which decisions about specification are made.

The similarities become more striking with an examination of common problems. If the directional guides are so broad and nebulous that wide agreement is achieved simply because of their vagueness, we have the usual problems of poorly articulated goals, and it is hard to see how incentives would work. If the goals are more specific, the problems of disagreement already discussed are likely to emerge. Further, these broad directions usually will have to pass through a bureaucratic structure, a factor which the incentive mechanism must take into account. Conversely, the more structured approach that has been used in the past has failed in part because it has not faced up to the complex issue of the kinds of incentives needed to motivate lower levels in the desired direction.

A fundamental assumption of the unseen-hand approach drawn from economics is that firms, in their self-interest, will seek and find efficient and effective means of production. The underlying model is one of a relatively homogeneous product for which the production process is well known. The big problem is to determine the appropriate incentives. But when the product is something like improved education or higher reading scores, where the means of production are not known and may be subject to much controversy, incentives may not lead to the desired outcome. The producer simply may not know how to get the desired outcome, as the recent performance-contracting experience indicates so vividly. Even where the strategy calls for giving those in the field wide latitude in reaching a desired future state, it still may make sense to seek detailed packages so that there will be some options to choose from. Again, the overlapping nature of the issues is striking.

Implementation Success

At some point there should be a determination of the degree to which an innovation has been implemented successfully. What should the im-

[8]The Levine quotation's mention of "broad-brush programs" may seem to contradict any notion of detailed specificity. But it is not unusual to find broadly conceived national programs embracing closely detailed projects. For example, while the national Head Start program is cast in terms of general educational objectives for preschool children, the *individual* Head Start projects may involve the detailed development of treatments.

plemented activity be expected to look like in terms of the underlying decision? For a complex treatment package put in different local settings, decisionmakers usually will not expect—or more importantly, *not want*—a precise reproduction of every detail of the package. The objective is performance, not conformance. To enhance the probability of achieving the basic program or policy objectives, the implementation should consist of a realistic development of the underlying decision in terms of the local setting. In the ideal situation, those responsible for implementation would take the basic idea and modify it to meet special local conditions. There should be a reasonable resemblance to the basic idea, as measured by inputs and expected outputs, incorporating the best of the decision and the best of the local ideas.

Learning how to determine whether an implementation has been successful is not enough. We must also be concerned with the factors associated with implementation success and with the likelihood that such success will yield successful outcomes as well. Implementation success can be conceived of as an intermediate stage in a process moving toward improved outcomes. But organizational change—even if specified—does not necessarily bring positive outcomes. Events of the last several years in the social policy areas have made this painfully obvious. What is less obvious is that the factors which are most likely to lead to organizational change may not be the ones most likely to lead to better outcomes. For example, an educational program with broad objectives that says, in effect, "here's some money with which to move forward" may be more likely to produce organizational change than is a tightly specified treatment making the money conditional on numerous stipulations. In the latter case, many prospective innovators may simply reject the offer. Which approach will be more likely to yield positive outcomes is not clear. And certainly in terms of conditional probability, given that significant organizational change has occurred, the more detailed specification may yield a clear winner. At this point, however, what needs to be stressed is that we know little either about the factors leading to implementation success or their relationship to positive outcomes.

Both the detailed-packaging and broad-directional-guide approaches envision an effort to elicit different organizational outputs that will lead to improved outcomes for participants. In its most simplistic form, detailed packaging has stressed the optimum solution, a super-technique for all seasons. *The* single best classroom approach for teaching disadvantaged preschool children can be found. At the other extreme, a focus on broad directional guides seems to imply that all one need to do to get people to find a means for producing positive outcomes for disadvantaged preschool children is to reward them for doing so. The detailed approach stresses the package; the other, the inducements. Both extremes may miss important elements of the truth.

These points are illustrated in an article by Silverman and Weikart that draws on their experience with preschool and regular school children.[9] Weikart had been successful in carrying out a series of carefully planned and executed preschool projects using Piagetian techniques. A later phase of the work compared the Piagetian approach with a Bereiter and Engelmann project and with a traditional approach that might be found in the usual classroom. Much to their surprise, Weikart and his colleagues found that all three approaches produced similar and significant learning gains. They had expected the traditional approach to be much like a control. These results have led them to abandon the notion that there is a single *best* approach and to push their own because they are comfortable with it.

It does now seem wrong to think in terms of a single best solution. At the same time, there is a need to seek methods that work better than those we have. For example, Weikart and his associates have searched for common elements in the several approaches they found successful. Silverman and Weikart observe:

> [We] find that each program had a consistent daily routine so that the children knew what was happening when; each had a strong commitment to its goals and methods on the part of the teaching team; each had paraprofessionals with teaching duties; and each demanded that a portion of the teacher's day be spent in planning and evaluation.[10]

Indeed, if there is a glimmer of hope in their work it is in the suggestion that a concern for details and structure may pay off; in education, such a concern would involve providing an articulated curriculum that lets teacher and pupil know what to do and what is expected, making relevant materials available, providing supervision, and so on.

The key point is that there may well be critical trade-offs between flexibility and conformance to specification. Detailed and inflexible specifications may stifle creativity or rule out an innovation when some elements are incompatible with local conditions. Yet a catchy program label with no concrete details may not be enough. There should be something to build upon and modify. As Weikart and Banet observe "it is difficult to train teachers and supervisors to implement a model that consists only of some basic hunches about good education." Combining elements of both the detailed-packaging and broad-directional-guide approaches—specificity, flexibility, and incentives—may be the preferred implementation strategy.

[9]Charles Silverman and David P. Weikart, "Open Framework: Evolution of a Concept in Pre-School Education," in *High/Scope Foundation Report*, Ypsilanti, Mich., 1973, pp. 14–19.

[10]*Ibid.*, p. 17.

TECHNIQUES OF IMPLEMENTATION ANALYSIS
AND ASSESSMENT

As we start to consider techniques, it is well to keep in mind that implementation is first and foremost a bureaucratic and political problem. Bureaucratic and political factors—not conventional technical or methodological problems per se—represent the main near-term deterrents to more effective implementation. By this I certainly do not mean that powerful techniques exist in the implementation area, but rather that considerably better results could be achieved with our present limited tools if political and bureaucratic factors fostered rather than impeded implementation activities. Further, technical questions often seem almost trivial when compared to such issues as whether or not political jurisdictions will cooperate or whether a teachers' union will be in favor of implementing a new idea. But as will be clear, the technical questions also are difficult and important.

Implementation Analysis

When considering major program innovations, decisionmakers in social agencies should have available ex ante analyses addressing the likelihood that an innovation (1) will produce positive outcomes, (2) will be accepted by higher-level decisionmakers, (3) can be put in place properly with available resources, and (4) will be accepted by those in the field who must either implement or operate the innovation. The first two are (or should be) the principal components of policy analysis; the second two, of implementation analysis. Asking ex ante whether a proposed policy alternative is likely to work has been fundamental to policy analysis. And now central analysts are getting more involved in determining whether the White House and the Congress will accept a new proposal and in developing an agency strategy for selling the idea.

It is important to realize not only that the two aspects of policy analysis are the counterparts of the two components of implementation analysis but also that the basic approaches to each set of questions are similar. Generally speaking, the big need in policy analysis has not been for overpowering techniques but rather for reasonableness, sensitivity, and the ability to order and synthesize diverse pieces of information that often are fragmentary and conflicting. The unfortunate tendency of early advocates of policy analysis to describe it in terms of such esoteric names as systems analysis (and worse) masked the truth that the better practitioners were seldom using much more than simple principles straight out of Paul Samuelson as a framework for formulating their inquiry. Nor in most cases were the analysts working with major research studies specifically performed to shed light on the main questions at issue; rather, they were usually trying to see if scattered research done for other purposes might provide a clue. Frequently the most useful information concerned existing programs and projects—some of it coming from formal reporting systems and some from discussions with people who had observed these activities. Over time, central analytic offices have supported relatively sophisticated research, such as the New Jersey negative income tax experiment, to develop information needed for decisionmaking. But it would be a great mistake not to recognize that the critical requirement in policy analysis continues to be for reasonable people asking sensible questions. The same can be said of implementation analysis. By this I do not mean to imply that implementation analysis is easy but rather that it involves activities which are much more familiar to us than might be thought.

Implementation analysis starts with a consideration of the clarity, precision, comprehensiveness, and reasonableness of the preliminary policy or design specifications. The analyst must ask if the proposal idea, rather than being merely a vaporous wish, addresses reasonable objectives cast in relatively specific terms, and if the treatment package is reasonably well specified. Specifications might include both physical and personnel inputs (equipment, skills) and expected outputs in terms of physical and behavioral changes. Some sketchiness can be expected because the analysis concerns preliminary specifications that will go through additional rounds before reaching a final product. At the same time, it seems that the absence of any concreteness in terms of either objectives or the delivery system should be taken as a clear indicator of grave trouble at the beginning.

Implementation analysis, then, should investigate (1) the technical capacity to implement, (2) political feasibility, and (3) the technical and political strategies for implementation. The question of technical capacity is twofold. First, does the organization have sufficiently developed lines of communication (the means of communicating a decision to the field), a good enough administrative structure, and sufficient numbers of individuals with requisite administrative and technical skills in specific substantive areas to have a reasonable probability of moving the innovation into the field? Second, do the local operating entities have, or can they obtain, the staff skills needed to administer the treatment package? These questions certainly are not easy ones, but simply posing them may uncover such grave deficiencies that either action on the innovation will be postponed or major corrective measures will be seen as required. Much the same may be said for issues of political feasibility. One hardly needs a political crystal ball to know with some certainty that individuals and groups will oppose certain actions.

Just as important as the technical and political problems is the question of whether or not the organization can develop an implementation strategy to overcome potential blockages. For example, an effort to implement an innovation may seem feasible only after extensive efforts are undertaken to train people. It may make sense to try out a new idea on a small scale before making a full commitment to a national program. And even if a national program has already been decided upon, it still might be useful to carry out the implementation in stages, "starting small" to develop information on implementation problems. Alternatively, a special team could be created for the one-time effort to implement a new program. Such a team might be drawn from several different parts of an agency and would be disbanded after the implementation was completed. The team would have responsibility and authority to cut across the many layers involved in the implementation process.[11]

In devising a strategy for surmounting political barriers, scenarios might be developed to look at such factors as the principal actors, their motivations, and their beliefs.[12] Once the nature of the opposition is determined, the problem is to figure out how to get around it or eliminate it. To expect any implementation strategy to yield a surefire means of overcoming technical blockages and political opposition is unrealistic. But it makes little sense not to investigate the various potential blockages and then develop a strategy so that at least the obvious blunders might be avoided. So whether a reasonable strategy exists is a critical final question in implementation analysis.

Implementation Assessment

Implementation assessment seeks to determine the extent to which the actual outputs of an organization have changed in the expected direction after the introduction of an innovation. How can it be determined whether or not the staff in an organization have changed their behavior, the way they interact with others, or their sentiments about the organization,

[11]Businesses sometimes use such an approach, usually labeled project management. A project manager and a small team of experts from various functional areas plan and coordinate a project that cuts across several departments. Once the project is deemed operational, the members of the project management team return to their regular jobs.

[12]See: Arnold J. Meltsner, "Political Feasibility and Policy Analysis," *Public Administration Review*, November/December 1972, pp. 859–66. This article provides a useful summary of approaches to the analysis of political feasibility that are relevant to the following discussion.

other staff, or clients? Apparently it can be done. O'Connell, for example, in a study of an outside consultant's effort to initiate changes in a life insurance company's selling (branch) offices, made such an assessment through direct observation and the investigation of detailed records. In the study he recorded and measured the activities, interactions, and sentiments of staff in a small number of branch offices before and after the consultant's intervention.[13] O'Connell was able to determine significant output changes in the desired direction by applying the techniques of a trained nonparticipant observer armed mainly with a stopwatch (the branch manager spoke 11.35 minutes at a sales conference) and lots of recording materials. It seems to me, admittedly not an expert in doing this form of research, that people with substantive knowledge of the situation being studied, reasonable knowledge of organizational behavior, and some sensitivity can carry out this type of study to yield useful implementation information.

As might be expected, however, implementation assessment presents a host of problems. There are technical and logistical difficulties in developing feedback mechanisms for intermediate implementation assessment. Seldom have organizations been able to construct reporting systems that provide useful information either for correcting or assessing a project. Equally difficult is the determination of appropriate points at which to assess implementation. One certainly can expect to hear the claim so frequently made in evaluations that it is much too early for an assessment. This claim should not necessarily be seen as an operator's rationalization for poor performances. The movement toward successful operations may not be along a straight path of improvement without setbacks. So even when the analyst knows how to assess implementation, he or she must still contend with judgmental issues concerning timing.

We can pursue issues of implementation analysis and assessment further by considering two techniques that may be used by social agencies to facilitate or carry out these activities—demonstration projects and monitoring. Historically, demonstration programs in the social agencies were often disguised operating efforts to meet political demands in a setting

---

[13]Jeremiah J. O'Connell, *Managing Organizational Innovations* (Homewood, Ill.: Richard D. Irwin, Inc., 1968). Even though direct applications from business to government are sometimes hazardous, the reader may find this volume useful for several reasons. First, it contains an extensive bibliography on earlier uses of the techniques employed. Second, it illustrates issues of implementation strategy through its description of the detailed planning of the implementation effort, which included the development of field instructions specifying both the physical and behavioral changes expected and the development of a multistage approach. Finally, O'Connell is able to obtain some outcome measures and presents an interesting discussion of output and outcome relationships.

unencumbered by the restrictions of regular programs. Even when the demonstration effort did try to test new ideas, the programs often were administered by action-oriented people who were both impatient with and distrustful of relatively rigorous assessment procedures. Moreover, these projects in the best of circumstances focused on inputs and outputs, not on the project outcomes that are so dear to the hearts of policy analysts. For these reasons, research-oriented analysts have looked down on demonstration projects and on the action-oriented people who developed and funded them. Such projects might have been tolerated to keep bureaucratic peace in an agency but were considered to be of little value for purposes of developing information.

It is now becoming clear that such projects can serve a useful function in the development of information. This is especially true when decisions about new programs have been made or have a high probability of being made in the near future. Once a planning or budgeting process indicates that program changes will be made in the upcoming fiscal year, an elaborate experimental project taking several years is out of the question. The political decision has already been made. However, it may be appropriate to carry out one or more demonstration projects that will provide both a test of administrative and political feasibility and useful implementing experience. Indeed, a most reasonable proposition is that the administrative bugs ought to be worked out in a small-scale effort before any complex, new program is launched full-scale.

This situation is different from the one in which a small-scale field testing program is undertaken in order to develop information concerning possible program alternatives *before* decisions are made. In the latter case, demonstration projects may be viewed in the same light as experiments. Time is available to develop and execute a research design, where it might not be in the case of demonstration projects for approved decisions.[14] While less severe than for experiments, the necessary conditions for a demonstration project to have a reasonable probability of yielding information useful for major program decisions are quite demanding. Moreover, the conditions are similar to those for experiments. This is hardly strange, as the reason for doing both kinds of projects is to generate information of sufficiently broad applicability to facilitate the *making* of major decisions. To provide such information, a demonstration project must be specified in operational terms and implemented in the field to meet these specifications. Further, the research design should support broad application and permit comparison with alternative concepts. If demonstration projects are to

[14]If time does permit, the requirements presented below would also apply generally to field testing of approved decisions.

provide information for future major decisions, they must be carefully designed to yield information that can be generalized to many projects.

It is important to recognize the limits of the information derived even from well-designed demonstration projects. The information *can* show that the project adhered to its specifications and overcame political or administrative problems to become a viable activity, but *not* that the project benefited the participants. Yet even with no information on outcomes, sound information about the degree to which a well-defined program strategy can be implemented, *plus experience in the actual implementation,* is so much better than what we now have that the only debatable point is whether it *can* be gotten, not whether it *should* be.

Whether useful demonstration projects can be carried out is moot. First, the technical requirements noted above are formidable although generally significantly less severe than in an experiment for the same activity. Second, political and bureaucratic timing problems loom large. For example, will decisionmakers take the time to allow for a good design and wait for its results? No one can say. However, the notion of sound demonstrations is so crucial to the improvement of implementation procedures in social policy organizations that it should be pushed. So while we must refrain from expecting too much, we must also see that some beginning efforts, even if halting, would be a great leap forward.

Agency monitoring generally involves site visits by teams composed of national and regional staffs, outside consultants, and/or local operators from other projects who consider such factors as administrative management practices, adherence to stated guidelines, and staff capability. In the past, monitoring efforts have focused far too much on inputs in a static sense, on relatively low-level administrative practices, or on issues of financial accountability. Yet monitoring has been the closest thing in the agency to an implementation assessment technique. A competent team of people with in-depth knowledge of both program substance and financial–administrative matters well may produce the kind of information needed to judge whether or not an activity is moving toward implementation success.

The main problems with monitoring have had less to do with techniques per se and more with a failure to ask the right questions. Again, perhaps the failure to specify substance has been a major culprit. The problem might be described as one of specification imbalance slanting concern toward financial and administrative practices. As Horst and her associates observe in discussing the development of social program guidelines,

> how-to-do-it rule making is the third kind of language that is commonly found. Here the terms are very concrete and specific. We find guidance on factors like the qualifications of project directors, the contents of affiliation agreements with other local agencies, report-

ing relationships, the use of consultants, and accounting practices. This guidance appears
to be definite and all inclusive. Closer examination shows that it usually tells how to run
the part of a project which does not deal directly with the intervention into society.
Guidance for the part of the project which actually produces effects in society is not
provided.[15]

However, if reasonable specifications about the program's operating elements exist, a monitoring team made up of relatively competent people
who have in-depth knowledge about programs and bureaucracy, and who
have not necessarily been trained as social scientists, should be able to
assess both compliance with specifications and the viability of the project.

The issue of assessing viability needs further comment. Assessment
in this case involves ex post facto judgments of whether an activity is
running well in bureaucratic/political terms, not ex ante statements about
which variables will yield smooth functioning. In the former situation,
people with well-honed bureaucratic sensitivities should be able to assess
within tolerable limits how well an activity is going and whether it is
beginning to fit into its institutional environment. Surely it ought to be
possible to spot the bad cases—but not necessarily to know what to do
about them, since that step requires ex ante prediction.

The central role of reasoned judgment in assessing implementation
should be clearly delineated. A static checklist of all the specified inputs
(one teacher, two teacher aides, three talking typewriters, and so on) will
not indicate the viability of the project. On the other hand, enough missing
pieces may spell trouble. The exercise of judgment or of a composite of
judgments of an activity in motion seems the only way to determine
viability. At the same time, technique may facilitate judgment. A set of
"dynamic" questions (e.g., does the principal support the project?), a
common scaling system, or a sampling frame may keep those carrying out
the assessment from missing important issues, provide a useful means of
comparing judgments, and avoid selectivity biases. Good judgment, however, remains the key element. Methodology simply does not appear to be
the big barrier. Nor do I see the need for highly trained social scientists to
carry out the various tasks. The biggest need is for competent, reasonable
people with sound substantive knowledge of programs and of bureaucracy.

RESEARCH ON IMPLEMENTATION

Little research has been done either on the implementation of social
policies, programs, or projects or on the implementation process in a social

[15]Pamela Horst and others, "Program Management and the Federal Evaluator,"
Public Administration Review, July/August 1974, p. 303.

policy organization such as a federal agency. The absence of studies is not explained by the nature of the topic itself. The question of implementation is one of the most fundamental of all the issues facing a large-scale organization. In its most general form, an inquiry about implementation seeks to determine whether an organization can bring together people and material in a cohesive organizational unit and motivate them in such a way as to carry out the organization's stated objectives. Implementation is such a basic issue that the failure to study it in the context of a social policy organization is most difficult to understand. This is especially true in light of the fact that the problem can be approached from several perspectives that cut across a number of academic disciplines.

The problem might be studied in terms of the development of a sound organizational structure by inquiring whether the organization has in place, or can be expected to develop quickly, the administrative and technical skills that will be required in operating a new program aimed at accomplishing specified objectives. It is the administrative science question of the soundness of a large bureaucracy's organizational structure and staff in terms of the administrative and technical demands of specific programs. Or, implementation could be looked at as a problem requiring the integration of a number of systems and subsystems, the kind of problem that might interest the sociologist with "macro" concerns or the systems analyst. Relatedly, the complex bureaucratic and political issues and their interface might pose questions of interest to political scientists.

The problem of implementing new programs might be looked at more from the perspective of interpersonal motivational factors. As Anthony observes: "The success or failure of the management control process depends on the personal characteristics of the manager: his judgment, his knowledge, and his ability to influence others."[16] In these terms the emphasis is on leadership—a blending of personal skill and experience that can get others to respond to direction in a dynamic situation. Viewed from this perspective, the implementation question is primarily one of the dynamics of interaction—the social psychological issue of how managers motivate others to carry out a program in line with stated objectives. One might cast this problem in terms of the individual manager or of an organizational unit with a focus on organizational development.

Another approach to the study of implementation might be in terms of incentives as discussed earlier. The incentive structure seems to be more the domain of the economist than of other social scientists. Finally, the social anthropologist might find observing the implementation process less crowded with other anthropologists and more rewarding than dropping in

[16]R. N. Anthony, *Planning and Control Systems: A Framework for Analysis,* Cambridge, Mass., Harvard University, Graduate School of Business Administration, 1965, p. 80.

on still another exotic island. A great deal might be gained from careful observation by a scientist trained to pick up the nuances of interpersonal relationships or the effects of mores on behavior.

In response to my statement that there has been little research specifically on problems of implementation in social organizations, some might call attention to a missing reference or question how little is little. But the general claim of the paucity of research on efforts to implement social programs and policies surely is well justified. However, any claim concerning the actual or potential relevance of social science techniques or past research to the study of implementation in social organizations is likely to be controversial. Take the organizational area, for example. There is a vast literature from each of the disciplines of sociology, political science, public and business administration, economics, and the emerging area of organizational development. Who considers himself sufficiently in command of all this literature to judge its actual or potential relevance? Further, as just discussed, the organizational approach is only one of several that might be relevant to the study of social policy implementation. Given such a wide sweep of disciplinary areas and substantive approaches, it is clearly premature to claim that no relevant work will be discovered.

A few cautious statements seem warranted. First, just as with the lack of implementation concerns in social agencies, the lack of specific research on social policy implementation is baffling—a Kafkaesque situation of ignoring fundamental issues for which there seems to be no explanation. Second, search in other areas yields no obvious candidates for a ready mining of research techniques or studies directly relevant to social policy implementation.[17] Third, at this point not enough is known about implementation in social organizations to do more than determine the lack of obvious relevance of available research. Scholars simply have not yet done enough research, including theory building, on social policy implementation to be good appraisers of the more subtle relevance of past work in the social sciences—and in saying this I recognize full well that more sophistication may show its irrelevance. Fourth, the biggest research need is to focus directly on social policy implementation, probably through careful case studies. At the same time, case material becomes more useful when ordered by a theoretical framework, but *probably* no single best theoretical framework will emerge. Rather, it is more likely that sound case material will be more valuable when approached by people with different disciplinary perspectives and frameworks that provide diverse interpretations. So let variety flower.

[17]For an excellent effort to determine the relevance of past work to the study of implementing educational innovation, see Paul Berman and Milbrey McLaughlin, *Federal Programs Supporting Educational Change,* vol. I, *A Model of Educational Change,* R–1589/1-HEW, Santa Monica, Calif., The Rand Corporation, September 1974, pp. 3–11.

I am relatively optimistic about implementation research, believing that it can yield results directly useful in program policy and analysis. Despite the limited amount of such research thus far, the findings take on some power because so often they are straightforward, logical, and intuitively appealing. For example, when we investigate why a project ended up not looking like its designers wanted it to, we so often find that they did not communicate what was wanted, that little or no support was provided, that no effort was made to monitor the implementation process, and so on in an obvious array of errors of commission and omission. Now it is true that our marvelous insights derived after the fact can mislead us as to how simple it would have been to do the thing right. But I still keep coming back to the feeling that a bit of common sense, a modicum of attention to implementation would reap many benefits. This point is well illustrated by some findings from a recent Rand study.[18]

Much in line with the Levine arguments presented earlier, the Rand study found that simple and straightforward sanctions—both positive and negative—including some bargaining and competition seem to improve the chances of implementation fidelity and significant organizational change. This was made apparent in the contrasting styles of the federal and state governments in administering projects. The former tended to support projects through nomination, usually by a state educational agency and *without a formal proposal*. In contrast the state-administered programs would require extensive proposals with the funding contingent upon a competitive process among applicants in which there could be some losers. The states also engaged actively in monitoring while the federal government did not. The states were willing to tell the individual projects where they thought they were going wrong and to indicate corrective actions. The federal government would hand out money and wait passively in their offices for results. Finally, the state agencies in some cases negotiated project evaluations that appeared to be methodologically sound. The federal government, in contrast, would send out written guidelines about the inclusion of an evaluation in a project and would get back evaluation designs that the Rand study group believed were usually useless and lacking in scientific rigor. It well may be that the great value of the sound evaluative design was in forcing both state and local people to specify objectives in measurable terms that they could agree on so that the project had a reasonable basis for its implementation.

As one might expect, the Rand study found the state projects to have been implemented more successfully than those administered by the fed-

[18]The study is summarized in Paul Berman and Milbrey McLaughlin, *Federal Programs Supporting Educational Change: The Findings in Review*, Volume IV, R–1589/4-HEW, The Rand Corporation, April 1975, and discussed in the McLaughlin chapter in this volume.

eral government. The research cannot tell us at this point whether this result flowed mainly from states' superior knowledge about local projects or competence or from some straightforward activities like going out to look at the project (practices one would think the federal officials also could carry out). However, I suspect the latter were the important ones since there is little evidence of state superiority, and, indeed, the opposite often seems true.

Three things stand out about the Rand study. First, it is by far the most ambitious effort to date to investigate social program implementation. Earlier work has been restricted to a single project or community, while the Rand study samples a variety of projects in different localities. Second, the results generally are consonant with the more limited (in a statistical sense) work of the past, including case materials from other areas. Third, and this is critical, the results in the main confirm our expectations. Most strikingly, the limited work on implementation to date, including the Rand study, has tended to verify what our eyes and common sense tell us are true. This should strengthen our confidence in the results, certainly to the extent of feeling we have some good road marks for further study. At a minimum we have some interesting hypotheses for investigating how better to implement social programs and what should be the key questions asked by implementation analysis and assessment.

If there is an overarching message that comes from the sum of research carried out thus far, it is that some reasonable thinking about implementation—call it a strategy, call it common sense, or what you will—is likely to pay off in projects of greater fidelity to design. It would be naive to expect wondrous improvements, but I do think we can avoid some of the most obvious mistakes of the past. Implementation will remain inherently difficult because it is ultimately a bureaucratic/political problem in which key actors are toting up structural benefits and costs. But the research of the past does suggest that a little forward planning, some sensitivity to individual needs, and a bit of real prodding rather than simply handing out the money as the federal government has done so often would seem to move us toward more successful implementation.

CONCLUDING OBSERVATIONS

Implementation is a difficult topic, partly because it embraces a number of seemingly paradoxical notions. On the one hand, the underlying theme of this book is the central importance of implementation for improving social program operations, policy analysis, and social experimentation. On the other hand, there is a mystifying neglect of implementation issues by social program people at all levels, by policy analysts, and by researchers.

In the same vein, much discussion has focused on the great complexity of implementation, especially in a many-layered setting, with some of the problems apparently well beyond our present capabilities. Yet it is also argued that the immediate need is not for methodological breakthroughs but for the application of simple techniques with some common sense.

The first paradoxical pair—the importance of implementation versus its neglect—is something we shall have to live with, but hopefully not for too long. The second, the matter of methodology, bears further discussion and provides some suitable concluding observations for this chapter.

How is the methodology issue to be reconciled? Both the systematic study of implementation and the development of better techniques for such study are needed. However, methodology may not be that much of a blockage during initial efforts to improve implementation in a social policy organization. This is so because the most basic descriptive information is in quite short supply. Under such circumstances, only the simplest methodological tools may be required to determine more precisely the structure of the implementation process (the level of technical competence, the degree of emphasis on administrative inputs, etc.) and the extent of communications between various levels and segments of an organization. Such studies often may produce mainly negative information showing deficiencies and misdirections. To recognize this fact, however, in no way negates the pressing need to fill these massive gaps in our knowledge. Moreover, the basic knowledge derived about implementation can help shape our understanding of what needs to be done if a social policy organization wants to improve implementation.

Beyond some point, progress will be difficult. Here the lack of techniques looms large. It is now beyond our ability in many cases to develop effective treatment packages through experimentation or other means and to determine effective means of implementation through the study of the dynamics of that process. Indeed, no one can be confident that research on the dynamics of implementation will yield major results in the near term. We must recognize both that implementation is where the research action ought to be and that progress is likely to be slow.

I would offer this as a single guiding rule: Always think about implementation problems, and always worry that others are not thinking about them, but do not expect major improvements to come quickly. This message—especially the stricture against expecting too much too fast—has particular relevance for the policy analyst. First, it has been argued that by far the most important step toward improvement is the strong commitment on the part of management (top decisionmakers) to deal with implementation problems. Since this commitment will require significant organizational changes with high bureaucratic costs, matters seem certain to proceed slowly. Analysts may work for such changes, but the changes must occur before their own efforts in the implementation process will have any large payoff.

Policy analysts should be realistic not only about their organizations but also about their own skills and techniques. They have suffered from a naive overconfidence that has resulted in disappointment with and disparagement of limited success. Like sports fans, analysts dream of the big change that will take the team to first place. First it was PPB; then evaluation and experimentation. Now we analysts may be boarding the implementation bandwagon, seeking again the sure technological fix. This would be a grave mistake. Implementation analysis and assessment should not become the new hope for technical ascendance. If we listen to history, we should anticipate neither rapid technical advances nor smooth sailing for recommendations based on implementation analysis and assessment. This is not to counsel despair but to recognize both that progress is likely to be slow and that it is more likely to occur if we formulate reasonable notions of success.

INDEX

QUANTITATIVE STUDIES IN SOCIAL RELATIONS

Consulting Editor: Peter H. Rossi

UNIVERSITY OF MASSACHUSETTS
AMHERST, MASSACHUSETTS

A 6
B 7
C 8
D 9
E 0
F 1
G 2
H 3
I 4
J 5

SOCIAL EXPERIMENTATION
A Method for Planning and Evaluating Social Intervention

Edited by HENRY W. RIECKEN
         ROBERT BORUCH

A Volume in the QUANTITATIVE STUDIES IN SOCIAL RELATIONS Series

1974, 350 pp. / ISBN: 0-12-588150-9

Based on meetings of a Social Science Research Council committee, this volume is a pragmatic guide to solving the technical and managerial problems that arise in social experimentation. The committee reviewed the current state of the art in social experimentation as an approach to social program development and evaluation.

The monograph provides a general orientation to social experimentation for the reader who is interested in the advantages, limitations, and practical possibilities of the method; but it also delves into the major scientific and technical issues of design and measurement. The management of experiments in the field is discussed from a practical point of view; and the decision to experiment as well as the utilization of experimental results in program planning are considered from a political and administrative perspective. The book features numerous illustrative examples drawn from planning and evaluation studies in economics, health rehabilitation, criminal justice, compensatory education, and manpower training. Most important, it is specifically designed for those actively engaged in conducting and managing social intervention programs. It includes a useful annotated bibliography on field experiments.

Needless to say, this is a useful and important book for graduate students in sociology, psychology, economics, statistics, community health, criminal justice and delinquency research; social researchers in profit-making or nonprofit research organizations; and middle and upper managers in Federal, state, and large local government agencies.

CONTENTS:
Experimentation as a Method of Program Planning and Evaluation. Why and When to Experiment. Experimental Design and Analysis. Quasi-Experimental Designs. Measurement in Experiments. Execution and Management. Institutional and Political Factors in Social Experimentation. Human Values and Social Experimentation. Epilogue. Appendix: Illustrative Controlled Experiments for Planning and Evaluating Social Programs. References.
Author Index—Subject Index.

DATE DUE

GAYLORD			PRINTED IN U.S.A.